INDICES AND INDICATORS
IN DEVELOPMENT

INDICES AND INDICATORS IN DEVELOPMENT

AN UNHEALTHY OBSESSION WITH NUMBERS?

Stephen Morse

Earthscan Publications Ltd

London • Stirling, VA

First published by Earthscan in the UK and USA in 2004

Copyright © Stephen Morse, 2004

All rights reserved

ISBN: 1-84407-011-5 paperback
      1-84407-012-3 hardback

Typesetting by TW Typesetting, Plymouth, Devon
Printed and bound in the UK by Cromwell Press Ltd, Trowbridge
Cover design by Susanne Harris

For a full list of publications please contact:
Earthscan
8–12 Camden High Street
London, NW1 0JH, UK
Tel: +44 (0)20 7387 8558
Fax: +44 (0)20 7387 8998
Email: earthinfo@earthscan.co.uk
Web: www.earthscan.co.uk

22883 Quicksilver Drive, Sterling, VA 20166-2012, USA

Earthscan publishes in association with WWF-UK and the International Institute for Environment and Development

A catalogue record for this book is available from the British Library

Library of Congress Cataloging-in-Publication Data

Morse, Stephen, 1957–Indices and indicators in development: an unhealthy obsession with numbers/Stephen Morse
        p. cm.
    Includes bibliographical references and index.
    ISBN 1-84407-011-5- (pbk)—ISBN 1-84407-012-3- (hbk.)
    1. Economic development–Statistical methods. 2. Economic indicators. 3. Social indicators. I. Title.

HD75.M667 2004
338.9'001'5195–dc22   2004013712

Printed on elemental chlorine-free paper

CONTENTS

List of Figures, Tables and Boxes   *vii*
List of Acronyms and Abbreviations   *x*
Acknowledgements   *xiii*
Preface   *xv*

1 Simplifying Complexity: Why Do We Need Indicators?   **1**
Introduction   1
Outline of book structure   4
Indicators and league tables   5
Modernist development   21
Modernization to dependency   24
Neopopulism, neoliberalism and anti-development   25
Sustainable development   27
Indicators of development   29
Summary   31

2 Development Indicators: Economics   **33**
Introduction   33
Economic activity: The Gross Domestic Product   34
Problems with the Gross Domestic Product   39
Gross National Product and other indicators   49
Gross Domestic Product and consumption   54
Summary   58

3 Development Indicators: Poverty   **60**
Introduction   60
Headcount Ratio   61
Income Gap Ratio   63
Poverty Gap Index   67
Income inequality   69
Summary   81

4 Integrating Development Indicators   **83**
Introduction   83
Human development   85
Birth of the Human Development Index   87

Calculating the Human Development Index   88
The 'HDI' family of human development indices   100
Critiques of the Human Development Index   106
Summary   114

5 **The Precarious Art of Simplifying Complexity**   **118**
Introduction   118
Indicators of sustainable development   119
Environmental Sustainability Index   121
Corruption and human development   132
Summary   148

6 **Taking Care with Development Indicators**   **150**
Introduction   150
Is the Human Development Index used by anyone?   151
Interpreting indices: Over-reduction?   156
Development indices and policy   171
Summary   173

7 **A Comparative Indicatorology**   **176**
Some meetings in Italy   176
People's indicators   180
Sense, fondness or obsession?   182

Notes   *184*
References   *185*
Appendix 1 Factor analysis: a brief introduction *194*
Index   *203*

LIST OF FIGURES, TABLES AND BOXES

FIGURES

1.1 Sustainable development encompassing concerns for the
community, economy and the environment 28
2.1 Simple model of an economy with only two components
(households and businesses) 35
2.2 GDP (billions £ sterling) and Real GDP (1995 set as 100) for
the UK economy between 1970 and 2000 40
2.3 The theory behind transfer price fixing, using Ireland (a low
corporate tax economy) as an example 52
2.4 Values of GDP and GNP (both adjusted for PPP) for the Irish
economy (1970–2000) 53
3.1 Illustration of depth of poverty 65
3.2 Illustration of average depth of poverty 66
3.3 Two different distributions of income below a notional
poverty line of $1/day 69
4.1 Effects of the two different transformations of GDP/capita
employed in the Human Development Reports 91
4.2 Percentage of countries included in the Human Development
Index tables between 1990 and 2003 categorized as low,
medium and high human development by the UNDP 99
5.1 The dashboard of sustainability 120
5.2 Hypothetical distributions of a corruption score found by
three separate surveys 139
6.1 GDP/capita ($) as a function of national intelligence 167
6.2 Logarithm (base 10) of GDP/capita as a function of national
intelligence 169
7.1 Relationships between indicators, data and information 181
A.1 GDP/capita as a function of life expectancy 194
A.2 Logarithm of GDP/capita as a function of life expectancy 195

TABLES

1.1 The Premier League table at the end of the 2002/2003
Football League season in England 6

1.2   Example university league table for the UK   7
1.3   League table of primary schools in Reading, UK, based on
      aggregate scores over 2 years (2002 and 2003)   14
1.4   League table of primary schools in Reading, UK, based on the
      difference between 2002 and 2003 aggregate scores   15
2.1   Example calculation of the Gross Domestic Product (GDP) for
      the US economy   37
2.2   'Openness' of economies measured in terms of inward and
      outward flows of goods and services as a proportion of GDP   38
2.3   Comparison of GDP/capita using current US$ exchange rate
      against GDP/capita adjusted for Purchasing Power Parity (PPP)   47
2.4   Suite of economic performance indicators for the US economy   50
2.5   Maximum tax rates applied to corporate income (2003)   52
2.6   Modifying the GDP   55
2.7   Some attempts to modify the GDP and GNP   55
2.8   An example of the components of the genuine progress
      indicator   56
3.1   Example of how depth of poverty varies between two
      populations   62
3.2   Example calculation of Income Gap Ratio   64
3.3   Second example calculation of Income Gap Ratio   65
3.4   Example calculation of Income Gap Ratio – a before and after
      scenario   66
3.5   Example calculation of Income Gap Ratio – a before and after
      scenario utilizing the Poverty Gap Index   68
3.6   Distribution of poverty amongst poor below the poverty line   68
3.7   Calculation of Index of Dissimilarity – Example 1   71
3.8   Calculation of Index of Dissimilarity – Example 2   71
3.9   Calculation of Index of Dissimilarity – real US Data   71
3.10 Some example Gini coefficients   73
4.1   Themes and main data years for the United Nations Human
      Development Reports and the calculation of the Human
      Development Index   85
4.2   Evolution of the calculation of the Human Development Index   92
4.3   Periods of relative consistency in the calculation of the Human
      Development Index   94
4.4   Average values of the HDI and its three components (life
      expectancy, education and GDP/capita) over the period
      2000–2003   94
4.5   Calculated values for the HDI and GDI (HDR 2002)   101
4.6   Number of 'hits' associated with five development indicators
      listed in the Human Development Reports (1990–1998)   106
4.7   Difference in scale between Human Development Index (HDI)
      and GDP/capita for three countries   107

4.8   Human Development Indices (1993, reported in the HDR 1996)
      for a sample of countries based on the use of life expectancy
      and happy life expectancy   110
4.9   The Life Product Index (LPI) compared with the HDI   115
5.1   Summary of indicators and components of the ESI   121
5.2   Components of the Environmental Sustainability Index (ESI) for
      2002   122
5.3   Variables for the air quality indicator of the environmental
      systems component of the ESI   124
5.4   Calculation of z-values for two of the indicators used in the
      Environmental Sustainability Index (2002)   127
5.5   Values of the Environmental Sustainability Index for 2002   129
5.6   Countries and sources of data for the 2002 Corruption
      Perception Index (CPI)   134
5.7   The highest and lowest scoring countries in the 2001 CPI
      league table   138
5.8   Values of the Corruption Perception Index reported by
      Transparency International in 2002   146
6.1   Data employed in the analysis of the relationship between real
      GDP/capita and national intelligence   164
6.2   Countries with the largest residuals following a regression
      analysis between GDP/capita and national intelligence scores   168
6.3   European development funds, 1959–2005   171
6.4   European Commission indicators towards Millennium
      Development Goals   173
7.1   Some issues regarding development indices designed for
      inter-country comparison   177
A.1   Observed and predicted life expectancy and residuals
      (observed – predicted life expectancy) for the countries
      included in the HDR 2000 (Data from 1998)   196
A.2   Factor analysis for the three components of the HDI in 2000.
      Extraction of the first factor   201

BOXES

1.1   The FTSE 100 Index   19
2.1   An explanation of Purchasing Power Parity (PPP)   42
3.1   The Gini coefficient   75
3.2   Sen's Poverty Index (P)   78
5.1   Skewness and the Environmental Sustainability Index (ESI)   125
5.2   The beta-transformation employed in the calculation of
      Transparency International's Corruption Perception Index (CPI)   141
6.1   Some regressions with the HDI   158

Acronyms and Abbreviations

ACP	African, Caribbean and Pacific
CHDI	Corporate Human Development Index
CPI	Corruption Perception Index
DSD	United Nations Division for Sustainable Development
EAW	Economic Aspects of Welfare
EDF	European Development Fund
EDP	Environmentally Adjusted Net Domestic Product
EIU	Economist Intelligence Unit
ESI	Environmental Sustainability Index
EU	European Union
Eurostat	Statistical Office of the European Union
FAO	United Nations Food and Agriculture Organisation
FTSE	Financial Times Share Index
GDI	Gender Related Development Index
	Gross Domestic Income
GEM	Gender Empowerment Measure
GDP	Gross Domestic Product
GI	Gallop International
GNI	Gross National Income (similar to GNP)
GNP	Gross National Product (similar to GNI)
GPI	Genuine Progress Indicator
H	Headcount Ratio
HDI	Human Development Index
HDR	Human Development Report (UNDP)
HLE	Happy Life Expectancy
HPI	Human Poverty Index (two forms: HPI-1 and HPI-2)
I	Income Gap Ratio
ICP	International Comparison Programme
ID	Index of Dissimilarity
ILO	International Labour Organization
IMD	Institute for Management Development
IMF	International Monetary Fund
IQ	Intelligence Quotient
ISD	Indicator of Sustainable Development
ISEW	Index of Sustainable Economic Welfare

LDC	less developed country
LPI	Life Product Index
MEW	Measure of Economic Welfare
MNC	multinational company
NDP	Net Domestic Product
NI	National Income
NNP	Net National Product
NGO	Non-Governmental Organization
NUT	National Union of Teachers
OECD	Organization for Economic Cooperation and Development
P_1	Poverty Gap Index
P	Sen's Index of Poverty
PCA	Principal Component Analysis
PERC	Political and Economic Risk Consultancy
PPA	Participatory Poverty Analysis
PPP	Purchasing Power Parity
PQLI	Physical Quality of Life Index
PwC	PricewaterhouseCoopers
SAP	Structural Adjustment Programme
SHDI	Sustainable Human Development Index
SNBI	Sustainable Net Benefit Index
SSA	Systemic Sustainability Analysis
TI	Transparency International
UN	United Nations
UNDP	United Nations Development Programme
UNEP	United Nations Environment Programme
UNESC	United Nations Economics and Social Council
UNRISD	United Nations Research Institute for Social Development
WBES	World Bank's World Business Environment Survey
WCED	World Commission on Sustainable Development
WDR	World Development Report (World Bank)
WEF	World Economics Foundation

ACKNOWLEDGEMENTS

I would like to take this opportunity of thanking my family (Maura, Llewellyn and Rhianna) for putting up with me during the year or so it took to write this book. This is a book I just had to write and it would not have been possible without their full encouragement and support – there were many indicators of these!

Preface

This book was born out of a number of nagging concerns I have had with development indicators for some years. In part this has arisen from the growing popularity amongst politicians, policy makers and managers for the 'target' culture applied to public services (including health and education) in the Western world. There is, of course, nothing wrong with accountability and the need for taxpayers to receive 'value for their money'. That is not the issue. Instead it is the mode in which these are achieved (or perhaps more precisely, 'attempted'). The tendency has been first to 'simplify' by the measurement of but a few 'key' indicators of achievement, and second to present the results in the form of a league table – an attempt to name and shame those who do not do well in the indicator stakes. It is this fashion for simplification, arguably over-simplification, that we also see in development.

In two previous books also published by Earthscan, Simon Bell (of the Centre of Complexity and Change, Open University) and myself made the case that indicators can be important tools within sustainable development, but they need to be handled with care. In our view, they are at their best when created and applied within a participatory approach that includes all the key stakeholders. Our first book suggested a methodology, Systemic Sustainability Analysis (SSA), for carrying out this participatory process, and suggested one way (a visual device called the AMOEBA) for presenting the results. Our second book took this further by discussing the results of a sustainable development project in Malta where SSA was applied. For us, one of the significant outcomes of this project was the power of 'learning', and particularly how those funding such projects tend only to be interested in the final outcome – the tangible deliverables. Unfortunately, stakeholder learning is often not seen by sustainable development project funders as a deliverable; instead it is seen as a means by which the deliverables are achieved. Yet we live in a projectified world, a world which demands 'value for money', impact and accountability. Try and argue otherwise, even if only as a Devils Advocate, to those who provide the funds for such projects, including taxpayers, and you will rapidly find yourself in a rather heated debate!

Here is the conundrum that prompted the writing of this book. Indicators can be powerful and useful tools. They summarize complexity, not by accident but by design, and speak with a quantitative and apparently objective authority that commands respect. But such power works both ways and can be used to support recommended action from all sorts of perspectives, including positions that are entirely contradictory. For example, much depends on who selects the indicators, the ways in which they are 'measured' and presented. The power held by those wielding indicators is rarely acknowledged, and instead the processes of creation and use are presented in benignly technical and, of course, objective language.

Love them or hate them indicators are here to stay. The question, I believe, is not so much whether or how we try to replace them, but how we use them. Development indicators are one species where this question is vital. Resources are inevitably limited and the problems of underdevelopment so acute that we can not afford to make bad decisions. People's lives and welfare, and not just those living in the underdeveloped world, are at stake. This is the starting point of the book and, in order to 'begin the beginning', it is as well to see where we are now and how we managed to get here. What are the development indictors currently in use, who created them, how and why? It is from here that we will explore some of the inherent problems that can emerge from such basic questions. But, as always, it is much easier to point out the problems than it is to provide solutions, and I certainly don't claim any privileged or even new insights.

I do need to stress that, while the book attempts to point out the problems with indicators, this does not mean that I am 'anti-indicators'! I am sometimes light-heartedly accused of this by colleagues and students alike. Paradoxically, no one would question the importance of safety when driving a car, flying an aeroplane or using a power tool. To argue for the highest standards by highlighting dangers is not necessarily the same as being anti-car, flying or DIY home improvements. There is obviously a balance, and my own view is that development indicators are necessary tools but need handling with care. However, as I will discuss in this book I also feel that we have been far too cavalier with indicators.

For the most part, of course, development indices are numerical (quantitative), and this can send shudders down the spine of those with an innate fear of anything that looks like mathematics. While they may be more than willing to 'consume' indices and use them to formulate and defend policy, they may come out in a sweat if asked to dissect the calculations and assumptions involved in arriving at the indicators. With some justice, it has to be said, they may point out that the very reasons such indicators exist is so that busy managers and policy makers do not have to get involved in such technical detail – it is best left to others. I do have some sympathy with this perspective, but unfortunately it is not possible to fully understand the limitations of development indicators unless you know something about how they are derived. It is in the derivation that most of the key assumptions are made. To refuse to engage with the assumptions is to hand over power to others. Policy makers and managers in development may feel that, after all, they are the ones with the power to make change, not the 'indicator technocrats'. But it is the latter group that define how 'change' is to be assessed.

With that in mind and in order to best illustrate the issues, I am not going to apologize for including a degree of technical detail. Some of this will be in boxes and an appendix, but much will also be in the text. I would urge the reader, even the most number-allergic, to please persevere.

If not for their sake then for the sake of those they serve.

1 SIMPLIFYING COMPLEXITY: WHY DO WE NEED INDICATORS?

INTRODUCTION

What does the term 'development indicators' mean to you?

- complicated
- technical
- mathematics and numbers
- politicians
- boring.

These are some of the terms that were used by a group of students on one of my courses when asked to summarize what they felt the term 'development indicators' signified to them. As can be guessed from the above list, the typical association is with numbers, maths and 'things which are highly technical; for experts only'. In part, it has to be said, this is true. For example, while there are many technical definitions of an indicator (Gallopin, 1997), a typical description is that they are: 'an operational representation of an attribute (quality, characteristic, property) of a system' (Gallopin, 1997). This doesn't sound very user-friendly, and would appear to have all the hallmarks of the above list. In fairness, there are less technical sounding definitions, such as the following referring specifically to 'social indicators':

> *A social indicator represents and measures wherever possible certain aspects of the progress or retrogression of such processes or activities as industrialization, health, welfare and educational services, areas of special concern to society.*
>
> *Interpreted in this broad sense, 'social indicators' as a measurement of the social aspects of life become an integral part of 'development indicators'* (Kao and Liu, 1984).

Nevertheless, the fact that, for the most part, development indicators are numbers derived from complex, or at least apparently complex, methodologies, can generate sympathy with students, and can be a serious disincentive for attempting to understand how they were created. Consider two more comments from the same group of students:

> *Let someone else (without a life!) worry about their calculation. I certainly don't want to.*

> *I don't want or need to know the details. All I want to see is the final number and what it means.*

Again it is hard not to sympathize with these views. After all, the whole point of generating such indicators is that they are meant to simplify. They exist so that we, the ordinary souls who need such information to 'do something', do not have to know or worry about the detail. They are there to make things easier for us – not by accident but by design.

When the students were asked for examples of such indicators, the following emerged:

- Gross Domestic Product (GDP) and Gross National Product (GNP)
- indicators of poverty
- access to and quality of health and education services
- quality of life and well-being
- the Human Development Index (HDI).

The list is not a surprising one. The first, GDP and GNP, are indicators of national economic achievement, and development (as will be seen later) has stubbornly been equated with economic progress. They are often referred to in the popular press, as well as being the foci for discussion (along with unemployment, interest rates, exports etc) by politicians at election times. Indicators of poverty, frequently expressed in terms of monetary income per day, are also a reasonable response to the request for examples. Indeed development is sometimes almost defined as the process by which we reduce or eliminate poverty. Today poverty is seen more broadly than just monetary income, and terms such as 'social exclusion' are commonly applied. Included here is access to good quality services such as health and education. Quality of life and well-being are perhaps the least tangible of all in the list, given the subjectivity involved. Quality of life encompasses everything important to us – income, health, education, opportunity, housing, transport, peace, leisure, happiness and so on. You name it. Yet here is the quintessential contradiction with development indicators. The above list begins with seemingly highly technical sounding terms that apparently fulfil the views of the students that indicators are 'technical', 'boring' and the stuff of people 'without lives', but, as we move down the list, they strike at the very heart of what probably all of us would see as vital – a job, our happiness, our health, our children. It's true that indicators are but one window onto these, but they are the window that is increasingly being used by those with the power to influence. Indeed the final item in the above list, the Human Development Index, is an example of a single index that encompasses but a few of these 'essentials' – health, education and income.

For example, as individuals we would see the quality of education given to our children through the eyes of our personal experience, but those charged with providing resources increasingly see quality through the window of indicators. Our experience would be partly based on an experience that includes exposure to quantitative (numerical) indicators (pass rates, results achieved in exams, class sizes etc) but also to qualitative (non-numerical) indicators (appearance of classrooms, location of school, how friendly the teachers appear to be etc). All of this information is put together (integrated or aggregated) in our brains without us realizing it is happening. Indeed, indicators are increasingly being seen as a tool within a broader policy of facilitating 'informed choice' by a much wider group than just policy makers and managers. As part of this process, indicators are often presented in a 'league table' format. We can compare one school against another simply by looking at their relative positions within the table.

Those creating and presenting indicators have great power as they can influence high level policy makers and managers, as well as the consumers of a service (Gill and Hall, 1997). The indicators they select and measure will set the agenda not only as to how a service is implemented but even how it is perceived. Rather than being just a limited topic relevant only for technocrats, there are deep issues of power at play:

> *Indicators are not necessarily collected or used in a purely 'objective', 'scientific' manner. Power politics and creative accounting frequently influence these practices as power holders try to look their best* (de Greene, 1994).

This book will focus on some of the issues surrounding development indicators and indices (an index is a number gained by combining indicators; Liverman et al, 1988; Quarrie, 1992). At one level, the reader will be provided with examples of such indicators and how they are rationalized and created, but, at another level, it takes this technical narrative and places it into a broader context of power. While at times the discussion may be technical, I would urge the reader to persevere. After all it is the methodologies used to get to the indicators that frame what the indicators are, who they were intended for and how they are intended to be 'used'. As such, like it or not, the devil can really be in the detail, and we ignore this to our peril! In order to facilitate this digestion, much of the technical material has been placed in boxes within the chapters, and some in an appendix at the end of the book.

OUTLINE OF BOOK STRUCTURE

The structure of the book is as follows.

Chapter 1 will begin by providing some examples of the use of indicators (and the 'league table' format of presentation) in our lives. It is impossible to provide examples relevant to all who will read this book, such is the pervasiveness of indicators, so I have had to be selective. Indeed I have selected three examples relevant to my own life: a soccer league table (the English Premier League), an example of a university performance league table (I work at a university in the UK) and the primary school league tables for England (my two children attend a primary school in England).

The remainder of Chapter 1 will briefly summarize the contested meaning and theories of development. It is within this evolution of theory and practice that indicators and indices have been created and used. As the reader will appreciate, it is impossible to do justice to the full range of ideas and debates in development spanning at least half a century; there are many other books that attempt just that. The intention here is to provide only a flavour of the trends and issues so as to set out the space within which people have tried to create and apply development indicators.

Chapters 2 and 3 will look at two commonly used sets of indicators and indices in development; economic performance (Chapter 2) and poverty (Chapter 3). Development is often seen in terms of a progression, such as the improvement in economic performance, but is also sometimes seen in the inverse, as the negation of an absence. In simple terms, development can equate to the reduction or elimination of poverty.

Chapter 4 will explore perhaps the most well known example of a development index, the Human Development Index (HDI). The HDI, first created by the United Nations Development Programme (UNDP) in 1990, attempts to pull together indicators from a range of factors typically regarded as important: education, health and income. It has had its successes and failures, and these will be discussed.

Chapter 5 will present other examples of indicators that are important in development. The ones I have selected are the Environmental Sustainability Index (ESI) and the Corruption Perception Index (CPI). The intention here is not to present the reader with what I think are necessarily the 'best' or indeed the 'only' such indices, but rather to provide examples which illustrate some of the problems involved. The ESI and CPI are more complex than the HDI and, while this can be seen to have advantages, there are trade-offs and these indices are interesting examples for that very reason.

Chapter 6 will look at the danger of oversimplification by exploring how some workers have tried to use indicators. There are a number of dimensions here, depending in part upon who is defined as the 'user'. First there is a discussion as to how indicators, more specifically the HDI, have been reported in the popular press. The second part of the chapter will look at how specialists have attempted to use indicators to analyse processes and constraints within development. The issue of cause–effect rises to the fore here. Indices such as the HDI, ESI and even CPI can almost be seen as benign and harmless. It may be the case that they simplify (perhaps oversimplify) reality, but is that necessarily a problem? Does it matter? The discussion in Chapter 6 will hopefully alert the reader to the fact that it does matter – it can matter a great deal! The third part of the chapter will explore how development indices are used in terms of setting and implementing policy.

In time honoured fashion, Chapter 7 will summarize the main messages of the book and draw out some conclusions.

INDICATORS AND LEAGUE TABLES

We are all familiar with league tables, particularly in competitive sports. An example is provided in Table 1.1 for English soccer clubs. This is the final placement of the 20 clubs that comprise the English Premier League at the end of the 2002/2003 season. Each team plays the others twice (once at home and once away), and points are allocated depending upon whether a team wins (3 points), draws (1 point each) or loses (0 points). Clubs with the same number of points are ranked by goal difference (between the number of goals scored and the number conceded). Clearly the points (and goal difference) are indicators (or measures) of how well a team has performed over the course of a season, and there are rewards for doing well. The team that finishes top of the league is crowned the 'champion', while the three that finish bottom are relegated to the division beneath this one (three teams from that lower division are promoted to the Premier League). Prestige is clearly important, as the higher a team finishes in the league the better it is from the point of view of its supporters, but there are also financial rewards. The higher a club finishes, the more money it receives at the end of the season. In addition, finishing in the top four of the table allows the club to enter financially lucrative European competitions the following season. The team I support, Chelsea (located in West London), came fourth and qualified for the European Champions League competition in the 2003/2004 season. At the time of writing, the club is doing well and I'm keeping my fingers crossed! Where Chelsea finish in the league table does matter to me, and no doubt supporters of the other clubs in Table 1.1 feel the same. Here, the league table is an essential part of the competitive process upon which the sport is based, and the balance of incentives (positive or negative) has been designed to encourage competition for as long as possible throughout the football season. As a device in this context the table is undoubtedly successful. Indeed, the English Premier League is one of the richest and most competitive soccer leagues in the world.

Table 1.1 *The Premier League table at the end of the 2002/2003 Football League season in England*

Position	Team	Goal difference (goals scored–goals conceded)	Points
1	Manchester United	40	83
2	Arsenal	43	78
3	Newcastle United	15	69
4	Chelsea	30	67
5	Liverpool	20	64
6	Blackburn Rovers	9	60
7	Everton	−1	59
8	Southampton	−3	52
9	Manchester City	−7	51
10	Tottenham Hotspur	−11	50
11	Middlesborough	4	49
12	Charlton Athletic	−11	49
13	Birmingham City	−8	48
14	Fulham	−9	48
15	Leeds United	1	47
16	Aston Villa	−5	45
17	Bolton Wanderers	−10	44
18	West Ham United	−17	42
19	West Bromwich Albion	−36	26
20	Sunderland	−44	19

Notes: Each team plays the other twice (home and away). Therefore each team plays 38 games. Three points are given for a win and one for a draw. The team that comes top (in bold) is crowned the 'champion' while the three at the foot (also in bold) are relegated to the division under this one.

If teams tie in terms of points, such as Middlesborough and Charlton Athletic, then ranking depends upon 'goal difference' (goals scored over the course of the season minus goals conceded). Middlesborough is ranked higher than Charlton because their goal difference is higher (+4 as opposed to −11).

The team I support, Chelsea, came fourth.

The same clubs in this table also compete in competitions that are not 'league table' based, such as knock-out cups. However, it is the league competition that is the most lucrative for most clubs over the course of a season, and indeed for most it is their 'bread and butter' source of income.

But league tables are not only applied in competitive sports.

The 'competitive spirit' that league tables engender has been applied to a host of other scenarios. In the UK a favoured sphere for applying such tables has been in education. Table 1.2 is an adaptation of a recently published (September 2003) league table of the performance of universities in the UK. This is not a table from an obscure management report, but has been adapted from a major and well-respected weekly newspaper, the *Sunday Times*, published in the UK.

A total of 121 universities appear in Table 1.2, and assessment has been based on a variety of characteristics that the newspaper deems to be important to its readers. The first six columns contribute a maximum of 1,000 points. The 'teaching quality' of the university is given a score out of 250 while 'research quality' is given a score out of 200, together comprising a

Table 1.2 *Example university league table for the UK*

Rank 2003	Rank 2002	University	Teaching quality (max 250)	Research quality (max 200)	A-level/higher points (max 250)	Employment (max 100)	1st/2.1 awarded (max 100)	Student/staff ratio (max 100)	Sub-total (max 100)	Dropout rate	Total
1	1	University of Cambridge	241	185	244	97	89	100	956	15	971
2	2	University of Oxford	214	178	246	93	87	100	918	5	923
3	3	London School of Economics	219	179	236	91	72	84	881	10	891
4	4	Imperial College London	205	167	234	94	73	100	873	−15	858
5	8	University College London	194	156	214	90	74	100	828	0	828
6	7	University of York	219	158	209	94	72	64	816	10	826
7	12	University of Bristol	164	148	225	96	82	92	807	15	822
8	5	University of Warwick	184	161	222	94	78	75	814	5	819
9	6	University of St Andrews	167	152	220	94	74	74	781	30	811
10	9	University of Nottingham	184	142	219	94	76	78	793	10	803
11	16	University of Edinburgh	164	143	221	95	76	87	786	−10	776
12	10	University of Bath	172	148	208	95	74	67	764	10	774
13	27	Loughborough University	237	123	180	95	66	55	756	10	766
14	22	Umist	167	147	192	91	58	100	755	10	765
15	11	University of Southampton	163	154	198	92	67	72	746	10	756
16	25	Cardiff University	179	142	197	94	68	65	745	10	755
17	13	University of Durham	167	149	208	94	65	66	749	5	754
18	21	King's College London	159	134	202	92	69	100	756	−5	751
19	18	University of East Anglia	181	143	178	94	64	70	730	20	750
20	25	University of Birmingham	167	122	201	95	69	76	730	10	740
20	29	University of Exeter	170	133	188	93	74	72	730	10	740
22	17	University of Manchester	146	144	196	93	71	90	740	−5	735
22	24	University of Newcastle upon Tyne	173	125	183	95	69	80	725	10	735
24	19	University of Leicester	175	129	173	93	66	78	714	20	734
25	20	University of Sheffield	158	129	206	95	72	73	733	0	733
26	31	University of Sussex	167	147	188	95	69	62	728	5	733
27	28	Royal Holoway, London	135	150	184	89	66	90	714	5	719

Table 1.2 *Continued*

Rank 2003	Rank 2002	University	Teaching quality (max 250)	Research quality (max 200)	A-level/higher points (max 250)	Employment (max 100)	1st/2.1 awarded (max 100)	Student/staff ratio (max 100)	Sub-total (max 100)	Dropout rate	Total
28	15	Lancaster University	153	154	174	93	64	59	697	20	717
29	23	University of Leeds	153	127	198	96	70	65	709	5	714
30	14	School of Oriental and African Studies	179	151	175	91	75	97	768	−60	708
31	30	University of Glasgow	167	121	183	94	70	87	722	−15	707
32	34	University of Liverpool	142	131	176	95	62	80	686	15	701
33	37	University of Essex	192	136	149	93	49	66	685	10	695
34	35	Queen's University Belfast	152	122	198	95	59	70	696	−5	691
35	43	Goldsmiths College, London	150	139	160	89	59	56	653	20	673
36	40	University of Dundee	162	120	144	96	64	81	667	5	672
36	32	University of Reading	121	139	172	94	64	82	672	0	672
38	49	Aston University Birmingham	167	111	176	95	70	57	676	−5	671
39	44	Keele University	147	115	150	94	59	69	634	35	669
40	40	University of Wales, Swansea	163	125	152	92	53	71	656	5	661
41	42	Queen Mary, London	107	135	167	89	60	95	653	0	653
42	54	Brunel University	176	89	158	91	58	50	622	15	637
43	33	University of Surrey	103	134	166	97	58	66	624	5	629
44	56	Herriot-Watt University	139	120	146	94	50	88	637	−10	627
45	53	University of Aberdeen	132	114	149	96	65	79	635	−10	625
46	36	University of Hull	163	91	134	97	61	53	599	15	614
47	45	City University	89	107	165	95	63	68	587	20	607
48	39	University of Wales, Aberystwyth	111	114	153	91	61	55	585	20	605
49	51	University of Strathclyde	132	103	170	95	61	73	634	−30	604
50	47	University of Wales, Bangor	117	111	139	93	54	62	576	20	596
51	51	University of Kent	100	115	166	97	58	49	585	5	590
52	48	University of Ulster	135	68	150	90	63	68	574	15	589
53	46	University of Stirling	125	111	144	93	69	63	605	−20	585
54	58	Oxford Brookes University	167	47	138	96	56	43	547	15	562

55	50	The London Institute	175	50	143	90	54	36	548	10	558
56	57	University of Bradford	107	96	140	93	55	61	552	−5	547
56	61	Northumbria University	155	32	133	95	52	55	522	25	547
58	68	University of Brighton	156	48	136	93	55	45	533	10	543
59	62	Nottingham Trent University	150	39	138	97	58	50	532	10	542
60	59	Bath Spa University College	143	44	118	92	61	46	504	25	529
61	64	University of Plymouth	143	44	128	92	53	55	515	5	520
62	55	University of Wales, Lampeter	100	124	118	87	52	59	540	−25	515
63	75	Kingston University	167	34	110	93	54	55	513	0	513
64	68	College of St Mark and St John	188	9	111	94	38	47	487	20	507
64	65	University of the West of England	163	46	126	91	44	47	517	−10	507
66	63	Sheffield Hallam University	119	31	134	93	51	48	476	30	506
67	67	University College Chichester	125	49	106	97	45	43	465	40	505
68	71	Manchester Metropolitan University	135	34	131	92	47	50	489	10	499
69	78	University of Hertfordshire	119	39	113	95	52	59	477	10	487
69	80	University of Salford	92	60	123	96	52	59	482	5	487
71	60	University of Portsmouth	109	49	120	93	49	50	470	15	485
72	70	Canterbury Christ Church	115	31	114	95	46	53	454	30	484
73	72	Bournemouth University	107	20	152	92	57	40	468	10	478
74	76	University of Wales Institute Cardiff	125	21	130	95	50	49	470	5	475
75	96	Middlesex University	147	37	98	87	55	40	464	5	469
76	73	King Alfred's College Winchester	100	42	130	93	52	35	452	15	467
77	86	Queen Margaret University College	63	42	130	96	68	52	451	5	456
78	88	Leeds Metropolitan University	79	24	137	93	54	47	434	20	454
79	89	University of Surrey Roehampton	91	56	121	93	50	42	453	0	453
80	84	Liverpool John Moores University	120	35	118	92	52	50	467	−15	452
80	79	Staffordshire University	139	32	112	91	45	48	467	−15	452
82	93	University of Glamorgan	150	37	83	95	54	42	461	−10	451
83	77	University of Luton	179	18	75	93	52	56	473	−25	448
84	92	University of Central Lancashire	141	24	116	94	56	47	478	−35	443
84	104	The Robert Gordon University	91	24	124	97	60	62	458	−15	443
86	85	Coventry University	107	29	119	92	46	49	442	−5	437
88	82	University College Chester	91	14	129	95	42	50	421	5	426

Table 1.2 *Continued*

Rank 2003	Rank 2002	University	Teaching quality (max 250)	Research quality (max 200)	A-level/higher points (max 250)	Employment (max 100)	1st/2.1 awarded (max 100)	Student/staff ratio (max 100)	Sub-total (max 100)	Dropout rate	Total
89	94	University of Wolverhampton	94	18	97	90	51	55	405	20	425
90	65	University College Worcester	83	22	116	96	44	49	410	10	420
91	101	De Montfort University	68	39	115	92	50	55	419	0	419
92	91	Edge Hill	100	12	102	93	39	49	395	20	415
93	103	University of Huddersfield	103	25	117	92	44	48	429	−25	404
94	100	University of Central England	44	22	123	92	56	60	397	5	402
94	102	University of Teesside	96	21	113	92	39	46	407	−5	402
96	96	University of Sunderland	83	49	105	93	54	49	433	−35	398
97	113	Southampton Institute	67	16	113	92	43	41	372	25	397
98	115	Bolton Institute	109	22	88	87	52	60	418	−25	393
98	87	Liverpool Hope University College	91	19	99	96	46	42	393	0	393
100	74	St Martin's College	36	15	114	96	43	63	367	25	392
101	106	St Mary's College	63	21	110	96	50	50	390	0	390
102	94	University of Gloucestershire	36	48	119	97	47	52	399	−10	389
103	112	University of Derby	66	25	106	92	50	59	398	−10	388
104	81	Napier University	71	22	46	91	65	50	345	35	380
105	99	University of Lincoln	38	20	118	89	51	50	366	10	376
106	116	London South Bank University	52	38	98	94	44	58	384	−10	374
107	107	Buckinghamshire Chilterns	56	24	102	93	43	39	357	10	367
108	110	University College Northampton	78	29	107	93	55	45	407	−45	362
109	114	Swansea Institute of Higher Education	125	8	100	97	40	40	410	−55	355
110	96	Trinity and All Saints	0	8	131	95	51	48	333	20	353
111	109	University of Greenwich	54	33	97	90	49	43	366	−15	351
112	83	York St John College	0	12	128	94	46	39	319	25	344
113	111	Anglia Polytechnic University	45	15	113	91	52	42	358	−30	328
114	118	Glasgow Caledonian University	15	33	119	92	60	57	376	−60	316
115	n/a	London Metropolitan University	86	28	91	90	34	44	373	−60	313

116	120	University of Abertay Dundee	25	19	90	91	51	60	336	−35	301
117	108	University of East London	14	40	99	83	40	54	330	−35	295
118	117	North East Wales Institute	0	14	103	91	46	43	297	−15	282
119	123	Thames Valley University	31	12	105	92	40	36	316	−35	281
120	122	University of Paisley	23	19	101	87	45	65	340	−70	270
121	119	University of Wales College, Newport	0	14	103	93	50	29	289	−25	264

Note: Adapted from the *Sunday Times* (14 September, 2003).

maximum of 450 points out of the 1,000. Other factors regarded as important are:

- **Qualifications required to enter the university (A-level or Higher Exam results).** The higher this score, the more demanding the entrance requirements.
- **Employment rates upon completion of the degree programme**. The higher the score, the greater the demand for students from that university once they graduate.
- **Number of first and upper second class degrees awarded**. Seen to be an indicator of the 'quality' of the education at university. However, this could also be seen as an indicator of the 'quality' of the students who enter the university.
- **Student:staff ratio**. Normally low values are better as they indicate that class sizes are smaller. In this case, the indicator has been scaled so that the higher the value the better, with a maximum value of 100.

The sum of all these values provides the subtotal to the right of the table. These subtotals are adjusted to allow for the dropout (or accretion) rate: this score is based on the number of students leaving the university (negative values) before the end of their degree or entering the university (positive values) from somewhere else. The final scores after adjustment are presented in the column to the extreme right of the table, and it is these that are used to rank the institutions. The table also compares the rank in 2003 against the rank in 2002.

There are a number of features of interest concerning the university league table. To begin with, unlike the Premier League of football clubs, there are no direct rewards for finishing as high up the table as possible, and neither are there direct negative repercussions for finishing at the bottom. Government in the UK, still the major source of funds (for research or teaching) for the university sector, does not use tables such as these for allocating resources, although it does employ various indicators of its own. Instead the raison d'être of the table is to inform choice amongst those opting to go to university in the UK, be they from the UK or from outside. Therefore, the indirect consequence of being at the top of the table is that more people would want to opt for that institution and hence provide that university with a better choice of which applicants to select. Quite frankly, not everyone opting to go to Cambridge (the university at the top) will be offered a place there. Universities would obviously want to be as high up the table as possible, and this can be a powerful driver for institutional policy and management.

Second, and on a more technical level, notice how the scores are weighted differently. For example, teaching quality has a maximum of 250 points, whereas research quality has a maximum of 200 points. Together these comprise nearly a half (450) of the total of 1,000 points, but why should teaching be higher than research? The rationale is a logical one given that the table is intended for those choosing a university for a degree course and hence it is assumed that they would be more interested in teaching than research quality. Research is included as it is a key activity of universities and also because there is an assumed link between the quality of research and the quality of the teaching so that better research is associated with better teaching. Please note that this is an assumed relationship, and one which is disputed. Also, why the balance of 200 and 250? Why not 100 and 350? Similarly, note the emphasis on entry requirements (maximum of 250 points), while the remaining three indicators included in the table (employment rate, degree class awarded, student:staff ratio) only accrue a maximum of 300 points together.

The key point is that the weighting of the various components is a subjective decision, based in part upon the intended consumer of the table. Different weightings of the components will alter the ranking in the league table. Indeed, unlike the Premier League table for football, there are many such 'league tables' for universities in the UK published in the media, and institutions could find themselves being ranked very differently depending upon what is included, how it is measured and how the components are weighted. Football clubs just play football and everyone (players, managers, shareholders, supporters etc) knows exactly what they want – to win – even if they don't quite agree how to achieve it! By way of contrast, universities have to do many things (teach, research, engage with the local community), and what is desirable for the 'consumer' (government, industry, students etc) can change over time and indeed space.

University league tables can be dismissed by some given that the majority of the age group (18–21 year-olds) in the UK who make up the bulk of the university population still do not go to university. The government wishes to raise the proportion of 18–21-years-olds going to university to 50 per cent (one in every two), but at the time of writing the figure is around 30 per cent (less than one in every three). For the majority of the population, university tables probably do not matter a great deal. However, other levels of education in the UK also use league tables to measure performance and inform choice. For example, there are league tables for primary schools aimed at everyone who has a child of school age in the country. The primary school league tables are compiled on the basis of scores allocated by teachers to pupils in three subject areas deemed important by the government: English, mathematics and science. The figures are aggregated for all the pupils taking the tests and reported on a scale where the maximum achievement is 100 per cent. In the 2003 tables, the national averages were 75 per cent for English, 73 per cent for maths and 87 per cent for science

An example of a primary school league table for the town in which I live (Reading, Berkshire) is provided as Table 1.3, and my children attend one of these schools. In Table 1.3 the results of the 2002 and 2003 assessments are provided, along with the average over the two years, which forms the basis

Table 1.3 *League table of primary schools in Reading, UK, based on aggregate scores over 2 years (2002 and 2003)*

Rank	Name of primary school	2002 E	2002 M	2002 S	Aggregate	2003 E	2003 M	2003 S	Aggregate	Average (2002 to 2003)
1	Caversham	92	95	97	284	94	87	98	279	282
2	Churchend	90	81	97	268	95	93	98	286	277
3	Caversham Park	69	69	100	238	100	97	100	297	268
4	St Anne's Catholic	87	77	90	254	91	85	97	273	264
5	Park Lane	82	86	91	259	86	85	96	267	263
6	The Hill	79	85	98	262	84	80	97	261	262
7	St John's C of E	89	89	97	275	86	66	97	249	262
8	St Mary and All Saints Church of England	75	75	89	239	90	83	93	266	253
9	Alfred Sutton	80	85	86	251	81	76	93	250	251
10	Coley	77	73	95	245	82	76	94	252	249
11	St Martin's Catholic	75	70	90	235	83	87	91	261	248
12	Emmer Green	67	73	86	226	80	86	93	259	243
13	Katesgrove	53	93	97	243	68	80	92	240	242
14	Christ The King Catholic	83	83	94	260	71	71	81	223	242
15	Ranikhet	77	65	100	242	68	79	93	240	241
16	Redlands	71	77	84	232	74	77	84	235	234
17	Manor	71	71	93	235	70	76	85	231	233
18	English Martyrs' Catholic	83	81	96	260	65	61	73	199	230
19	E P Collier	68	60	80	208	95	70	85	250	229
20	Micklands	73	69	71	213	83	68	93	244	229
21	Southcote	77	68	90	235	68	63	91	222	229
22	Battle	67	65	88	220	58	53	95	206	213
23	Moorlands	77	50	86	213	70	54	80	204	209
24	Thameside	67	49	76	192	72	57	89	218	205
25	Wilson	76	62	90	228	50	50	80	180	204
26	Geoffrey Field Junior	54	66	92	212	61	45	87	193	203
27	Upcroft	64	66	84	214	68	45	78	191	203
28	St Michael's	47	34	81	162	76	67	88	231	197

Rank	Name of primary school	2002 E	M	S	Aggregate	2003 E	M	S	Aggregate	Average (2002 to 2003)
29	Oxford Road Community	53	53	66	172	64	56	60	180	176
30	New Christ Church Church of England	68	37	68	173	59	41	59	159	166
31	New Town	43	47	70	160	61	45	64	170	165
32	Whitley Park Junior	38	49	68	155	51	44	69	164	160
33	The Ridgeway	54	51	68	173	54	39	54	147	160
34	Coley Park	32	27	55	114	63	47	63	173	144
35	George Palmer	38	20	47	105	41	26	52	119	112

Notes: E = score for English; M = score for mathematics; S = score for science.
The score for each school in the table is the average of the scores for English, maths and science.

Table 1.4 League table for primary schools in Reading, UK, based on the difference between 2002 and 2003 aggregate scores

Rank	Name of primary school	2002 E	M	S	Aggregate	2003 E	M	S	Aggregate	Average (2002 to 2003)
1	St Michael's	47	34	81	162	76	67	88	231	69
2	Caversham Park	69	69	100	238	100	97	100	297	59
3	Coley Park	32	27	55	114	63	47	63	173	59
4	E P Collier	68	50	80	208	95	70	85	250	42
5	Emmer Green	67	73	86	225	80	86	93	259	33
6	Micklands	73	69	71	213	83	58	93	244	31
7	St Mary and All Saints Church of England	75	75	89	239	90	83	93	266	27
8	St Martin's Catholic	75	70	90	235	83	87	91	261	26
9	Thameside	67	49	76	192	72	57	89	218	26
10	St Anne's Catholic	87	77	90	254	91	85	97	273	19
11	Churchend	90	81	97	268	95	53	98	286	18
12	George Palmer	38	20	47	105	41	26	52	119	14
13	New Town	43	47	70	160	61	45	64	170	10
14	Whitley Park Junior	38	49	68	155	51	44	69	164	9
15	Oxford Road Community	53	53	66	172	64	56	60	180	8
16	Park Lane	82	86	91	259	86	85	96	267	8

Table 1.4 *Continued*

Rank	Name of primary school	2002			Aggregate	2003			Aggregate	Average (2002 to 2003)
		E	M	S		E	M	S		
17	Coley	77	73	95	245	82	76	94	252	7
18	Redlands	71	77	84	232	74	77	84	235	3
19	Alfred Sutton	80	85	86	251	81	76	93	250	−1
20	The Hill	79	85	98	262	84	80	97	261	−1
21	Ranikhet	77	65	100	242	68	79	93	240	−2
22	Katesgrove	53	93	97	243	68	80	92	240	−3
23	Manor	71	71	93	235	70	76	85	231	−4
24	Caversham	92	95	97	284	94	87	98	279	−5
25	Moorlands	77	50	86	213	70	54	80	204	−9
26	Southcote	77	68	90	235	68	63	91	222	−13
27	Battle	67	65	88	220	58	53	95	206	−14
28	New Christ Church Church of England	68	37	68	173	59	41	59	159	−14
29	Geoffrey Field Junior	54	66	92	212	61	45	87	193	−19
30	Upcroft	64	66	84	214	68	45	78	191	−23
31	St John's C of E	89	89	97	275	86	66	97	249	−26
32	The Ridgeway	54	51	68	173	54	39	54	147	−26
33	Christ The King Catholic	83	83	94	260	71	71	81	223	−37
34	Wilson	76	62	90	228	50	50	80	180	−48
35	English Martyrs' Catholic	83	81	96	260	65	61	73	199	−61

Notes: E = score for English; M = score for mathematics; S = score for science.
The score for each school in the table is the average of the scores for English, maths and science.

of the ranking. In practice, a separate table is produced for each year, and one can rank the schools depending upon the difference in score over the two years. The results of this change are shown in Table 1.4, where positive values mean that the school has 'improved' while negative values mean that the school has 'worsened'. In Table 1.4, 18 of the schools have 'improved' while 17 have worsened, and note that the ranking is quite different from that of Table 1.3. Different schools can claim to be the 'best' depending upon whether 'best' is based on absolute rank in one year, the average of two years or the extent of improvement over the two years. But of course with such a time-series style, much depends upon whether the form of the tests has been kept uniform between the two years. If there have been changes in the way the tests were applied or assessed, then this can result in an apparent improvement or worsening as an artefact rather than being due to any real change in the quality of education.

While university league tables have their critics and supporters, and the arguments on both sides can be fierce, the debates are often more intense when it comes to primary school tables. Perhaps this is because they impact upon more families or perhaps it is because they are based on assessments of young children at a critical stage in their personal development. The following quotations are taken from just one media story accompanying the release of the 2003 primary school tables[1]. Note that the quotations are from both 'winners' (such as a primary school in Newcastle-upon-Tyne) and those more hostile to the use of such tables:

> *It's the most wonderful acknowledgement of everything that we do . . . And it defeats the stereotype that people in inner-city Newcastle have low aspirations and low attainment* (Sandra Marsden, headteacher, Delaval Community Primary School, Newcastle-upon-Tyne).

> *It's boosted the whole school's morale* (parent, Delaval Community Primary School in Newcastle-upon-Tyne).

> *I think personally that I could do without them. Teacher assessment is pretty spot-on now and I think it is more realistic than tests done on one day* (Sandra Jones, Werrington Primary, Cambridgeshire).

> *It doesn't tell you anything about the true performance of the school. [League tables] fail to show the strengths of the school and are misleading because some people will read them and think this isn't a good school . . . If they are here to stay, they have to be reformed* (Cecelia Davies, headteacher at Moor Nook Community Primary School, Preston).

> *Value added tables shuffle the winners and losers without addressing the fundamental flaws behind the tables in the first place. A school can receive a glowing inspection report and yet be at the bottom of the tables and suffer as a result* (Doug McAvoy, National Union of Teachers (NUT)).

However, despite the views of the teaching community, the government's view is that such tables are here to stay, and the discussion is about how they can be improved rather than how they can be replaced:

> We have always said that we will listen to the views of heads, teachers and parents about how the performance tables can provide a more comprehensive and rounded picture of school performance (David Miliband, School Standards Minister).

The above three examples of different forms of league tables illustrate how indicators of performance and league tables are increasingly being used in important aspects of our lives (although admittedly these examples relate to my life). They do have a basic appeal in that they crystallize complex information about complex issues into single numbers that conveniently allow a ranking. Parents and university aspirants can look at the tables and use them as an input into their decision making. It is not intended by those compiling such indicators and tables that they be the only such input. Aspiring students are encouraged to visit universities and assess for themselves other features such as location, education, sports facilities and accommodation. Similarly, parents visit schools to see how it 'feels' to them, whether the staff are friendly and what facilities are available. Indicators are a tool, but they can be a powerful one.

While the three examples have been selected on the basis of their importance to me, it would not be difficult to come up with examples relevant to someone else. The school and university league tables would apply to many others who have children or relatives attending or due to attend these institutions, but there are many other examples including applications in measuring performance of local government and in health care (eg hospital performance, residential homes for the elderly). Even if not expressed in a 'league table' format, indicators of performance can be found in many aspects of our lives.

Lest those working in the private sector think that indicators do not apply to them, I would point out that company share price is an important (if not critical) indicator of performance. Many (not all) companies will sell shares and these are traded on the stock exchange. Investors will expect to see an annual return on their shares, and if the price of shares falls below and remains below what they initially paid, shareholders' concern would be understandable. The value of a share is driven by supply and demand, and poor company performance (ie poor profits) will be reflected in the share price. At an aggregate level, there are indices such as the FTSE 100 (pronounced 'footsee 100') for the London stock exchange which gauge the share values of a number of companies deemed by experts to be important in an economy (Box 1.1). Such indices can provide a barometer of the business environment, but, of course, in part, share values are based on people's perception of how companies are performing and may not necessarily reflect their actual performance. A company's share price can be overvalued if expectations do not match performance.

Box 1.1 *The FTSE 100 Index*

The FTSE 100 Index based on the share price of the largest 100 companies (by market capitalization) listed on the London Stock Exchange. It is produced by a company called the FTSE Group, a leading producer of financial indices, which describes itself as:

> *FTSE Group is the index provider of choice for the world's leading investors. Indices are our specialty.* (FTSE Group website www.ftse.com).

The FTSE 100 is a barometer of the performance of these 100 companies and through them the UK economy. It was first calculated in January 1984, and began with a 'base level' of 1000 points. Prior to 1984 there were other indices such as the FT30 (created in the 1930s) and the FTAW All-Share (created in 1962 and still used). Values of the FTSE 100 since April 1984 are shown in the graph.

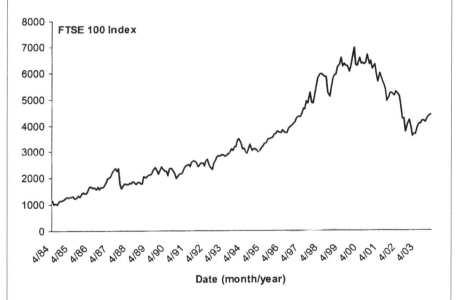

Over this period the highest value of the FTSE 100 Index was 6930.2 points (achieved on the 30th December 1999), but note the marked downturn between 2000 and 2003.

The theory behind the calculation of the FTSE 100 (and similar indices of stock value) is shown below for five companies (A to E) with different numbers of shares per company being traded on the stock exchange. The table shows changes in total market value of the shares (number of shares multiplied by the value of each share) over just 3 days. The index is calculated for days two and three, and reflects the change in market value of the shares for these six companies.

▶

Company	Number of shares	Value of each share (£)	Market value (£)
A	40	5	200
B	20	10	200
C	10	8	80
D	30	6	180
E	50	4	200
		Aggregate market value end day 1 (£)	**860**

Company	Number of shares	Value of each share (£)	Market value (£)
A	40	6	240
B	20	12	240
C	10	10	100
D	30	7	210
E	50	6	300
		Aggregate market value end day 2 (£)	**1,090**
		Index value	**1,267**

Company	Number of shares	Value of each share (£)	Market value (£)
A	40	8	320
B	20	17	340
C	10	12	120
D	30	10	300
E	50	9	450
		Aggregate market value end day 3 (£)	**1,530**
		Index value	**1,778**

The sum of these for the five companies gives us the 'aggregate market value' at the end of the day. Assuming that the starting point of the index is '1000' points then we find the index at the end of each day as follows:

$$\text{Index} = \frac{\text{Aggregate market value at end of day}}{\text{Aggregate market value at end of previous day}} \times \text{previous value of index}$$

Therefore, at the end of day 2 we have:

$$\text{Index} = \frac{1090}{860} \times 1000 = \textbf{1267 points}$$

and at the end of day 3:

$$\text{Index} = \frac{1530}{1090} \times 1267 = 1778 \text{ points}$$

The increase in the index from 1267 to 1778 points suggests that the value of the companies is growing rapidly, and given that these companies are major players in the economy then it suggests that the economy as a whole is also doing well. If the aggregate market value is lower than that of the previous day then the index will decline.

However, this explanation is highly simplistic. In practice there can be a number of complicating factors, including the companies that are included in the index. Some of these may merge, go out of business or no longer be deemed important in terms of their capitalization. New businesses may emerge, and there is constant need to review the constituents of the index. With the FTSE 100 these are reviewed four times a year – in March, June, September and December.

Given the popularity of indicators to reduce complexity, it is not surprising to see them being applied in development. But much depends here upon what development means, and before we can explore the creation and use of development indicators in the following chapters, we first need to explore some of the changing fashions in development theory. The following sections will briefly explore some of the contested meanings and theories of development.

MODERNIST DEVELOPMENT

'Development' as we know it today is a post-World War II phenomenon that has passed through various forms and fashions. There were a number of reasons for the birth of development with the end of World War II, besides the obvious soul searching as to the causes and after-effects of the war. There were perhaps three main factors at play, and these no doubt interacted:

- the rise of the US as the dominant industrial, political and military power
- the rise of the USSR as a competing power to the US
- agitation for political independence in colonized countries.

The post-war period saw increasing concerns in the capitalist West over the growing power and influence of the form of communism espoused by the USSR and its satellites. An obvious 'battle ground' for this competition was the colonies of Britain, France, Belgium, Portugal and others, most of whom were in the capitalist bloc. These colonies were beginning to campaign for their independence, and the US response was to use development assistance programmes to prevent the spread of communism by making it less appealing. It is often convenient to talk of 'starting points' for ideas, and there is a commonly expressed notion that the starting point of what we know as development was the inaugural speech of President Truman on 20 January 1949. However, while Truman's speech may be regarded as a turning point in development, it should be remembered that development is much older than this. In previous centuries, theories of development were based, to a greater or lesser extent, on economic growth. Protagonists in these debates were typically labelled as 'political economists' and 'neoclassical economists'. Before 1870, the political economy approach held sway, with its emphasis on a distribution of wealth between the different socio-economic classes of society. After 1870, the neoclassical theory dominated. Here the emphasis was not so much on the social relations of production, but on how to distribute scarce resources among unlimited consumers. Neoclassical approaches use mathematics to develop predictive universal theories, and goods must be valued with a view to future utility not past labour. Neoclassical economics is seen by its proponents as a science, and indeed can almost be thought of as a branch of pure mathematics. This view is still dominant and has grown dramatically over the past century.

Truman's 1949 speech[2] is replete with statements addressing the perceived dangers from communism:

> . . . the United States and other like-minded nations find themselves directly opposed by a regime with contrary aims and a totally different concept of life.
>
> That regime adheres to a false philosophy which purports to offer freedom, security and greater opportunity to mankind. Misled by that philosophy, many peoples have sacrificed their liberties only to learn to their sorrow that deceit and mockery, poverty and tyranny, are their reward.
>
> That false philosophy is communism.

Following this there is a statement of Truman's programme for peace and freedom, which stresses four major courses of action that his presidency will pursue during his tenure. The fourth one of these is often taken to be the starting point of modern development:

> Fourth, we must embark on a bold new program for making the benefits of our scientific advances and industrial progress available for the improvement and growth of underdeveloped areas.
>
> More than half the people of the world are living in conditions approaching misery. Their food is inadequate. They are victims of disease. Their economic life is primitive and stagnant. Their poverty is a handicap and a threat both to them and to more prosperous areas.
>
> For the first time in history, humanity possesses the knowledge and skill to relieve the suffering of these people.
>
> The United States is pre-eminent among nations in the development of industrial and scientific techniques. The material resources which we can afford

to use for assistance of other peoples are limited. But our imponderable resources in technical knowledge are constantly growing and are inexhaustible.

I believe that we should make available to peace-loving peoples the benefits of our store of technical knowledge in order to help them realize their aspirations for a better life. And, in cooperation with other nations, we should foster capital investment in areas needing development.

Note the emphasis on applying technical knowledge and capital investment. This period of development following the war is equated with what we now call the 'modernization' approach, and has an underlying and pervasive assumption that industrialization of developing countries should follow the path of the West. While it was acknowledged that wealth may be unevenly distributed in the societies being 'developed', the riches would percolate down to all strata of the society. The result, at least in theory, was a sort of progressive movement towards technologically and institutionally more complex and integrated forms of 'modern' society (Cowen and Shenton, 1996).

While Truman regarded the dismantling of colonial rule as important:

The old imperialism – exploitation for foreign profit – has no place in our plans. What we envisage is a program of development based on the concepts of democratic fair-dealing.

there is resonance with the notion of trusteeship expressed by the Imperialist powers. These powers had increasingly rationalized their empires in terms of a sort of enlightened management, until the local populations were ready to take the reins. Modernization was seen as a means for accelerating this process, and from the late 1940s through the 1960s there was a wave of independence from colonial rule.

Modernization was implemented through an encouragement of trade in commodities and through a series of interventions involving the transfer of technology, knowledge, resources and organizational skills from the more 'developed' world to the less 'developed' parts. There were a number of 'multilateral' institutions that played an increasingly important role in this process, and continue to do so today. The 'Bretton Woods' institutions (named after the conference venue in New Hampshire where their creation was agreed), the International Bank for Reconstruction and Development (the World Bank) and International Monetary Fund (IMF), were born on 22 July 1944 and became operational in 1946. The United Nations, the replacement for the pre-World War II 'League of Nations', was created in 1945, and has various specialist sections such as the United Nations Development Programme (UNDP), Food and Agriculture Organization (FAO) and the United Nations Environment Programme (UNEP). The US paid the largest contribution to these institutions and, as a result, had much influence over what they did and how. The US's support for colonial disengagement backed up with development assistance was thought by them to be entirely consistent with a mutually beneficial expansion of trade, the pursuit of humanitarian goals, and the fostering of democratic political institutions.

MODERNIZATION TO DEPENDENCY

It rapidly became clear that the 'modernization' approach to development, while appealing in its relative simplicity, had its problems. Various experiences from the 1950s onwards indicated that the expected prosperity was not materializing and indeed the poor were sometimes becoming poorer. While some developing economies did experience growth, this was often not sustainable.

An alternative theory for development was proposed, which was in many ways the mirror image of modernization – dependency. Many of the originators of Dependency Theory were influenced by Marxist theories of capitalist imperialism, and the emphasis shifted more to an understanding of disparities in levels of development by examining how certain regions or sections of the economy are transformed and exploited for the benefit of outside interests. The argument is that, although the colonial pattern of direct exploitation of territories for the benefit of the imperial power had been ostensibly dismantled, what had replaced it was a sort of neocolonialism with exploitation and notions of core–periphery still very much intact. Wallerstein (1974), in his 'world system' theory variant of dependency theory, traced the origins of the world market and argued that the core areas of the system exploit the peripheral areas by a process of unequal exchange. In effect 'the dependency school of thought ... holds that the rich are the cause of the problems of the poor, and that under-development is a historical process, not an original condition' (Othick, 1983, p68).

However, while dependency theory offers a plausible, although incomplete, explanation of underdevelopment, it provides no workable solution to the problems of addressing it, other than promoting sometimes vaguely worded notions of self-sufficiency. Perhaps this is not surprising given that the focus is upon nation states and world systems as units for analysis rather than upon people. Nevertheless, dependency theory has been helpful in highlighting the situation whereby the power is at the centre while the periphery is weak, and has had significant political impact, especially among the so-called peripheral countries where it has provided theoretical justification for nationalistic struggles against imperialism.

There were two major attempts in the 1970s to use the lessons offered by dependency theory to build new and more independent economies: Julius Nyerere's Tanzania and Michael Manley's Jamaica. Tanzania, during the 1970s, became something of a development strategy 'laboratory', which strongly emphasized the 'self-reliant' and 'socialist' aspects propounded by dependency theorists. Industrialization was a key feature of the government's new policy that would lead to national 'self reliance'. The ideology and process was referred to as *Ujamaa* (Brotherhood), and its ethos can be summarized as follows:

> Both the rich and the poor were completely secure in [precolonial] African society. Nobody starved, either of food or of human dignity, because he lacked personal wealth; he could depend on the wealth possessed by the community of which he was a member. That was socialism. That is socialism. (Julius Nyerere, 1966)[3]

The experiment included the resettlement of people to new communally owned villages with communally owned land for agriculture. Between 1967 and 1976 more than 90 per cent of Tanzania's rural population was resettled, largely voluntarily at first, but later this became coercive (especially between 1974 and 1976; Schraeder, 2000). The Tanzanian experiment eventually failed (Blomstrom and Hettne, 1984).

NEOPOPULISM, NEOLIBERALISM AND ANTI-DEVELOPMENT

While dependency theory has been influential in allowing a better understanding of core–periphery relationships, modernization theory continued to dominate up to the 1980s and, some would say, to the present day (Simon, 2003). The 1970s and early 1980s witnessed a rapid spread of so-called 'development projects', designed to deliver development to an area in a relatively short period of time (often 5 years). These were typically referred to as 'blueprint projects', largely because the objectives and tasks were set out in a detailed blueprint before the onset of the project and were expected to be mechanically followed during its lifetime. Such projects were modernist in soul. Many of the projects were 'integrated' in the sense that although they were focused on agriculture, for example, they also had elements that dealt with infrastructure, water supply, primary health care etc. This broader and more interdisciplinary vision of development also fed through into new perspectives on issues such as poverty. For example, 1976 saw the rise of the 'basic needs' approach promoted by the International Labour Organization (ILO) and others encompassing access to key resources such as water, education and health care, and moving away from seeing poverty purely in monetary terms. In the 1970s a key conference on the human environment was held in Stockholm, spurred by increasing concerns over resource depletion, particularly energy resources following a significant increase in oil prices.

The 1980s and 1990s were marked by the retreat of the state, often manifested by a reduction in the public sector and the rise of accountability and 'value for money' in the remaining services kept in the public sphere.

This was a time when free market philosophies (neoliberalism, with 'neo' meaning 'new') came to dominate the development agenda. The 1980s saw the introduction of Structural Adjustment Programmes (SAPs) designed to force through free market philosophies and push back the borders of the state. Yet, while SAPs were applied at the national level, there was a parallel emphasis at the micro-level, with issues such as the importance of participation, credit and gender coming to the fore. This period also saw the rise of the non-governmental organization (NGO) as a significant player in development, with a variety of NGOs often taking over from the state in areas of service provision.

The 1980s and 1990s were the age of 'micro-intervention' and 'people orientated' (neopopulist) approaches as opposed to grand development theories. The actor oriented theory (Long and Long, 1992) stressed the obvious fact that society is composed of people (actors) who are thinking agents capable of strategizing and finding space for manoeuvre in the situations they face and of manipulating resources and constraints. Terms such as 'empowerment' and 'partnership' became fashionable. The outcome is that people are allowed to play a role, not just in the 'doing' of a development project but in setting the agenda as to what development means. This allowance for deconstruction of meaning at local levels is a radical departure from the structural approaches to development, and especially from the top-down and technocratic assumptions that rest behind modernization. Stakeholder participation became a central requirement of any development activity. It even began to be re-exported back to the developed world which had promoted it in the first place (Buhler et al, 2002). Terms such as post-structuralism, post-modernism and even post-development (the 'postist' school of Blaikie, 2000) became popular.

Within this maelstrom, and responding to the perceived lack of success of many of the development projects, some went further and began to deconstruct power relationships in development to a greater extent than even the dependency theorists had suggested. They came to the conclusion that development itself can almost be seen as tyrannical with resistance to it being necessary. This is referred to as the anti-development school of thought (Escobar, 1992, 1995):

> *Development, thus, must be seen as a historically specific, even peculiar, experience; it must be defamiliarized so that its naturalness can be suspended in the eyes of theorists and practitioners. Resistance to development and the repeated failure of many development projects provide important elements for this task. Is it then possible to say that development is a 'historical necessity'?* (Escobar, 1991, p676)

Consider also, the following comment from the late Professor Claude Ake, one of Africa's most famous political scientists:

Development strategies in Africa, with minor exceptions, have tended to be strategies by which the few use the many for their purposes. They are uncompromisingly top-down. There is not, and never has been, popular participation in political and economic decision-making ... development has turned into concerted aggression against the common people, producing a theatre of alienation. (Prof. Claude Ake, cited in Davidson, 1992)

However, anti-development does have much in common with dependency theory – both offer little practical advice other than the need to stress the importance of local knowledge, interpretation of need and action. It also tends to oversimplify what are in practice a diverse range of development practices, at least some of which are founded on participatory approaches. The following quotation is replete with the need for local 'deconstruction':

The defense of the local as a prerequisite to engaging with the global; the critique of the group's own situation, values and practices as a way of clarifying and strengthening identity; the opposition to modernising development; and the formulation of visions and concrete proposals in the context of existing constraints, these seem to be the principal elements for the collective construction of alternatives that these [Third World] groups seem to be pursuing. (Escobar, 1995, p226)

Yet do 'local' actors always have the power to change matters and overcome 'existing constraints', and is it not a convenient form of justifying abstention on the part of the developed world (Buhler et al, 2002)? After all, 'adopting the privilege of being "anti-development" is not, in my view, politically or morally viable when sitting in an "over-developed" social and individual location' (Fagan, 1999, p180).

SUSTAINABLE DEVELOPMENT

The 1980s also saw the rise of another approach to development that spanned all of the above – sustainable development. While sustainable community projects such as 'Sustainable Seattle' rapidly gained popularity, in 1987 the highly influential World Commission on Environment and Development (WCED) produced perhaps the most widely quoted definition of sustainable development:

Development that meets the needs of current generations without compromising the ability of future generations to meet their needs and aspirations. (WCED, 1987)

This really was different. First it stressed the importance of the micro-level and the role of the individual in development, and in that sense was in tune

Figure 1.1 *Sustainable development, encompassing concerns for the community, economy and the environment*

with the general post-structural trend of the period. The individual was seen as central, but one could scale-up from that to, quite literally, the globe and thereby encompass the macro-theories as well as the post- and even anti-development schools! The idea is that we are all part of the same global village and, given this interaction, what meanings can we apply to 'local' or the 'West'? Unlike all of the other theories that are based on a developed–developing axis, the ideas encapsulated within sustainable development have as much application to the developed as to the developing world. Older ideas, such as modernization and dependency, did not disappear. Instead they became reframed within the notion of sustainability.

The all-encompassing nature of sustainable development – multi-scale, multi-disciplinary, multi-perspective, multi-definition – have combined to ensure that it is perhaps the ultimate culmination to development theories, and Figure 1.1 is the classic representation of sustainable development as the meeting point of three interlocking circles representing the economy, the community and the environment. However, despite the centrality of protecting resources and the environment for future generations, sustainable development does not imply stasis. Human societies cannot and must not remain static as our aspirations and expectations constantly shift. In human development terms, sustainability means that we meet these changing needs without reducing our capability to do so. Yet it can sometimes appear as if sustainable development is more about protecting the environment and natural resources than it is about people, and some have felt moved to make the priorities clear. The following is the UNDP's spin on the WCED definition given above:

> *the development process should meet the needs of the present generation without compromising the options of future generations. However, the concept of sustainable development is much broader than the protection of natural resources and the physical environment. It includes the protection of human lives in the future. After all, it is people, not trees, whose future options need to be protected.* (UNDP HDR, 1990, p61–62)

There have been two major UNEP sponsored 'Earth Summits' on sustainable development that have been highly influential. The first took place in Rio de Janeiro in 1992 and the second in Johannesburg in 2002, and governments from the developed and developing world signed up to concrete steps that must be taken to implement sustainable development. The following quotations have been selected from the website of the Johannesburg conference, and again note the emphasis on making peoples' lives better as well as protecting the environment.

> *The Summit reaffirmed sustainable development as a central element of the international agenda and gave new impetus to global action to fight poverty and protect the environment.*

> *The understanding of sustainable development was broadened and strengthened as a result of the Summit, particularly the important linkages between poverty, the environment and the use of natural resources.*

> *Governments agreed to and reaffirmed a wide range of concrete commitments and targets for action to achieve more effective implementation of sustainable development objectives.* (www.johannesburgsummit.org/)

INDICATORS OF DEVELOPMENT

Given the complex and evolving terrain of theories of development, what underlies them? Do they have anything in common? As David Simon (2003) points out, one could probably apply a broad definition of the type 'development constitutes a diverse and multifaceted process of predominantly positive change in the quality of life for individuals and society in both material and non-material respects'. But what exactly are 'positive changes' and 'quality of life', and who should define these? While one can try and pin these down further, ultimately it would appear that we are still left with a value judgement. Yet these are decisions that have to be made by someone, be it through a classic top-down modernization processes or via the local actions favoured by the anti-development group. To act effectively we have to have some idea where we want to get to and not just how we want to get there. In that sense, all of these development theories and all the means by which we try to 'do' them have one thing in common – they all have indicators of process (how we are getting there) and achievement (whether we have got there). Granted that many, if not the vast majority, of these will be qualitative in nature – it 'feels' that we have done the right thing – rather than quantitative – we can measure whether we have done the right thing –they are indicators nonetheless (de Greene, 1994).

> *Indicators are used by people on a day-to-day basis for making decisions. A blue sky in the morning indicates that we should wear a T-shirt because the weather will be good. All around us there are indicators that tell us something about the state of the world. The media and television are littered with indicators.* (Acton, 2000)

Indeed de Greene (1994) suggests that one of the 'most successful and useful indicators of socio-economic change appears to be the subjective index of consumer confidence or sentiment'.

Managers and policy makers tend to select indicators with characteristics such as the following:

- **Specific** – must clearly relate to outcomes that are being sought, although some also point out the advantages of indicators that reflect many more facets than those they directly measure (Kao and Liu, 1984).
- **Measurable** – implies that it must be a quantitative indicator, although 'scores' or 'ranks' of more qualitative attributes are also acceptable.
- **Usable** – indicator must facilitate usage in terms of guiding management and/or policy.
- **Sensitive** – must readily change as circumstances change; ideally there should be a minimum time lag so that as circumstances change the indicator will also change.
- **Available** – it must be a relatively straightforward task to collect the necessary data for the indicator, even if it has to be collected (primary data) rather than being already available (secondary data). There are dangers here though. Care needs to be taken that the indicator does not become 'data driven' (Bayless and Bayless, 1982; Wish, 1986).
- **Cost effective** – it should not be expensive to obtain the necessary data.

The indicator tables for primary schools and universities given earlier meet these requirements. However, clearly there are potential trade-offs over what is or is not a suitable indicator. It is not inconceivable that in a desire to find suitable indicators using a list of characteristics such as that above that compromises will be made. For example, with the final characteristic, which calls for cost-effectiveness, there may be a tendency to select indicators for which it is relatively cheap and easy to collect data rather than more technically appropriate yet expensive alternatives. In turn, this could shape the target that is being aimed for. The result is an interaction between what we want to achieve and the means by which we measure this achievement such that the former can influence the latter rather than vice versa.

A further obvious concern with the above list that has to be mentioned is the risk of falsification. There are various dimensions to falsification, including the corruption of data to present the picture as better or worse than it is. An alternative is not to falsify the data, but to select indicators and/or methodologies that it is known will prove success/failure in a particular endeavour. Biased (whether conscious or unconscious) sample selection, from either secondary or primary data sets, is one way of doing this, but it can also be achieved through selective analysis and presentation. When presentation of results is by league tables, there may be motives other than pride for aiming as high as possible. For example, contractors may wish to 'prove' their success in one development project in order to secure further funding. It is worth remembering that indicators reflect the people who create and use them, and can be imperfect and corruptible as a result.

SUMMARY

This chapter has shown how indicators can be used to simplify complexity. Universities and primary schools are complex institutions and education, be it at tertiary or primary level, is an intricate field with many dimensions. Yet people have to have information both to frame policy, to manage or simply to make choices. Condensing this complexity down to single numbers or, even better, to league table rankings is attractive. Tables 1.2 to 1.4 may look complex, but there are many institutions presented here and each institution only occupies a single line of the table. The University of Cambridge (www.cam.ac.uk) is one of the oldest in the world, has 31 colleges, over a hundred departments, employs approximately 7,000 people, has even more students (16,500) from all over the world, teaches a wide variety of degree programmes (undergraduate and postgraduate) and is engaged in a wealth of research activity that responds to the demands of many different funding agencies. This is a complex, diverse, flexible and evolving institution, yet in Table 1.2 its performance is measured by only six figures and ultimately these have been condensed down to one: 971.

Indicators, quantitative and qualitative, are obvious tools to employ in development. Again we are dealing with complexity and a pressing need to simplify in order to act. This is true whether the process is top-down and based on modernization or bottom-up and locally led. In all these situations we need to know when we have achieved what we want to achieve, and expressed in those terms it is clear that even the anti-development school will have their indicators of process and impact. Neoliberal economic indicators will stress levels of imports, exports, government expenditure as a proportion of GDP etc, while neopopulist indicators could include extent of participation and more local achievements. While all of the approaches to development will incorporate indicators, they will obviously need to be different. There are numerous options, but what separates the various approaches is not just the need for indicators, but who makes the decisions over what to chose? This is of critical importance, as those who control the means by which success or failure is acknowledged set the agenda for the whole process. The examples provided in Chapters 2, 3 and 4 are all widely-publicized examples of 'top-down' development indicators and indices, and have been purposely selected to tease out the issues involved.

2 DEVELOPMENT INDICATORS: ECONOMICS

INTRODUCTION

As discussed in the previous chapter, many of the early theories of development were in essence theories centred on notions of economic growth and, in the 1950s, development was synonymous with economic growth. The idea was a simple one – economic growth leads to more income for people, which in turn leads to less poverty and a better standard of living (Veenhoven, 1996). While distribution of wealth may not necessarily be a direct concern in economic growth, there is an assumption that it will 'trickle down' within the economy. The result was that up to the late 1960s, development was measured largely in terms of income per member of the population (income/capita; Othick, 1983).

An apparent obsession with economic indicators is perhaps understandable given the impact that economic depressions have had on people's lives. Prior to the 1930s, policy makers had to manage economies with limited and fragmentary information. The Great Depression (early 1930s, with the worst year in 1932) underlined the problems of attempting to manage an economy with incomplete data, and it is very easy for us living at the start of the 21st century to forget how bad the Great Depression was for those who lived through it. It was much worse than the earlier depression of 1873–1896 and no continent was untouched. The result was high unemployment and a steep rise in the cost of living, with the inevitable outcome of poverty. Indeed, the Great Depression was one of the precursors of the coming to power of the Nazi Party in Germany, with all the horrors that were unleashed in the 1930s first in Germany, and in the 1940s throughout Europe and the world.

One of the other outcomes of the Great Depression was a realization amongst those charged with managing economies that they needed a system of national accounting. The following quotation is a poignant one:

> *One reads with dismay of Presidents Hoover and then Roosevelt designing policies to combat the Great Depression of the 1930s on the basis of such sketchy data as stock price indices, freight car loadings, and incomplete indices of industrial production.*

The fact was that comprehensive measures of national income and output did not exist at the time.

The Depression, and with it the growing role of government in the economy, emphasized the need for such measures and led to the development of a comprehensive set of national income accounts (Richard T Froyen)[1]

The Nobel Prize winner Simon Kuznets (1901–1985), a Professor of Economics at the Universities of Pennsylvania, Johns Hopkins and Harvard, is usually given the credit for the creation of our modern system of national accounting (de Greene, 1994). It is not possible here to go into systems of national accounting in any depth, and instead only a few indicators designed to measure economic performance will be covered in this chapter.

ECONOMIC ACTIVITY: THE GROSS DOMESTIC PRODUCT

Perhaps the most well known of the indicators used to gauge economic performance of a country are the Gross Domestic Product (GDP) and the Gross National Product (GNP; also known as Gross National Income, GNI). It is perhaps no exaggeration to say that:

While the GDP and the rest of the national income accounts may seem to be arcane concepts, they are truly among the great inventions of the 20th century (Paul A. Samuelson and William D. Nordhaus).[2]

These terms have become familiar to us through their wide reporting in the popular press, and are the centre-piece of the World Bank Development Reports (World Bank, various dates) published in September each year, as well as those of other institutions. The GDP is a basic, 'work horse', economic growth indicator that measures the level of total (domestic) economic output. A technical definition, taken from the World Development Report (2000/01) is as follows: 'GDP is the gross value added, at purchaser prices, by all resident producers in the economy plus any taxes and minus any subsidies not included in the value of the products'. Note that 'resident' includes nationals and foreigners. The GDP is expressed in a variety of forms. As it is a gross value of economic activity within a country, it will have some relationship with the size of the population living in that country – generally the larger the population, the larger will be the GDP. Therefore, a common format is to consider GDP/capita (GDP divided by size of the population).

There are various ways of calculating the GDP, but perhaps the most intuitively straightforward is to estimate the expenditure in an economy. The expenditure approach to GDP measures total economic activity by adding the amount spent by all final consumers of products and services.

$$GDP = C + I + G + (EX - IM)$$

where:

GDP = Gross Domestic Product
C = consumer expenditure on goods and services
I = investment
G = government expenditure on goods and services
EX = exports
IM = imports.

In this equation, expenditure is the sum of what is spent by consumers (C) and the government (G) on productive goods and services along with expenditure on investment. This may seem odd given that the expenditure of some is the income of others, but in a simplified model of an economy which is 'closed' (ie the money circulates between groups), we only need to estimate one of the flows of money to arrive at the flows within the system as a whole. The idea is represented in Figure 2.1 with a model which includes only two components – households and business. Notice that all the loops (arrows) are closed and assuming that money does not accumulate in households or businesses to a significant extent, or pass outside the system, then we only need to know 'C' to have an idea of the scale of monetary flow.

In practice, of course, money can be saved (or invested) in Figure 2.1 by both households and businesses. The investment (I) component of GDP is complex. It refers to 'private domestic investment' since government investment in infrastructure, such as roads, is included within G. Also note

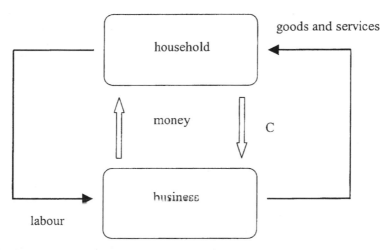

In a closed economy where the money circulates between households and businesses, the arrow 'C' (household expenditure) will estimate the output of the economy.

Figure 2.1 *Simple model of an economy with only two components (households and businesses)*

that non-productive expenditures (social security benefits, unemployment compensation, welfare benefits, interest payments on the national debt) are not included in G.

The final term (EX − IM) allows for the country's trade balance (exports − imports) to be taken into account. Note that a good or service does not actually have to leave the country to be counted as an export. Tourists spend money on hotel rooms, local travel and food and, while these goods have been 'produced' locally, they are paid for by foreigners and hence are considered as an export.

An example of the calculation of GDP for the US economy in 2002 is presented in Table 2.1 (adapted from US Department of Commerce data sets). The table is a breakdown of the calculation of GDP along the lines given in the above equation. The four quarters (3 monthly periods) for the year are shown as well as the final values for the year (given by the average of the four quarters). There are a number of points of interest in Table 2.1. To begin with, note how there is variation in C, I, G and (EX − IM) between the four quarters, although, given the magnitude of the figures, this proportional difference is not substantial. For example, the difference in GDP calculated for the fourth quarter ($10,588.9 billion) and first quarter ($10,313.1 billion) is 'only' $275.8 billion! This may sound like a lot of money to you and me, but it is less than 3 per cent of the first quarter figure. Also, note how the 'C' component of the GDP calculation makes up 70 per cent of the total GDP, with the 'G' component comprising just under 20 per cent. Therefore some 90 per cent of GDP comprises personal and government expenditure, and the trade balance is a minor item (4 per cent of GDP), and in this case it is negative (imports are greater than exports). Even if imports and exports are added together, the result in 2002 ($2,453.4 billion) is still only 23 per cent of GDP. Monetary flow as a proportion of GDP is often used as an indicator of an economy's 'openness', and the higher the percentage then the more 'open' the economy. It may be surprising to see that the US economy is not as 'open' as that of many other countries. Table 2.2 provides some examples of the average 'openness' of economies measured between 1970 and 2000. Also provided in the table (as averages can hide variation) is the standard deviation of 'openness' for the sample of years. The higher the standard deviation of 'openness' for a country, the greater the variation in 'openness' over the period. Using this measure, the Irish economy has an average 'openness' between 1970 and 2000 of 115 per cent, a figure more than double that of the UK (53 per cent) and nearly six times higher than that of the US (20 per cent). Indeed, the 'openness' of the Irish economy measured with this indicator is one of the highest in the world.

Clearly, given that consumer and government expenditure is such a major component of GDP, much depends upon what is included under 'goods and services'. For the US economy we can glean some clues by looking at the headings within Table 2.1. The bulk (nearly 60 per cent) of 'C' is taken up with 'services' (housing, medical care, recreation, transport), while most (65 per cent) of 'G' is under the 'state and local' category. This

Table 2.1 *Example calculation of the gross domestic product (GDP) for the US economy*

Expenditure	Quarter of 2002 I	II	III	IV	Average for 2002	% of total GDP
PERSONAL CONSUMPTION (C)						
(a) Durable goods						
Motor vehicles and parts	365.8	362.1	400.7	375.9	376.1	
Furniture and household equipment	317.1	319.1	319.2	319.4	318.7	
Other	176.1	175.8	177.9	178.6	177.1	
Total durable goods	**859.0**	**857.0**	**897.8**	**873.9**	**871.9**	
(b) Non-durable goods						
Food	1,025.0	1,023.9	1,024.8	1,043.9	1,029.4	
Clothing and shoes	325.8	323.9	321.0	326.6	324.3	
Gasoline and oil	142.3	160.7	163.5	167.4	158.5	
Fuel oil and coal	13.9	14.0	14.7	17.3	15.0	
Total energy goods	156.2	174.7	178.2	184.7	173.5	
Other	578.0	585.6	592.9	594.8	587.8	
Total non-durable goods	**2,085.0**	**2,108.1**	**2,116.9**	**2,150.0**	**2,115.0**	
Housing	1,051.7	1,066.0	1,078.0	1,090.1	1,071.5	
Electricity and gas	143.9	144.9	147.4	156.5	148.2	
Other household operation	255.4	256.1	258.9	257.7	257.0	
Household operation	399.3	401.0	406.3	414.2	405.2	
Transportation	273.3	275.6	276.1	278.3	275.8	
Medical care	1,119.0	1,139.3	1,158.8	1,176.9	1,148.5	
Recreation	279.0	283.8	285.9	291.8	285.1	
Other	1,107.8	1,123.8	1,140.9	1,150.2	1,130.7	
Total services	**4,230.1**	**4,289.5**	**4,346.0**	**4,401.5**	**4,316.8**	
Personal consumption expenditures	**7,174.1**	**7,254.6**	**7,360.7**	**7,425.4**	**7,303.7**	**70**
INVESTMENTS (I)						
(a) Non-residential						
Structures	288.3	275.2	259.4	254.2	269.3	
Equipment and software	838.5	840.7	850.4	863.0	848.1	
Non-residential total	1,126.8	1,115.9	1,109.8	1,117.2	1,117.4	
(b) Residential	462.6	468.7	469.9	486.5	471.9	
Residential and non-residential total (fixed investment)	1,589.4	1,584.6	1,579.7	1,603.7	1,589.3	
Change in private inventories	−29.9	3.4	17.6	24.5	3.9	
Gross private domestic investment	**1,559.5**	**1,588.0**	**1,597.3**	**1,628.2**	**1,593.2**	**15**
GOVERNMENT EXPENDITURE (G)						
(a) Federal						
National defence	431.7	442.1	451.2	464.7	447.4	
Non-defence	240.3	246.1	246.5	252.2	246.3	
Total federal	672.0	688.2	697.7	716.9	693.7	
(b) State and local	1,267.5	1,271.6	1,283.3	1,294.4	1,279.2	
Government consumption expenditures and gross investment	**1,939.5**	**1,959.8**	**1,981.0**	**2,011.3**	**1,972.9**	**19**
TRADE BALANCE (EX-IM)						
(a) Exports						
Goods	679.8	709.4	722.6	702.6	703.6	
Services	297.7	308.8	316.0	322.8	311.3	
Total exports	977.5	1,018.2	1,038.6	1,025.4	1,014.9	

Table 2.1 *Continued*

| Expenditure | *Quarter of 2002* | | | | *Average* | *% of* |
	I	*II*	*III*	*IV*	*for 2002*	*total GDP*
(b) Imports						
Goods	1,102.3	1,202.9	1,220.9	1,242.5	1,192.1	
Services	235.2	240.8	250.6	258.9	246.4	
Total imports	1,337.5	1,443.7	1,471.5	1,501.4	1,438.5	
Trade balance	−360.0	−425.5	−432.9	−476.0	−423.6	−4
Gross Domestic Product (GDP)	10,313.1	10,376.9	10,506.1	10,588.9	10,446.2	
C + I + G + (EX − IM)						

The table provides a breakdown of the year 2002 into four quarters with an overall value for the year (the average of the four quarters). Figures are in billions of $US.
Source: US Department of Commerce. Bureau of Economic Analysis (www.bea.doc.gov/beahome.html)

Table 2.2 *'Openness' of economies measured in terms of inward and outward flows of goods and services as a proportion of GDP*

| | *Exports plus imports as a % of GDP* | | *Ratio of standard deviation to* |
	Average	*Standard deviation*	*average*
Ireland	115	21	0.18
Saudi Arabia	86	13	0.15
Malawi	61	10	0.16
Kenya	60	8	0.13
Nigeria	57	22	0.39
UK	53	4	0.08
Ecuador	53	8	0.15
South Africa	50	6	0.12
Sierra Leone	48	15	0.31
Italy	44	5	0.11
France	43	5	0.12
Mozambique	42	14	0.33
Spain	39	9	0.23
Nepal	38	13	0.34
Uganda	30	7	0.23
China	26	14	0.54
Japan	21	4	0.19
USA	20	3	0.15
India	18	6	0.33
Brazil	17	2	0.12

'Openness' assessed in terms of exports plus imports as a % of GDP. The figures are the average 'openness' over the period 1970–2000 and the standard deviation (measure of year-on-year variation). As year-on-year variation could be greater with higher 'openness', the table also provides the ratio of standard deviation to the average. The lower this ratio, the lower the year-on-year variation in the 'openness' indicator.
In this data set Ireland has the most 'open' economy and Brazil the most 'closed'. The UK has a relatively high openness, which is consistent over the period. Note that the US economy is relatively 'closed'.

may be surprising, as expenditure on durable (cars, washing machines, TVs) and non-durable (food, drink) goods may intuitively be thought of as the largest part of private expenditure, and federal expenditure (for example, on defence) as the greater part of government expenditure. While the items (electricity, gas, transport, medical care, recreation) listed here under services are logical, if we change these items the 'C' component will also change.

How does the agency responsible for calculating GDP actually collect these data? Presumably one can get figures for 'G' relatively easily from government accounts, but what about 'C'? In an economy where monetary transactions are recorded on paper or electronically for purposes of tax, it would not be difficult to derive estimates of personal expenditure. In economies where such transactions are not recorded to the same extent as they are in the US, this may be far more difficult.

PROBLEMS WITH GROSS DOMESTIC PRODUCT

While GDP is a popular measure of economic performance, and indeed has been the bedrock of assessing a country's progress in development terms for many years (higher GDP = higher economic development), it is not without its problems as a comparative device. One of these can probably be immediately gleaned from the earlier discussion – the quality of the data upon which the calculation is based. Poor quality inputs into Table 2.1 will give an unreliable output (an under- or overestimate of GDP). Faced with a calculation such as that of Table 2.1, it is all too tempting to accept the figures at face value and not question the quality of the information upon which the whole edifice is based. Indeed, perhaps surprisingly, the quality of data for such national accounting has not been the priority it should have been over the years, although the World Bank, United Nations and others have been attempting to address this key issue. However, as important as this is, there are other concerns.

An obvious problem that arises with GDP is comparison over time given that all countries suffer an element of inflation (Maddison, 1983). The prices of goods tend to increase with time, albeit more slowly in some countries than others. As the GDP in Table 2.1 is based on expenditure and, as expenditure is a product of quantity of goods sold and the price for each of these goods, then one can get an increase in GDP purely by increasing the price of goods and not the quantity being traded. An increase in GDP, for example as shown in Figure 2.2 for the UK economy between 1970 and 2000, may not represent any fundamental increase in economic activity (and hence 'development' in a narrow sense) but may be an artefact of price inflation. There are ways around this problem. The usual approach is to calculate GDP based on a constant price taken from some sample year. This is referred to

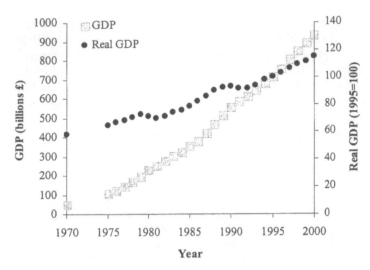

Figure 2.2 *GDP (billions £, sterling) and Real GDP (1995 set as 100) for the UK economy between 1970 and 2000*

GDP values will be a combination of change in value (as a result of inflation) as well as change in output. Therefore, is the gradual increase in GDP caused by a real increase in output or has it been caused by inflation? If the former then the economy has grown, if the latter then the economy may have been static or even contracted.

Real GDP keeps the value of goods and services constant (in this case set at 1995 figures) so the change reflects output from the economy. Note the fall in output in the late 1970s and early 1990s that corresponds to a contraction in the UK economy. This cannot be detected using GDP at current prices.

as 'real GDP' with the year used in the calculation stated. In Figure 2.2 the second line is the real GDP for the UK economy over the same period calculated on the basis of 1995 prices. It would not matter which reference year had been selected, the main point is that prices have been kept constant so differences in real GDP reflect changes in output. Note that the increase in GDP over these years is less than it was using current prices. Indeed for some years (around the late 1970s and early 1990s, for example) there were downturns (the economy shrank) that are not readily apparent from the GDP figures based on current prices. If growth in GDP is being used here as an indicator of economic development, then clearly the real GDP will provide a much lower estimation of growth than would the GDP based on current prices. I will leave it to the reader's imagination as to how those using such figures for the purposes of increasing their popularity with constituents are likely to make decisions over which estimates of GDP in Figure 2.2 they would wish to highlight, particularly during the downturns!

A second problem is with comparison across space (between countries, for example). This is an issue that is familiar to anyone who has spent time in another country either on vacation, for work or after retirement. Compared to one's home country, another country may appear to be either more expensive or cheaper. We all instinctively make such comparisons when confronted with the goods or services we are used to. But if, say, $1 buys a different quantity of a good across different countries, then what use is GDP as an international indicator of economic performance? In theory the size of two economies may be identical in terms of the type and quantity of goods being traded, but if prices are higher in one country relative to the other then the higher prices will generate a higher GDP. Also, the GDP in one country could be lower than the other even when there is a greater volume of goods and services being exchanged. This is a thorny problem, but one that had to be solved if we were really going to compare different economies. It is important to realize that this is not just a currency exchange rate issue. Even when a currency is converted, there can still be very different prices across national borders for the same good. After all, money is easily traded across the globe, and it is this trade that sets the benchmark for exchange rates. But many goods are not so easily traded across borders – there are market frictions which induce a 'band of inaction' (Peel and Venetis, 2003). This may be due to a number of factors such as their bulk-to-price ratio making transportation uneconomical; perishability, or because of inducements to production (such as tariffs) that provide advantages for local producers. Just using currency exchange rates will overstate intercountry variation (Ram, 1992).

One answer to this problem is to apply the notion of 'purchasing power parity' (PPP), first articulated by scholars in 16th century Spain, but in its modern form is said to originate from the collapse of the world economy during and following World War I (Taylor, 1995; Rogoff, 1996). PPP has been viewed in various ways (Taylor, 1995), but in its simplest form we can start with an assumption (referred to as the Law of One Price; Rogoff, 1996; Odedokun, 2000) that the price of a commodity should be identical irrespective of where in the world it is sold (ie that there are no market frictions), once we allow for monetary exchange rates. In such a ideal case (Absolute PPP; Holmes, 2000), change in the local prices for the same product will mirror the change in monetary exchange rate, allowing for a transitory deviation (a time lag) as the economic system readjusts (Boyd and Smith, 1999). Armed with this assumption we can then look for longer-term (non-transitory) deviations (Box 2.1).

PPP is one of the most widely tested economic hypotheses (Holmes, 2000) and is a commonly employed method for calibrating GDP to allow for comparison across countries (Dowrick and Quiggin, 1997). It is usually estimated by collecting the prices of specified items (typically grouped within categories, or 'basic headings') that are representative of typical expenditure but at the same time are comparable across countries. Given the diversity in normal household purchases between cultures, this is certainly not a straightforward feat. It is also important to sample outlets where the prices paid by a household are typical. The PPP is carried out for the components of GDP before aggregation to provide the 'PPP adjusted GDP'. The PPP

Box 2.1 *An explanation of Purchasing Power Parity (PPP)*

Two families (A and B), one living in New York (A) the other in London (B), agree to a house swap for a weeks vacation.

Amongst the goods that they will need to purchase while on holiday are milk and rice, but they each set a budget constraint on these goods of $20 and £10 in New York and London respectively. Given these budget constraints there are two factors which determine how much of these goods the families will purchase while on their exchange holiday:

● **prices of the goods in London and New York (these will differ).**

For example (using the old imperial measures still very much in vogue in the two locations) we have the following unit prices for a pint of milk and a pound (lb) of rice:

Place	Milk (pint)	Rice (lb)
New York ($)	0.40	2.0
London (£)	0.25	1.0
Price ratio ($/£)	1.60	2.0

Why do these goods not cost the same in both the UK and US? This may hold true for commodities that are readily traded across national borders, like gold for example, but for many items there is little if any trade across borders. Fresh milk, for example, is produced locally in both the UK and US but has high bulk and low monetary value as well as being perishable. Therefore most of the consumption in those countries is from local production, and prices paid will be subject to differing production, transportation and processing costs in those countries.

● **preferences of the 2 families for these goods.**

This is the same whether they are at home or on holiday. For example, let us assume the relative preference values (in terms of expenditure) for milk and rice are as follows:

Family	Milk	Rice	Sum
A	0.2	0.8	1.0
B	0.8	0.2	1.0
Sum	1.0	1.0	

All this table is saying is that family A prefers to spend its money on rice rather than milk (rice is preferred 4 times more than milk), and the opposite is true for family B. This is, of course, a major simplifying assumption given that preferences can change with time and indeed place.

Now let us take the optimal consumption and expenditure of each family while at home and abroad (assuming the preferences are constant).

Family A. Normally resident in New York but spent a week in London. This family prefers to spend its money on rice rather than milk.

| | Quantities purchased/week | | Expenditure/week | | Total |
	Milk (pint)	Rice (lb)	Milk	Rice	
Home ($)	10	8	4	16	**$20**
London (£)	10	8	2.50	8	**£10.50**

Family A have to spend £10.50 in London to buy the same goods (10 pints of milk and 8 lb of rice) they purchased for $20 at home. To them, with a 'New York basket' of goods it would appear that the exchange rate is $1 = £0.53 (ie 10.5/20).

Family B. Normally resident in London but spent a week in New York. This family prefers to spend its money on milk rather than rice.

| | Quantities purchased/week | | Expenditure/week | | Total |
	Milk (pint)	Rice (lb)	Milk	Rice	
Home ($)	32	2	8	2	**$10**
London (£)	32	2	12.80	4	**£16.80**

Family B normally spends £10 at home for their goods but they have to spend $16.80 in New York on the same 'London' basket of goods. To them the exchange rate is $1 = £0.60 (ie 10/16.8).

These exchange rates (individual purchasing power parities) reflect the value of the same basket of goods in two locations. They are different as the price ratios for the two goods between London and New York differ and the basket of goods the families purchase differ. A difference of £0.07 between £0.53 and £0.60 may not sound all that much, but for every £100 spent this equates to a difference of £7.

Taking the geometric mean (ie the square root of their product) of these two individual PPPs provides Fishers Ideal Index of PPP:

$$PPP = \sqrt{0.53 \times 0.6} = 0.56 \ (\$1 = £0.56)$$

Note that if the price ratios were identical:

Place	Milk (pint)	Rice (lb)
New York ($)	0.4	2.0
London (£)	0.2	1.0
Price ratio ($/£)	2.0	2.0

Then the individual PPPs would be identical (0.5) no matter what the preferences.

▶

Note that the exchange rates for dollars and pounds paid by the two families in banks, hotels and *Bureau d'Change* are based upon the trade in the two currencies, and this can be volatile. It can happen that over the period of a few days the exchange rates may vary significantly, but provided the preferences remain constant and there is no hyper-inflation rapidly pushing up local prices of the goods to differing extents the PPP will remain constant.

Another example is provided by *The Economist* 'Big Mac Index'. Prices of the 'Big Mac' hamburger, a commodity that can be purchased in many countries, can be compared. The table on pages 45 and 46 is an adaptation of *The Economist* 'Big Mac Index' data presents the price of one 'Big Mac' in terms of the local currency.

Assuming that one 'Big Mac' in the US is $2.49 (an average figure calculated by *The Economist* from outlets in a number of US cities) it is possible to calculate a US$ exchange rate based on the 'Big Mac'. In South Africa, for example, one 'Big Mac' costs Rand 9.70 while the same 'Big Mac' in the US costs $2.49. The exchange rate appears to be $US 1 = Rand 3.90 (9.70/2.49). This 'Big Mac' based exchange rate can be compared to the actual US$ exchange rate based on currency trade (as of the 23 April 2002), and for many countries the two do not match. The table also shows how many hamburgers can be purchased for the US price of $2.49 with actual exchange rates. In South Africa it is possible to buy nearly three hamburgers by changing $2.49 to Rand! Only in Peru and Costa Rica is there apparent equality between the PPP and actual exchange rates. In some European countries $2.49 will not even purchase one hamburger. Again, as with milk and rice, there are all sorts of local costs that come into play to vary the price (local beef production, taxes, wage rates etc).

This milk and rice example uses only two commodities and two countries. The International Comparisons Programme (ICP) has to work with the prices of many commodities over many countries, and software has been developed to help facilitate this process. An example is the 'ICP ToolPak' developed by the Statistical Advisory Service of the World Bank, and is available for download (Excel worksheet format) from the World Bank. The 'ToolPak' software allows various 'versions' of PPP to be calculated depending upon the way in which the individual price comparisons are aggregated (The Fisher Index described earlier is but one of them). The data required are basically prices of the various commodities in the ICP, and of course much depends on the quality of these. No matter how good the software, poor quality data will yield poor results.

adjusted GDP values are normally given in terms of some international monetary unit such as 'international dollars', and lists of PPP adjustments are published on a regular basis (Vachris and Thomas, 1999).

The result of adjusting GDP in this way can be dramatic. Table 2.3 gives the ratio of GDP/capita adjusted for PPP to GDP/capita without adjustment for a sample of economies (the same economies as in Box 2.1). The greatest shift in this table is for the Russian Federation with a GDP/capita of US$1,725 and a PPP adjusted GDP/capita of International $8,377; almost a fivefold increase. For some countries, such as Japan, the adjustment is downwards.

As can perhaps be imagined, PPP adjustment is not an easy task in practice, although some countries do routinely collect price data as a part of their calculation of consumer and producer price indices (Vachris and Thomas, 1999). Much depends on the balance of items included in the 'basket' of

Economy	Local currency	Price of one 'Big Mac' in local currency	Dollar exchange rate based on 'Big Macs' (local price/US price)	Actual dollar exchange rate (as of 23/4/02) (local currency for $1)	Number of 'Big Macs' that can be purchased for the US price of $2.49 at the actual $ exchange rate
Argentina	Peso	2.50	1.00	3.13	3.12
South Africa	Rand	9.70	3.90	10.90	2.80
Russia	Rouble	39.00	15.66	31.20	1.99
Yugoslavia	Dinar	85.00	34.14	67.80	1.99
China	Yuan	10.50	4.22	8.28	1.96
Thailand	Baht	55.00	22.09	43.30	1.96
Philippines	Peso	65.00	26.10	51.00	1.95
Malaysia	M$	5.04	2.02	3.80	1.88
Hong Kong	HK$	11.20	4.50	7.80	1.73
Poland	Zloty	5.90	2.37	4.04	1.71
Brazil	Real	3.60	1.45	2.34	1.62
Australia	A$	3.00	1.20	1.86	1.54
Czech Rep.	Koruna	56.28	22.60	34.00	1.50
Uruguay	Peso	28.00	11.24	16.30	1.49
Hungary	Forint	459.00	184.34	272.00	1.48
Indonesia	Rupiah	16,000.00	6,425.70	9,430.00	1.47
New Zealand	NZ$	3.95	1.59	2.24	1.41
Singapore	S$	3.30	1.33	1.82	1.37
Morocco	Dirham	23.00	9.24	11.53	1.25
Taiwan	NT$	70.00	28.11	34.60	1.24
Japan	Yen	262.00	105.22	130.00	1.24
Canada	C$	3.33	1.34	1.57	1.17
Chile	Peso	1,400.00	562.25	655.00	1.16
Mexico	Peso	21.90	8.80	9.23	1.06
South Korea	Won	3,100.00	1,244.98	1,304.00	1.05
Saudi Arabia	Riyal	9.00	3.61	3.75	1.04

Economy	Local currency	Price of one 'Big Mac' in local currency	Dollar exchange rate based on 'Big Macs' (local price/US price)	Actual dollar exchange rate (as of 23/4/02) (local currency for $1)	Number of 'Big Macs' that can be purchased for the US price of $2.49 at the actual $ exchange rate
Peru	New Sol	8.50	3.41	3.43	1.00
USA	US$	2.49	1.00	1.00	1.00
Costa Rica	Colon	875.00	351.41	351.00	1.00
Israel	Shekel	12.00	4.82	4.79	0.99
Columbia	Peso	5,700.00	2,289.16	2,261.00	0.99
Sweden	SKr	26.00	10.44	10.30	0.99
Jamaica	Jamaican $	120.00	48.19	47.40	0.98
Venezuela	Bolivar	2,500.00	1,004.02	857.00	0.85
Denmark	DKr	24.75	9.94	8.38	0.84
Turkey	Lira	4,000,000.00	1,606,425.70	1,324,500.00	0.82
UK	Pound £	1.99	0.80	0.64	0.80
Switzerland	SFr	6.30	2.53	1.66	0.66
Norway	Kroner	35.00	14.06	8.56	0.61
Iceland	Krona	399.00	160.24	96.30	0.60

Table 2.3 *Comparison of GDP/capita using current US$ exchange rate against GDP/capita adjusted for Purchasing Power Parity (PPP)*

Economy	GDP/capita		Ratio
	Current US$	PPP International$	
Russian Federation	1,725	8,377	4.86
China	855	3,976	4.65
Indonesia	728	3,043	4.18
Philippines	989	3,971	4.02
Colombia	1,922	6,248	3.25
South Africa	2,941	9,401	3.20
Thailand	2,012	6,402	3.18
Morocco	1,162	3,546	3.05
Czech Republic	4,943	13,991	2.83
Hungary	4,553	12,416	2.73
Malaysia	3,853	9,068	2.35
Peru	2,084	4,799	2.30
Turkey	3,062	6,974	2.28
Poland	4,081	9,051	2.22
Brazil	3,494	7,625	2.18
Costa Rica	4,159	8,649	2.08
Chile	4,638	9,417	2.03
Korea, Rep.	9,671	17,380	1.80
Argentina	7,695	12,377	1.61
New Zealand	13,026	20,069	1.54
Mexico	5,864	9,023	1.54
Uruguay	5,908	9,035	1.53
Jamaica	2,812	3,639	1.29
Australia	20,337	25,693	1.26
Canada	22,370	27,840	1.24
Venezuela	4,985	5,794	1.16
Israel	17,710	20,132	1.14
Hong Kong	23,928	25,153	1.05
Singapore	22,960	23,356	1.02
UK	23,679	23,509	0.99
US	34,940	34,142	0.98
Iceland	30,338	29,580	0.98
Sweden	25,631	24,277	0.95
Denmark	30,424	27,627	0.91
Switzerland	33,393	28,769	0.86
Norway	36,021	29,918	0.83
Japan	38,162	26,755	0.70

Data are taken from the World Development Report (2002), and relate to the year 2000. The countries selected for this sample are the same as those of Box 2.1, and have been ranked in terms of the ratio of GDP/capita (PPP) over GDP/capita (current US$).

goods which are being compared (as seen in Box 2.1 with the New York and London baskets having different quantities of milk and rice) and the quality of the data collection process (UNESC, 1999) as many countries have to do special pricing surveys (Rogoff, 1996; Vachris and Thomas, 1999). For example, it is logical to suppose that the preferences of consumers can shift, for example by substituting towards goods that are locally cheap (Dowrick and Quiggin, 1997). Also, even within the same country, city or street the same good can be available at different prices on the same day of shopping (Rogoff, 1996).

An International Comparison Programme (ICP) was established in 1968 as a joint venture between the United Nations and the University of Pennsylvania, funded by the Ford Foundation and the World Bank. In 1970 the ICP compared 10 countries, and subsequent rounds in 1975, 1980, 1985, 1990 and 1993 have gradually taken on a wider global coverage. The OECD and the Statistical Office of the European Union (Eurostat) collect price data for their member states and operate on a 3 year cycle (1993, 1996, 1999, 2002), while the World Bank coordinates data collection for non-OECD countries. The number of 'basic headings' of goods included in the comparison has varied between 150 and 250 for different country groupings within the ICP.

The ICP has from time to time been subject to reviews, and these have covered a range of issues, including whether PPP is needed in a policy context (see for example, UNESC, 1999). The general consensus is that PPP is needed for at least four main reasons (UNESC, 1999):

1   To provide better assessments of poverty and its distribution. As we will see in the next chapter, poverty assessments have often been based on a notional 'poverty line' (minimum income needed for subsistence). This may be set, for example, at $1/day and expressed in terms of PPP to allow for differing purchasing power.
2   To better inform decision making in organizations such as the International Monetary Fund and the World Bank.
3   To better inform decision makers in countries that are opening up their economies to foreign trade and investment.
4   To provide a clearer understanding of competitiveness in foreign trade.

There is inevitably a time lag between the collection of the data within the ICP process and the time the PPP conversions are made available (Rogoff, 1996; UNESC, 1999). Even so, PPP does have resilience given the trading frictions that exist across borders, even in this increasingly globalized world (Rogoff, 1996). Similarly some have questioned whether using PPP data from the ICP to correct GDP makes any real difference when compared with less demanding approaches, such as the use of exchange rates:

> *Without doubt correct PPPs are to be preferred to exchange rates for conversions directed at output comparisons, but it is at least possible that available ICP estimates of the PPPs are of such poor quality that they are less accurate estimates of the correct PPPs than exchange rates* (Summers and Heston, 1997; quoted in UNESC, 1999, p21).

As we will see in Chapter 4, despite the above concerns over the quality of ICP data, the PPP corrected GDP/capita is routinely used as a component in perhaps the most widely quoted and used development index – the Human Development Index of the UNDP.

GROSS NATIONAL PRODUCT AND OTHER INDICATORS

Gross Domestic Product is the basis for a host of other economic performance indicators normally published in national accounts. Table 2.4 illustrates a number of these for the US economy in 2002, with the GDP from Table 2.1 as the starting point at the top of the table.

The first significant variant is the Gross National Product (GNP), the total value of income from domestic and foreign sources claimed by nationals of the country. In effect, this is the GDP adjustment for money which leaves the economy and which comes into the economy from outside.

GNP = GDP + income from the rest of the world −
                              payments to the rest of the world

GNP acknowledges that the simple model of the economy in Figure 2.1 is misleading, as money can enter and leave the system in ways other than the trade balance. Foreign residents and companies based overseas but with a subsidiary in the economy may transfer money out of the system. Similarly, nationals earning income overseas and companies based in the economy but with overseas subsidiaries may bring money in. The GNP for the US economy in 2002 was lower than GDP by approximately $10 billion.

There are occasions when it may be better to use the GNP as a measure of national economic performance than the GDP. Ireland, for example, has a relatively small economy with significant levels of investment from multinational companies (MNCs), largely as a result of having the lowest company tax regime in Europe. The Irish company tax rate is less than half the figure for the UK, a country often considered to have a low tax regime (Table 2.5). This has resulted in substantial inward investment and many MNCs have set up regional offices and assembly plants in Ireland. Understandably MNCs would prefer to register their profits in Ireland as they would pay less tax, with the result that money can flow into the country for purposes of tax declaration before being exported out of the country. One mechanism for achieving this is called transfer-price fixing (Figure 2.3). An MNC subsidiary in a high tax country pays the subsidiary based in Ireland for any transfer of goods and services between them. But the Irish subsidiary does not pay for goods and services it receives from subsidiaries in the high tax country. The result is an accumulation of profits in Ireland, which are declared. While this is good news for the MNC, there is the danger of transfer-price fixing inflating the GDP of the Irish economy. Sweeney (1999, p53) suggests using the 'more modest GNP rather than GDP' for

Table 2.4 *Suite of economic performance indicators for the US economy*

	Quarter of 2002				Average for 2002
	I	II	III	IV	
Gross Domestic Product	10,313.1	10,376.9	10,506.2	10,588.8	10,446.3
Income receipts from the rest of the world	264.7	276.0	287.3	284.2	278.1
Income payments to the rest of the world	262.8	296.1	298.2	293.4	287.6
Income balance	1.9	−20.1	−10.9	−9.2	−9.6
Gross National Product (GDP+income balance with rest of the world)	10,315.0	10,356.8	10,495.3	10,579.6	10,436.7
Private capital consumption allowances	1,324.0	1,322.0	1,317.9	1,315.9	1,320.0
Private capital consumption adjustment	187.0	160.8	143.1	133.3	156.1
Consumption of fixed capital: Private (allowances adjustment)	1,137.0	1,161.2	1,174.8	1,182.6	1,163.9
Capital consumption: General government	192.5	194.1	195.7	197.6	195.0
Capital consumption: Government enterprises	34.0	34.4	34.8	35.1	34.6
Consumption of fixed capital: Government (general+enterprises)	226.5	228.5	230.5	232.7	229.6
Consumption of fixed capital: Total (private+government)	1,363.5	1,389.7	1,405.3	1,415.3	1,393.5
Net Domestic Product (GDP − consumption of fixed capital)	8,949.6	8,987.2	9,100.9	9,173.5	9,052.8
Net National Product (GNP − consumption of fixed capital)	8,951.5	8,967.1	9,090.0	9,164.3	9,043.2
Indirect business tax and non-tax liability	786.2	795.1	806.9	813.3	800.4
Business transfer payments	43.8	43.9	44.4	44.3	44.1
Subsidies less current surplus of government enterprise	37.0	35.1	29.1	29.0	32.6
Gross private saving	1,578.3	1,616.1	1,570.3	1,614.5	1,594.8
Gross government saving (Federal, State and local)	24.9	−12.1	−34.7	−65.6	−21.9
Gross saving (private+government)	1,603.2	1,604.0	1,535.6	1,548.9	1,572.9
Gross private domestic investment	1,559.4	1,588.0	1,597.3	1,628.1	1,593.2
Gross government investment	355.5	348.2	351.7	352.2	351.9
Net foreign investment	−421.7	−497.2	−495.6	−541.0	−488.9
Gross investment (private+government+foreign)	1,493.2	1,439.0	1,453.4	1,439.3	1,456.2
Statistical discrepancy (gross investment − gross saving)	−110.0	−165.0	−82.2	−109.6	−116.7
Sub-total 1 (business tax and transfer payments − subsidies + discrepancy)	683.0	638.9	740.0	719.0	695.2

National Income (NNP-subtotal 1)	**8,268.5**	**8,328.2**	**8,350**	**8,445.3**	**8,348.0**
Corporate profits with inventory valuation and capital	797.6	785.0	771.0	796.1	787.4
Net interest	672.8	678.1	687.6	698.3	684.2
Contributions for social insurance	740.4	746.1	748.8	754.9	747.6
Wage accruals less disbursements	0	0	0	0	0
Sub-total 2 (profits + interest + social insurance + wage balance)	**2,210.8**	**2,209.2**	**2,207.4**	**2,249.3**	**2,219.2**
Personal interest income	1,069.9	1,082.3	1,080.7	1,080.9	1,078.5
Personal dividend income	423.7	430.3	437.3	443.8	433.8
Government transfer payments to persons	1,217.4	1,247.7	1,263.1	1,283.5	1,252.9
Business transfer payments to persons	34.6	34.9	35.3	35.6	35.1
Sub-total 3 (personal income + transfers)	**2,745.6**	**2,795.2**	**2,816.4**	**2,843.8**	**2,800.3**
Personal Income (NI – subtotal 2 + subtotal 3)	**8,803.3**	**8,914.2**	**8,959.0**	**9,039.8**	**8,929.1**
Gross Domestic Income (GDP – statistical discrepancy)	**10,423.1**	**10,541.9**	**10,588.4**	**10,698.4**	**10,563.0**
Gross National Income (GNP – statistical discrepancy)	**10,425.0**	**10,521.8**	**10,577.5**	**10,689.2**	**10,553.4**

The table provides a breakdown of the year 2002 into 4 quarters with an overall value for the year (in bold). Figures are in billions of $US. The various economic indicators are in bold.
Source: US Department of Commerce. Bureau of Economic Analysis (www.bea.doc.gcv/beahome.html)

Table 2.5 *Maximum tax rates applied to corporate income (2003)*

Country	Maximum tax rate (% income)
Ireland	12.50
Switzerland	24.50
Sweden	28.00
Australia	30.00
UK	30.00
China	33.00
Brazil	34.00
Netherlands	29.00/34.50
France	34.33
Spain	35.00
Canada	36.60
Italy	38.25
Germany	39.58
Japan	40.00
US	40.00
Belgium	40.17
Italy	40.25

In some countries, the corporate tax regime is complex and the figures presented here are averages. Note that Ireland has the lowest tax regime in Europe, with a rate less than half that of the UK.

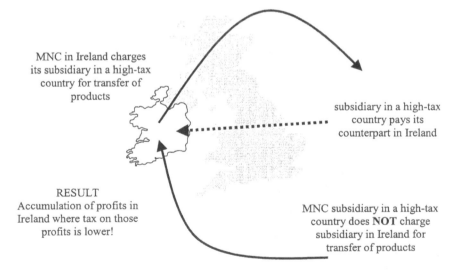

MNC in Ireland charges its subsidiary in a high-tax country for transfer of products

subsidiary in a high-tax country pays its counterpart in Ireland

RESULT
Accumulation of profits in Ireland where tax on those profits is lower!

MNC subsidiary in a high-tax country does **NOT** charge subsidiary in Ireland for transfer of products

Figure 2.3 *The theory behind transfer price fixing, using Ireland (a low corporate tax economy) as an example*

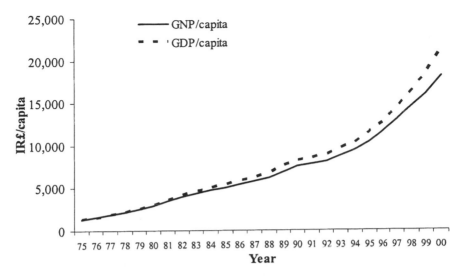

Note the gradual increase in difference between Irish GDP and GNP per capita from the early 1980s as the economy improved. By the turn of the century, GDP/capita was 17 per cent higher than GNP/capita. In the Irish economy, GDP tends to be higher than GNP partly because of the declaration of multinational corporate profits.

Figure 2.4 *Values of GDP and GNP (both adjusted for PPP) for the Irish economy (1970–2000)*

gauging economic performance in Ireland, and the marked difference between the two (both adjusted for PPP) is shown in Figure 2.4. The Irish GNP would include the MNC money which ultimately leaves the country and hence would be lower than GDP.

The GDP and GNP can also be adjusted to allow for the consumption of fixed capital (Net Domestic Product, NDP, and Net National Product, NNP, respectively). This allows for a flow of money into the economy arising from a depreciation of fixed capital by both the private and government sectors. Because it takes account of capital depreciation, some commentators have suggested that NNP can be seen as an indicator of sustainability (Asheim, 1994). Taking such depreciation into account for the US economy reduces both GDP and GNP by $1,393.5 billion.

Following the NDP and NNP, there is National Income which adjusts for business tax and transfer payments, subsidies, a 'statistical discrepancy' (difference between investment and savings) and Personal Income. The two indicators at the foot of the Table 2.4 are further refinements of the GDP and GNP allowing for the difference between investment and saving (Gross Domestic Income and Gross National Income respectively).

The point being made here is not to overwhelm the reader with terminology but to illustrate that a reliance on only one (GDP) or even two (GDP and GNP) indicators may not tell the full picture of economic activity, hence the need for such a menagerie of indicators. This is a theme we will continue to come across.

GROSS DOMESTIC PRODUCT AND CONSUMPTION

The GDP is limited in other ways which the suite of variants in Table 2.4 does not address. For example, while NDP and NNP do take into account capital consumption, they do not include the social and environmental costs of production. A high NDP may have been achieved through widespread pollution, or perhaps been accompanied by a massive imbalance in wealth distribution leading to poverty for most of the population. It is possible to adjust the NDP to allow for environmental costs, and an example is the Environmentally Adjusted Net Domestic Product (EDP). The EDP is the NDP minus the environmental costs incurred, such as degradation of water, air, forests etc. EDP is an example of what some term 'green accounting', and can include entries in the standard systems of national accounting alongside the more familiar entries in Tables 2.1 and 2.4 (Hueting and Bosch, 1991; Solow 1993; Mitchell, 1996; Bartelmus, 1997). The assumption is that as long as the depreciation of natural resources are made up for by replacement with other assets of equal value then the system will be sustainable. It is a sort of 'colonization' of the economy by the environment (Bartelmus, 1999) summarized by the phrase 'the cardinal sin is not mining; it is consuming the rents from mining' (Solow, 1993). While the idea of locating an economy into the broader context of what is happening to the natural resource base and the environment may be appealing, the problem is that degradation has to be 'valued' in monetary terms. However, this may not be easy, given that 'value' may be subjective (the loss of a good view for instance). One possibility is to cost what it would take to get the environment back to some notional baseline (ie what would it cost to regain the good view?).

It is also possible to modify the GDP type of indicator in other ways so as to take on board wider social and environmental costs (Khan, 1991; Dowrick et al, 2003). All of these have similar attributes in that they seek to adjust GDP or GNP to bring in expenditures that add 'value' to a community; basically they add 'desirables' and deduct 'regrettables'. Even so, what is to be added or left out in each case is a value judgement made by those who developed the indicator. The idea is illustrated in Table 2.6 with a simplified GDP based on just seven goods and services (a to g). In the 'new' version of the GDP it may be decided to keep a to c but replace d to g with different goods and services (w to z). The new components may be deemed 'better' for society than the ones they replace.

There have been various attempts to modify the GDP to make it an indicator that is more representative of what is 'valued' by a community; some examples are provided in Table 2.7 (Hamilton, 1999; Neumayer, 2000, Lawn,

Table 2.6 *Modifying the GDP*

Current GDP 'goods and services'	'New' GDP 'goods and services'
a	a
b	b
c	c
d	−d but +w
e	−e but +x
f	−f but +y
g	−g but +z

The current GDP has seven elements to 'goods and services' (a to g). The 'new GDP' removes some of these (d to g) and replaces them with others (w to z). Items w to z could be positives (such as valuing volunteer work or child care) or negatives (costs of pollution or degradation)

Table 2.7 *Some attempts to modify the GDP and GNP*

Period	Index	Notes
Early 1970s	Measure of Economic Welfare (MEW)	Economic welfare said to be related to consumption not production. Started with GNP but excludes costs for: • education • health • police • sanitation • road maintenance • defence • health services Includes cost of commuting
Early 1980s	Economic Aspects of Welfare (EAW)	Similar to MEW, but includes costs of: • pollution control • environmental and health damage arising from pollution • natural resource depletion Even includes half of advertising costs
Late 1980s	Index of Sustainable Economic Welfare (ISEW) Opschoor (1991) Mayo et al (1997)	Includes expenditure on: • education • health • household labour But not for commuting or advertising Also considered is the distribution of income within the population
1995	Genuine Progress Indicator (GPI) 'Redefining Progress' (www.rprogress.org/projects/gpi/)	Includes costs of: • volunteer work • cost of crime • family breakdown • underemployment • environmental damage But excludes defence

2003). For example, the Measure of Economic Welfare (MEW) created in the 1970s included costs of commuting but excluded other costs such as education, health and sanitation. The most recent, and perhaps best known, example of this family of community-value modified GDPs is the Genuine Progress Indicator (GPI) produced by the organization 'Redefining Progress' (based in the US)[3]. The GPI includes, amongst other things, volunteer work, the cost of crime and family breakdown, underemployment and environment-al damage. Table 2.8 is an example of the type of changes typically made to the GDP to generate the GPI. The table has been created from two sources, one of which is an example for the Australian economy (Hamilton, 1999).

Table 2.8 *An example of the components of the Genuine Progress Indicator*

Item included in GPI	Effect on GDP (+increases; −reduces)	Description (where applicable taken from the Australian example of Hamilton, 1999)
Personal consumption	+	Private final consumption expenditure
Income distribution	(adjusts consumption)	Share of lowest quintile in total income
Weighted personal consumption	+	Personal consumption weighted by index of changing income distribution
Value of household work and parenting	+	Value of hours of household work performed each year
Value of volunteer work	+	Value of volunteer work performed each year
Services of consumer durables	+	
Public consumption expenditure (non-defence)	+	Value on non-defence government consumption spending
Services of public capital	+	Contribution of public investment in non-defence works (eg roads)
Cost of crime	−	Measured by property losses and household spending on crime prevention
Cost of consumer durables	−	
Cost of commuting	−	Time spent commuting valued at opportunity cost
Private spending on health and education	−	Health and education spending that offsets declining conditions
Cost of family breakdown	−	
Cost of overwork	−	Value of hours of work done involuntarily
Loss of leisure time	−	
Cost of unemployment	−	Value of psychological costs of unemployment greater than 1.7%
Cost of underemployment	−	Value of psychological costs of underemployment of part-time employees who want to work full-time
Cost of transport accidents	−	Costs of repairs and pain and suffering
Cost of industrial accidents	−	Costs of pain and suffering
Cost of household pollution abatement	−	
Cost of water pollution	−	Damage to the environment measured by the control costs of improving water quality

Table 2.8 *Continued*

Item included in GPI	Effect on GDP (+increases; −reduces)	Description (where applicable taken from the Australian example of Hamilton, 1999)
Cost of air pollution	−	Damage to humans and environment from noxious emissions measured mainly by health costs
Cost of noise pollution	−	Excess noise levels valued by cost of reducing noise to acceptable level
Costs of irrigation water use	−	Damage to the environment measured by the opportunity cost of environmental flows
Costs of farmland degradation	−	Costs to current and future generations from soil erosion etc, measured by forgone output
Loss of old growth forests/loss of native forests	−	Environmental values denied to future generations measured by willingness to pay
Depletion of non-renewable energy resources	−	Costs of shifting from oil and gas to renewables
Other long-term environmental damage	−	
Cost of ozone depletion	−	Annual emissions valued by future impacts on humans and environment
Cost of climate change	−	Annual emissions valued by future impacts on humans and environment
Net capital investment/growth	+	Growth in net capital stocks per worker
Net foreign lending or borrowing	−	Change in net foreign liabilities

The above table is a list of components that may be included in the GPI rather than a definitive list of those that must be. Note the inclusion of 'environmental' costs in the GPI as well as 'quality of life' issues (crime, family breakdowns, leisure time).
Source: Table adapted from Hardi et al (1997) and Hamilton (1999).

As a result of the adjustments illustrated in Table 2.8, the GPI tends to be significantly lower than the GDP. For example, Hamilton (1999) estimates that while the GDP/capita in Australia increased from $9,000 to more than $23,000 between 1950 and 1996 the GPI/capita over the same period increased from $9,000 to $16,000. However, note the inclusion of a correction for income inequality (personal consumption) in Table 2.8. There are various methods that can be used to adjust for inequality, but the result is that the GPI will have such an adjustment while the GDP will not. This makes an absolute comparison between the two invalid, and instead the emphasis should be upon the trend over time (Neumayer, 2000). In Hamilton's Australian example, while the GDP/capita showed a steady increase between 1950 and 1996, the GPI/capita actually had a marked decline in the 1980s before increasing. The result has been a noticeable divergence in GDP/capita and GPI/capita by the mid-1990s. This has been explained by Hamilton (1999, p26) as being due to:

- unsustainable levels of foreign debt
- the growing costs of unemployment and overwork
- the combined impact of a number of environmental problems including greenhouse gas emissions
- the escalating costs of energy resource depletion; and
- a failure to maintain investments in national stock.

In effect the Australian economy reached a threshold – a point beyond which increases in wealth as measured by GDP/capita did not necessarily translate into better 'quality of life' as proxied by the GPI/capita (Neumayer, 2000). Similar increases in GDP/capita and GPI/capita (or indeed the ISEW/capita) followed by a levelling of the latter have been seen in other economies (Lawn, 2003).

While it is intuitively appealing, the GPI methodology has its critics given the numerous assumptions it makes about the valuation of resources and environmental damage (Neumayer, 2000; Lawn, 2003). This may in part explain the continued dominance of the GDP and related economic indices. As Lawn (2003) says:

> *Indeed, unless a robust and consistent set of valuation techniques can be established along similar lines to the way in which the United Nations System of National Accounts is used to calculate GDP, the results of the ISEW, GPI and SNBI [Sustainable Net Benefit Index] will forever be open to criticism.* (Lawn, 2003, p116)

Another reason for the popularity of the GDP family is that it may be much easier for a country to improve these economic indicators than to make progress with social indicators such as public health and housing (Kao and Liu, 1984).

SUMMARY

Economic indices such as the GDP continue to be seen as important indicators of a country's development. The GDP is but one of a suite of indicators, including the GNP, which all take into account various aspects of an economy, such as consumption of fixed capital.

As indicators of development, the GDP family has its limitations. It is possible for an economy to have a high GDP while incurring significant damage to its environment and natural resource base. Such an economy will not be sustainable and, even if the damage were aesthetically and morally defensible at some stage, there will be a need for realignment. Similarly, an economy that results in prosperity for a relative few and poverty for the rest could hardly be considered 'developed'. Other indicators have been developed, such as the Environmentally Adjusted GDP and the GPI, to include some of these costs, but these still do not have the wide appeal and 'headline' capturing ability of the GDP.

Despite the technical and apparently objective appearance of the tables and figures in this chapter, it should be noted that with all of the indicators discussed so far there is an element of human (and thereby subjective) choice. Just what should be left out and included in the GDP, GPI etc? How is environmental damage to be valued? How do we define and measure poverty? These are themes that will be highlighted in subsequent chapters, but in the next we will concern ourselves with just one of issues discussed so far and which is obviously of major relevance in development: poverty.

3 DEVELOPMENT INDICATORS: POVERTY

INTRODUCTION

Poverty is obviously an important element to consider in development, and indeed stated 'goals of development' often emphasize a reduction in poverty as a main measure of success (Anand and Ravallion, 1993). However, poverty means very different things to different people. There have been many ways of formally identifying poverty over the last few hundred years. An early example is the notion of 'subsistence' (Poor Laws, early 19th century); people are said to be in poverty if their incomes are not sufficient to maintain a minimum level of subsistence, typically defined in terms of essential requirements for life such as food, rent and clothing. Another view is the 'basic needs' approach adopted by the International Labour Organization (ILO) in the 1970s (Streeten, 1979; Khan, 1991; Brinkerhoff et al, 1997). This is a broader based definition that includes shelter, drinking water, sanitation, education, health care etc, as well as food and clothing. Also included in this 'basic needs' perspective are issues such as social participation, right to work, self-reliance and a voice in decision making. The 'basic needs' approach is more relative than 'subsistence' as it may change with time and place. The 'basic needs' approach lead to the creation in the 1970s of a set of performance indicators by which attainment could be measured, and these in turn, along with parallel work by the social-indicators movement, have helped spawn the current interest in development indicators (Hicks and Streeten, 1979; Ogwang and Abdou, 2003).

Given its importance, the measurement of poverty has long been a major concern, but due to differences in meaning there are problems (Townsend, 1954). A commonly applied approach, albeit highly simplified, is to consider the notion of a 'poverty line'. This defines poverty in terms of an income below which people are deemed to be in poverty (ie not able to afford all the requirements for subsistence or basic needs). It can be determined in various ways, but the typical approach is to set it in terms of financial income (usually daily). The line may be relative or absolute. If relative then the line is determined in relation to the country context (for example 50 per cent of the mean income in the country). If absolute then the line is fixed over space and/or time.

The 'poverty line' is a useful conceptual device that is easily understood. It is also widely applied, and pre-dates the modern era of development. For example, a pre-World War II example for the UK can be found in George (1937), and this author also makes the valid point that 'under no circumstances can the "Poverty Line" be regarded as a desirable level'. The magnitude of the poverty line depends upon assumptions regarding what items are important to life (Townsend, 1954). George's (1937) example assumes that the minimum costs of food, clothing, fuel, lighting, cleaning materials, compulsory insurance, travel to and from work and rent are included, but within these categories there can be significant variation. What do we include under 'food' and 'clothing' for example?

The notion of a 'poverty line' can also suffer from political interference. Governments may wish to present themselves in a good light, and one easy and extremely cheap way of achieving this is simply to lower the poverty line so that the proportion classified as 'poor' is reduced. Therefore, there is something of a conundrum in that using a common 'poverty line' across countries is problematic (different conditions exist in each country), but using different 'poverty lines' for countries can also be suspect if one relies upon 'official' figures that are open to political interference. In terms of international figures for the poverty line, the notional values of US$ 1 and US$ 2 per day (adjusted for PPP of course) are often used by aid agencies and the media.

In order to provide continuity with Chapter 2, this chapter will explore four 'income based' indicators of poverty which employ the poverty line as a standard:

1   Headcount Ratio (or Headcount Index) (H)
2   Income Gap Ratio (I)
3   Poverty Gap Index (P_1)
4   Sen's Poverty Index (P)

While the poverty line may be a convenient intuitive device, it does have its problems, and in fact the evolution demonstrated by the four indicators above, from the simplest (Headcount Ratio) to the most complex (Sen's Index of Poverty), reflects some of these problems and the ways in which they are addressed. Indeed the fourth indicator is an example of a composite index comprising a number of separate indicators, and therefore it, in turn, begins to raise complex issues of presentation and interpretation.

HEADCOUNT RATIO

The Headcount Ratio (H) is the simplest of the four indicators. It is the proportion of the population below the poverty line.

$$H = \frac{\text{number of poor}}{\text{total population}}$$

It ranges from 0 (no one is poor – the ideal) to 1 (everyone is poor – far from ideal).

The Headcount Ratio obviously depends upon the level of the poverty line. The lower this is set, the lower will be the value of H. Of course if it is set too low, it becomes meaningless.

The Headcount Ratio is a simple measure of poverty, and there are variations on this theme. For example, it is possible to differentiate between the proportion of rural and urban populations below the national poverty line. Similarly, the figures can differentiate by region within a country. The relative simplicity and ease of calculation of the Headcount Ratio has ensured its wide use (Sen, 1976).

The main problem with the Headcount Ratio is that it does not take into account the depth of poverty (how far below the poverty line people are). For example, consider two populations with 10 people in each population and a poverty line of $1/day (Table 3.1).

Table 3.1 *Example of how depth of poverty varies between two populations ($N = 10$; $Z = \$1.0/day$)*

Population 1		Population 2	
Person (i)	y_i ($)	Person (i)	y_i ($)
1	2.0	1	4.0
2	1.9	2	3.8
3	1.9	3	2.5
4	1.8	4	2.5
5	1.2	5	1.5
6	0.8	6	0.9
7	0.6	7	0.9
8	0.5	8	0.8
9	0.5	9	0.7
10	0.4	10	0.7
H	0.5		0.5

Headcount Ratio (H) is the same for both populations, but depth of poverty appears to be greater in population 1 compared to population 2.

In each case the value of the Headcount Ratio is 0.5 (half the population is below the poverty line of $1/day), but the depth of poverty is greater in population 1 than in population 2. In our example this is readily apparent from only a cursory glance at the figures. The maximum depth below the poverty line for population 2 is $0.30, and this only applies to two of the people. There are four individuals in population 1 whose depth below the poverty line is greater than $0.30. Another way of analysing this is to find the average deviation from the poverty line. For population 1 this is $0.44 (0.2 + 0.4 + 0.5 + 0.5 + 0.6, all divided by 5) while for population 2 the average deviation from the poverty line is $0.2 (0.1 + 0.1 + 0.2 + 0.3 + 0.3, all divided by 5). Therefore, while our Headcount Ratio suggests that the level of poverty is the same for both populations, the position is clearly worse for population 1 than population 2.

INCOME GAP RATIO

The next indicator in the series, Income Gap Ratio (I), was designed to focus on the depth of poverty below a nominal poverty line. It is the average deviation from the poverty line for people who are *below* the poverty line. Therefore, by definition it does not include those above it (ie those deemed not to be in poverty).

For each individual in the population the deviation from the poverty line can be found as:

Deviation of per capita income relative to the poverty line $= \dfrac{Z - y_i}{Z}$

where

$Z =$ poverty line

$y_i =$ income of person i (by definition, $y_i < Z$).

If $y_i = \$0.8$ and Z (poverty line) $= \$1.0$:

deviation relative to poverty line $= \dfrac{1.0 - 0.8}{1.0} = 0.2$

(deviation is 20 per cent of the poverty line for this individual).

Summing this for all the individuals (or households) below the poverty line and dividing by the number of people included will give an average deviation from the poverty line:

$$I = \frac{\text{total deviation from poverty line (relative to poverty line)}}{\text{number of people below poverty line}}$$

The higher the value of the Income Gap Ratio, the greater the average depth of poverty, but note that average deviation is expressed relative to the value of the poverty line. It is a proportional shortfall in income. The reason for this is that absolute deviation from the poverty line may be misleading. For example, if the poverty line is $1/day and two individuals have incomes of $0.80/day, the average depth of poverty is $0.20/day. Setting the poverty line at $2/day and incomes at $1.80/day will give us the same average depth of poverty as before ($0.20/day), but arguably the situation is not as bad. With a poverty line of $1/day our two individuals have an average depth of poverty 20 per cent that of the poverty line, while in our second example, the average depth of poverty is only 10 per cent of the poverty line of $2/day. For the individuals concerned, a gap of 20 per cent from what is deemed to be an acceptable income for subsistence is probably worse than a gap of 10 per cent.

The calculation of the Income Gap Ratio is illustrated in Table 3.2 with the same data as before ($Z=\$1/day$ and the population size is 10 in each case).

As expected, the Income Gap Ratio is more than twice as large for

Table 3.2 *Example calculation of Income Gap Ratio (N= 10; Z=$1.0/day)*

Person (i)	Population 1 $y_i(\$)$	$\frac{(Z-y_i)}{Z}$	Person (i)	Population 2 $y_i(\$)$	$\frac{(Z-y_i)}{Z}$
1	2.0		1	4.0	
2	1.9		2	3.8	
3	1.9		3	2.5	
4	1.8		4	2.5	
5	1.2		5	1.5	
6	0.8	0.2	6	0.9	0.1
7	0.6	0.4	7	0.9	0.1
8	0.5	0.5	8	0.8	0.2
9	0.5	0.5	9	0.7	0.3
10	0.4	0.6	10	0.7	0.3
H	0.5			0.5	
Total		2.2			1.0
Number below poverty line		5			5
I	2.2/5 =	0.44		1.0/5 =	0.2

I is greater for population 1 indicating that this population has a greater depth of poverty than population 2.

population 1 than population 2, suggesting that the depth of poverty is much greater for population 1 (Figure 3.1).

However, there is another problem in that, like all averages, the Income Gap Ratio can hide the variation in the gap. Another dataset illustrates this problem (Table 3.3); two populations, numbered 3 and 4 to avoid confusion with the previous example, with $Z=\$1.0$ and a total population$=10$.

In this example, the values of the Income Gap Ratio are the same (0.34), and therefore the average depth of poverty for the two populations is the same (Figure 3.2).

However, while the average depth is the same for both populations, there is greater variation in the depth of poverty for population 4 than population 3. The range of the depth of poverty for population 3 is 20–50 per cent of the poverty line, while the range for population 4 is 10–70 per cent of the poverty line.

While this matters a great deal to the individuals concerned, does it matter in a policy context? Well, yes it does. For example, because it is an average, the Income Gap Ratio can be a dangerous measure of the success of poverty

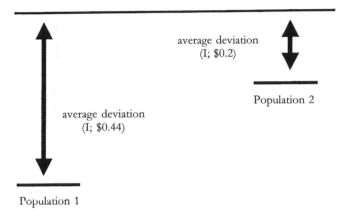

POVERTY LINE ($1.0; 100%)

average deviation
(I; $0.2)

Population 2

average deviation
(I; $0.44)

Population 1

Figure 3.1 *Illustration of depth of poverty*

Table 3.3 *Second example calculation of Income Gap Ratio (N= 10; Z=$1.0/day)*

| | Population 3 | | | Population 4 | |
Person (i)	y_i($)	$\frac{(Z-y_i)}{Z}$	Person (i)	y_i($)	$\frac{(Z-y_i)}{Z}$
1	2.0		1	4.0	
2	1.9		2	3.8	
3	1.9		3	2.5	
4	1.8		4	2.5	
5	1.2		5	1.5	
6	0.8	0.2	6	0.9	0.1
7	0.7	0.3	7	0.9	0.1
8	0.7	0.3	8	0.8	0.2
9	0.6	0.4	9	0.4	0.6
10	0.5	0.5	10	0.3	0.7
H	0.5			0.5	
Total		1.7			1.7
Number below poverty line		5			5
I	1.7/5 =	0.34		1.7/5 =	0.34

In this case the value of I is the same for both populations, but there is greater variation in the depth of poverty for population 4 compared to population 3.

reducing programmes. This can be illustrated as shown in Table 3.4 for population 3, only in this case the two columns can be thought of as a 'before and after' set of results following a poverty reduction project. Those above the poverty line, even if just above it, are not targeted, hence there is no change in their daily income. But individual six has moved above the poverty line ($0.8/day to $1.1/day, a change of $0.3). The Headcount Ratio does

POVERTY LINE ($1.0; 100%)

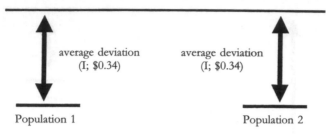

Figure 3.2 *Illustration of average depth of poverty*

Table 3.4 *Example calculation of Income Gap Ratio – a before and after scenario (N= 10; Z=$1.0/day)*

Person (i)	Population 3 Before project $y_i(\$)$	$\frac{(Z-y_i)}{Z}$	Person (i)	Population 4 After project $y_i(\$)$	$\frac{(Z-y_i)}{Z}$
1	2.0		1	2.0	
2	1.9		2	1.9	
3	1.9		3	1.9	
4	1.8		4	1.8	
5	1.2		5	1.2	
			6	1.1	
6	0.8	0.2			
7	0.7	0.3	7	0.7	0.3
8	0.7	0.3	8	0.7	0.3
9	0.6	0.4	9	0.6	0.4
10	0.5	0.5	10	0.5	0.5
H	0.5			0.4	
Total		1.7			1.5
Number below poverty line		5			4
I	1.7/5 =	0.34		1.5/4 =	0.38

While H has improved the value of I worsens, suggesting that project has worsened the depth of poverty!

bring out this success (H declines from 0.5 to 0.4), but the value of I actually gets worse (0.34 to 0.38). In this example, $Z=\$1.0$ and the total population $= 10$.

Taking individual six out of the equation, so to speak, has increased the average depth of poverty. This should not be surprising given that individual six was near the poverty line to begin with and hence the depth of poverty for that individual was relatively small. In effect that individual was pulling the average downwards. Removing him/her from the sample without changing any of the other figures would inevitably raise the average. The result is good news for individual six, but no difference for the other four people. This may not be a brilliant success, but it is nonetheless an improvement. If the policy makers go only by the Income Gap Ratio, it would appear to them that their intervention had worsened matters rather than improved them.

POVERTY GAP INDEX

One way of handling the lack of sensitivity of the Income Gap Ratio to the proportion of people below the poverty line is to modify it using the Headcount Ratio. This brings us to our third stage in the evolution of the poverty line based indicators – a combination of the Headcount Ratio and the Income Gap Ratio.

The Poverty Gap Index (P_1) is found by multiplying the Headcount Ratio by the Income Gap Ratio.

P_1 = proportion of people below poverty line ×
average deviation below the poverty line

P_1 = Headcount Ratio × Income Gap Ratio

The Poverty Gap Index adjusts or weights the value of the Income Gap Ratio to take into account the proportion of the population that are classified as poor in terms of the poverty line being used. Therefore, as with the other two indicators, the lower the value of P_1 the better, and a P_1 value of zero means that nobody is poor. Using our 'before' and 'after' example (population 3) as before gives us the results shown in Table 3.5 (with Z still equal to $1.0):

Here the reduction in the Poverty Gap Index from 0.17 to 0.15 reflects an improvement in the aftermath of the poverty reduction programme. Although the Income Gap Ratio increased, the value of the Headcount Ratio declined. As the Poverty Gap Index is found by multiplying H and I, in this case its value declined.

While the Poverty Gap Index looks like the final answer to our problem of providing a measure of poverty upon which policy makers and managers can act, it does have a further disadvantage. The Poverty Gap Index does not cover the nature of the distribution of the income of poor people (ie those below the poverty line). Are these people uniformly poor or are some poorer than others? The Income Gap Ratio only tells us about the average depth of poverty and the Headcount Ratio only informs us about the proportion of the population below the poverty line (ie the proportion defined as poor). Multiplying them together has provided a correction to I allowing for H, but that is all.

Consider two populations of ten poor people (ie only those people below a poverty line of $1/day) out of a total population of 20. I have labelled them in Table 3.6 as populations 5 and 6 to avoid confusion with the previous tables.

Table 3.5 *Example calculation of the Poverty Gap Index ($N=10$; $Z=\$1.0/day$)*

Person (i)	Population 3 Before project $y_i(\$)$	$\dfrac{(Z-y_i)}{Z}$	Person (i)	Population 4 After project $y_i(\$)$	$\dfrac{(Z-y_i)}{Z}$
1	2.0		1	2.0	
2	1.9		2	1.9	
3	1.9		3	1.9	
4	1.8		4	1.8	
5	1.2		5	1.2	
			6	1.1	
6	0.8	0.2			
7	0.7	0.3	7	0.7	0.3
8	0.7	0.3	8	0.7	0.3
9	0.6	0.4	9	0.6	0.4
10	0.5	0.5	10	0.5	0.5
H	0.5			0.4	
Total		1.7			1.5
Number below poverty line		5			4
I	1.7/5 =	0.34		1.5/4 =	0.38
P₁	0.5 × 0.34 =	0.17		0.4 × 0.38 =	0.15

Table 3.6 *Distribution of poverty amongst the poor ($N=20$; $Z=\$1.0/day$). Individuals presented in the table are all below the poverty line*

Category	Population 5 Individual (i)	Income $y_i(\$)$	Population 6 Individual (i)	Income $y_i(\$)$
Lowest earner	1	0.90	1	0.49
	2	0.80	2	0.48
	3	0.70	3	0.46
	4	0.50	4	0.44
	5	0.40	5	0.43
	6	0.30	6	0.42
	7	0.25	7	0.41
	8	0.20	8	0.40
	9	0.15	9	0.39
Highest earner	10	0.10	10	0.38
Total income		4.30		4.30
Average income		0.43		0.43
Range		0.1 to 0.9		0.38 to 0.49
Headcount Ratio (H)		0.50		0.50
Income Gap Ratio (I)		0.57		0.57
Poverty Gap Index (P1)		0.285		0.285

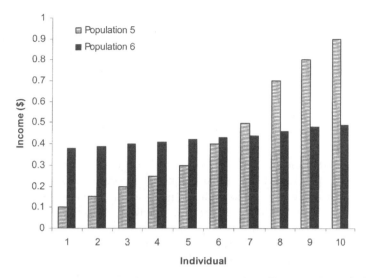

Population 6 has a more even distribution of income relative to population 5. The average income for both these populations is $0.43/day, and they have identical Income Gap Ratios of $0.57/day.

Figure 3.3 *Two different distributions of income below a notional poverty line of $1/day*

While the average income of the two populations is identical ($0.43) the distributions are very different (Figure 3.3). Population 6 has a more uniform income, while population 5 has a greater spread between the lowest and highest earners (remembering that all of these individuals are still defined as 'poor'). Also note that all three poverty indicators provide exactly the same result! Maybe we can argue that there is no difference between the two populations, after all the same proportions are below the poverty line and the average depth below the poverty line is the same. Does the distribution matter?

It can be argued that from a policy perspective it may matter whether we are dealing with a population of poor people with an unequal (5) or more equal (6) distribution. For example, maybe the more equal distribution suggests a common and pervasive cause of poverty, while the unequal distribution suggests a host of causes. It could be useful to consider the form of the distribution below the poverty line, but what we are missing in all three of the poverty indicators covered so far is a measure of inequality. That is the subject of the next section.

INCOME INEQUALITY

Inequality is an important consideration within development. After all:

> *To many social scientists, the ultimate goal of development is an improvement of the social welfare for all people, rather than merely raising the 'standard of living' for any particular group or groups.* (Kao and Liu, 1984)

There are, of course, moral dimensions to a discussion of inequality, but there are also material concerns such as the potential for social tension (Quadrado et al, 2001). Here we will concern ourselves more with inequality within a population than between countries or regions (see Maasoumi and Jeong, 1985, for one example of the measurement of international inequality in GNP). While the focus here, and indeed for many studies of inequality, will be on income, it has to be stressed that inequality can be considered in terms of other factors such as education, health care, resources, quality of the natural environment, expenditure etc (Sen, 1985; Cohen, 2000). My intention is certainly not to imply that income is the only such factor important to development, and I have focused on income in order to provide continuity with the income-based poverty indices discussed in previous sections.

There are a number of measures of equality of distribution of income amongst individuals within a population, and there is a substantial literature which discusses their relative merits (Atkinson, 1970). Perhaps the simplest way of approaching this is to first rank the population in terms of income (or whatever) category and then consider the proportion of income associated with that category. The difference between the proportion of individuals in a category and the proportion of wealth in that same category will provide some idea as to the extent of equality. For example, the Index of Dissimilarity (ID) is given by:

$$\mathrm{ID} = 0.5 \Sigma X_i - Y_i$$

where X_i is the income category width (different categories are denoted with the subscript i) and Y_i is the proportion of income associated with that category width. The symbol Σ signifies that this difference has to be added up over all of the income categories and $|X_i - Y_i|$ means that we have to take the absolute value of the difference ($1 - 2 = 1$ not -1). Values of the ID range from a minimum of zero and a maximum of 1, and the higher the value of the ID then the greater the level of inequality.

Two theoretical examples illustrate the calculation. Both have income categories of 20 per cent (ie the population is divided into quintiles). In the first example (Table 3.7), all income categories have exactly the same share (20 per cent) of total income, and the ID in this case is zero.

In the second example (Table 3.8), four of the categories (covering 80 per cent of the population) have between them only 0.4 per cent of total income, whilst the richest 20 per cent have a massive 99.6 per cent of total income. Clearly there is inequality and the ID is 0.796.

An example with real data is shown in Table 3.9 (data from the US for 1999). Here there are differences between all five categories in terms of their share of total income, and they are ranked in terms of the poorest 20 per cent, second poorest 20 per cent etc up to the richest 20 per cent of the population. The value for the ID is 0.326 (somewhere between our two theoretical examples).

Table 3.7 *Calculation of Index of Dissimilarity – Example 1 where income is distributed equally amongst five categories*

Income category	Category width X_i	Proportion of total income Y_i	Absolute $X_i - Y_i$		
1st 20%	0.2	0.2	0		
2nd 20%	0.2	0.2	0		
3rd 20%	0.2	0.2	0		
4th 20%	0.2	0.2	0		
5th 20%	0.2	0.2	0		
Total	1	1		Total	0
				ID	0

Table 3.8 *Calculation of Index of Dissimilarity – Example 2 where income is unevenly distributed between the richest 20% of the population and the remaining 80%*

Income category	Category width X_i	Proportion of total income Y_i	Absolute $X_i - Y_i$		
1st 20%	0.2	0.001	0.199		
2nd 20%	0.2	0.001	0.199		
3rd 20%	0.2	0.001	0.199		
4th 20%	0.2	0.001	0.199		
Richest 20%	0.2	0.996	0.796		
Total	1	1		Total	1.592
				ID	0.796

Table 3.9 *Calculation of the Index of Dissimilarity – real US data*

Income category	Category width X_i	Proportion of total income Y_i	Absolute $X_i - Y_i$		
Poorest 20%	0.2	0.036	0.164		
2nd 20%	0.2	0.089	0.111		
3rd 20%	0.2	0.149	0.051		
4th 20%	0.2	0.232	0.032		
Richest 20%	0.2	0.494	0.294		
Total	1	1		Total	0.652
				ID	0.326

However, perhaps the best known and most widely used such measure of equality is the Gini coefficient. Like the Index of Dissimilarity, the Gini coefficient is not in itself a measure of poverty, but it is one that is often used in lists of development indicators. It is a summary measure of the extent to which the actual distribution of income differs from a hypothetical distribution in which each person receives an identical share. It is based on the Lorenz curve (Box 3.1), and like the ID has values ranging from 0 to 1. A Gini coefficient of 0 means that income, expenditure etc are equally distributed amongst all members of the population and a coefficient of 1 means that there is extreme inequality. Gini coefficients tell us nothing about living standards. Low values do not necessarily equate to higher standards of living, as everyone could be equally poor rather than equally rich! Hence quite different distributions can yield the same coefficient. Hence, the isolated reporting of simple indices of inequality such as the Gini coefficient, while widespread, have been criticized (Atkinson, 1970).

Another problem with the Gini coefficient is that while it is easy to calculate (as shown in Box 3.1), one must have good quality data to feed into the calculation. Table 3.10 provides a number of examples of the Gini coefficient for nations (data taken from the World Development Report 2002). Three of the countries in Table 3.1 have Gini coefficients above 0.6 and none above 0.7. But where do these figures come from? How reliable are they? The difficulty of doing this can perhaps be gleaned from the fact that four of these are based on data collected before 1990, 22 between 1990 and 1995 and 46 between 1996 and 1998. While it may be reasonable to suppose that little change in income distribution can occur over five years, evidence also suggests that change can be rapid (as with the US example in Box 3.1).

The Gini coefficient as discussed here is one-dimensional – only inequality in income is covered. There have been efforts to take a more multidimensional perspective on inequality, considering, for example, income alongside non-monetary variables (Atkinson and Bourguignon, 1982; Maasoumi, 1986). If these are correlated, and the likelihood is that many will be, the analyses and results can be complex and not simple extrapolations from the one-dimensional scenarios.

There have been efforts to use the Gini coefficient as a component of poverty indicators in order to address the problem highlighted in the discussion of the Poverty Gap Index, above. Perhaps the best known approach is Amartya Sen's Index of Poverty (P; Sen, 1976): a combination of the Headcount Ratio, the Income Gap Ratio and the Gini coefficient for the population classified as poor (ie those below the poverty line). The calculation of P is outlined in Box 3.2. This index is of interest in our story of development indicators for a number of reasons. First it is a composite index composed of three separate indicators designed to measure quite different features of a population. Indeed its derivation by Sen was influential and resulted in a surge of other efforts to produce poverty indices (Shorrocks,

Table 3.10 *Some example Gini coefficients*

Gini category	Country	Survey year	Notes	Gini coefficient (G)
>0.6 (most unequal)	Sierra Leone	1989	a b	0.629
	Central African Republic	1993	a b	0.613
	Brazil	1998	c d	0.607
0.5 to 0.6	South Africa	1993–94	a b	0.593
	Paraguay	1998	c d	0.577
	Colombia	1996	c d	0.571
	Chile	1998	c d	0.567
	Honduras	1998	c d	0.563
	Lesotho	1986–87	a b	0.560
	Guatemala	1998	c d	0.558
	Burkina Faso	1998	a b	0.551
	Mexico	1998	c d	0.531
	Zambia	1998	a b	0.526
	El Salvador	1998	c d	0.522
	Nigeria	1996–97	a b	0.506
	Mali	1994	a b	0.505
	Niger	1995	a b	0.505
	Gambia, The	1998	a b	0.502
	Zimbabwe	1995	a b	0.501
0.4 to 0.5	Venezuela, RB	1998	c d	0.495
	Russian Federation	1998	a b	0.487
	Panama	1997	a b	0.485
	Cameroon	1996	a b	0.477
	Dominican Republic	1998	c d	0.474
	Peru	1996	c d	0.462
	Costa Rica	1997	c d	0.459
	Kenya	1997	a b	0.449
	Bolivia	1999	a b	0.447
	Uzbekistan	1998	a b	0.447
	Armenia	1996	a b	0.444
	Ecuador	1995	a b	0.437
	Uruguay	1989	c d	0.423
	Tunisia	1995	a b	0.417
	Turkey	1994	a b	0.415
	Thailand	1998	a b	0.414
	Senegal	1995	a b	0.413
	Turkmenistan	1998	a b	0.408
	Ghana	1999	a b	0.407
	Moldova	1997	c d	0.406
	China	1998	c d	0.403
	Trinidad and Tobago	1992	c d	0.403
	Ethiopia	1995	a b	0.400
0.3 to 0.4	Mozambique	1996–97	a b	0.396
	Morocco	1998–99	a b	0.395
	Tanzania	1993	a b	0.382
	Madagascar	1999	a b	0.381
	Jamaica	2000	a b	0.379
	India	1997	a b	0.378

▶

Table 3.10 *Continued*

Gini category	Country	Survey year	Notes	Gini coefficient (G)
0.3 to 0.4	Estonia	1998	c d	0.376
(contd)	Mauritania	1995	a b	0.373
	Georgia	1996	c d	0.371
	Lao PDR	1997	a b	0.370
	Côte d'Ivoire	1995	a b	0.367
	Nepal	1995–96	a b	0.367
	Jordan	1997	a b	0.364
	Azerbaijan	1995	c d	0.360
	Portugal	1994–95	c d	0.356
	Kazakhstan	1996	a b	0.354
	Algeria	1995	a b	0.353
	Sri Lanka	1995	a b	0.344
	Bangladesh	1995–96	a b	0.336
	Yemen, Rep.	1998	a b	0.334
	Mongolia	1995	a b	0.332
	Latvia	1998	c d	0.324
	Lithuania	1996	a b	0.324
	Indonesia	1999	a b	0.317
	Korea, Rep.	1993	a b	0.316
	Poland	1998	a b	0.316
	Pakistan	1996–97	a b	0.312
	Romania	1998	a b	0.311
0.2 to 0.3	Croatia	1998	c d	0.290
	Ukraine	1999	a b	0.290
	Egypt, Arab Rep.	1995	a b	0.289
	Rwanda	1983–85	a b	0.289
	Slovenia	1998	c d	0.284
	Bulgaria	1997	c d	0.264
	Czech Republic	1996	c d	0.254
	Hungary	1998	a b	0.244
	Belarus	1998	a b	0.217
<0.2 (most equal)	Slovak Republic	1992	c d	0.195

a. Refers to expenditure shares by percentiles of population.
b. Ranked by per capita expenditure.
c. Refers to income shares by percentiles of population.
d. Ranked by per capita income.
The data have been extracted from the World Development Report (2002). The countries in this table have been ranked ('league table' style) with the highest (most uneven) distributions at the top.

1995). However, like all such indices the same value can be obtained from quite different balances of its three components, as outlined at the end of Box 3.2. Therefore, in order to make best use of such indices, we cannot just present the 'end' product, so to speak, but must also present the values of the indicators upon which it is based. The second point of interest is that Sen's work on poverty, and particularly the importance of increasing capability (options available to the poor) as a way of fighting poverty has also been highly influential in the creation of perhaps the best known and most quoted composite development indicators – the Human Development Index (HDI) of the United Nations Development Programme.

Box 3.1 *The Gini coefficient*

This graph shows a plot of the cumulative percentage of households ranked with the poorest households to the left and the richest to the right. The vertical axis is the cumulative proportion of the household income (or indeed any resource).

The graph has two 'theoretical' plots:

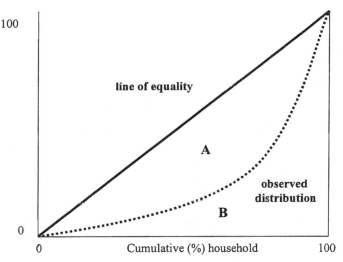

- **'line of equality'** assumes that there is an equal distribution of income amongst the households (45° angle to the 0 starting point). The addition of one household on the horizontal axis adds exactly the same amount of income each time.
- **'observed distribution'** is closer to what we see in practice (called a 'Lorenz Curve') and in this case more of the wealth is concentrated in relatively few households. Because the poorest households are ranked towards the left of the axis, as we add additional households there is little increase in cumulative income. However, as we reach the richer households to the right of the graph, the cumulative income rapidly rises.

To compute the Gini coefficient, we first measure the area between the Lorenz curve and the 45° equality line (A). This area is divided by the entire area below the 45° line (ie A+B; always taken to equal 0.5).

$$\text{Gini coefficient} = \frac{\text{area A}}{\text{area (A+B)}}$$

▶

For a perfectly equal distribution, there would be no area between the 45° line and the Lorenz curve (A = 0). This equates to a Gini coefficient of zero. For complete inequality, in which only one person has any income, the Lorenz curve would coincide with the straight lines at the lower and right boundaries of the curve. This equates to a Gini coefficient of one (ie A would more or less equal to A + B).

One formula for the Gini coefficient is as follows:

$$\text{Gini coefficient} = 1 - \Sigma(\sigma X_i - \sigma X_{i-1})\ (\sigma Y_{i-1} + \sigma Y_i)$$

Where:

$i =$ label for the categories along the x-axis
$\sigma X_i =$ cumulated values for the population up to category i
$\sigma Y_i =$ cumulated values for the income up to category i
$\Sigma =$ sum of all income categories

While the calculation of the Gini coefficient may look daunting, the calculation is in fact easily carried out with a program such as Microsoft Excel. An example is provided in the table opposite (data are for the US in 1999 and available at www.census.gov).

The income categories are provided on the left of the table (divided into categories of 20 per cent) along with the proportion of the population that falls into the income categories. For example, 3.6 per cent of the population are in the lowest 20 per cent income category while 49.4 per cent are in the highest 20 per cent income category. In this example the Gini coefficient is 0.424.

Note that, in this example, the Gini coefficient has been calculated for quite broad categories of 20 per cent (quintiles). Do we get the same Gini coefficient with other categories? Not necessarily. The second table is theoretical but uses the same quintile proportions as the US example for 1999. The difference is that the categories are based on tenths (10 per cent), but the methodology is exactly the same as before. The Gini coefficient this time around is 0.434 (a significant increase of 0.01).

Economies have Gini coefficients between zero and one. Generally, the distribution of income is considered to be relatively even if its value falls between 0.2 and 0.35. However, the Gini coefficient varies greatly from one country to another, depending on the level of development. In general, more highly developed countries tend to have a lower differentiation of income (0.28–0.35). A high differentiation of income is characteristic of developing countries. Here the Gini coefficient usually falls between 0.44–0.60.

The interpretation of why some Gini coefficients are higher/lower than others may not be straightforward. For example, within a country the Gini coefficient can change with time, and there may be various explanations. The following graph of Gini coefficients for the US (1967 to 1999) has been taken from the US Census Bureau.

There has been a steady tendency toward increased inequality between 1970 and 1997, although between 1997 and 1999 inequality appears to have levelled out. There are three possible explanations:

1   The distribution of wage income may have become more unequal.
2   The distribution of income from property may have become more unequal.
3   The functional distribution may have shifted, so that property incomes are a larger fraction of total incomes. This would make the personal distribution of income more unequal as

Calculation of the Gini coefficient (US, 1999). Income categories in quintiles

Category	Label (i)	Category width X_i	Proportion of total income Y_i	Cumulative categories σX_i	Cumulative income σY_i	$\sigma X_i - \sigma X_{i-1}$	$\sigma Y_{i-1} + \sigma Y_i$	$(\sigma X_i - \sigma X_{i-1})(\sigma Y_{i-1} + \sigma Y_i)$
Lowest 20%	1	0.2	0.036	0.2	0.036	0.2	0.036	0.007
2nd 20%	2	0.2	0.089	0.4	0.125	0.2	0.161	0.032
3rd 20%	3	0.2	0.149	0.6	0.274	0.2	0.399	0.080
4th 20%	4	0.2	0.232	0.8	0.506	0.2	0.780	0.156
Highest 20%	5	0.2	0.494	1.0	1.000	0.2	1.506	0.301
Total		1.0	1.000				Total	0.576
							Gini	0.424

Theoretical calculation of the Gini coefficient (based on the US 1999 example) with categories based on tenths (not quintiles)

Category	Label (i)	Category width X_i	Proportion of total income Y_i	Proportion of income in quintiles	Cumulative categories σX_i	Cumulative income σY_i	$\sigma X_i - \sigma X_{i-1}$	$\sigma Y_{i-1} + \sigma Y_i$	$(\sigma X_i - \sigma X_{i-1})(\sigma Y_{i-1} + \sigma Y_i)$
Lowest 10%	1	0.1	0.012		0.1	0.012	0.1	0.012	0.001
	2	0.1	0.024	0.036	0.2	0.036	0.1	0.048	0.005
	3	0.1	0.031		0.3	0.067	0.1	0.103	0.010
	4	0.1	0.058	0.089	0.4	0.125	0.1	0.192	0.019
	5	0.1	0.062		0.5	0.187	0.1	0.312	0.031
	6	0.1	0.087	0.149	0.6	0.274	0.1	0.461	0.046
	7	0.1	0.110		0.7	0.384	0.1	0.658	0.066
	8	0.1	0.122	0.232	0.8	0.506	0.1	0.890	0.089
	9	0.1	0.236		0.9	0.742	0.1	1.248	0.125
Highest 10%	10	0.1	0.258	0.434	1.0	1.000	0.1	1.742	0.174
Total		1.0	1.000					Total	0.566
								Gini	0.434

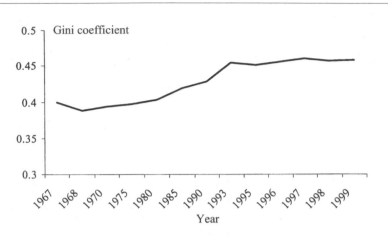

Property incomes are the more unequal component of the two. Increasing the weight on the more unequal component will increase overall inequality.

Evidence suggests that both of items 1 and 3 were responsible. One explanation is that there was a big decrease in the demand for unskilled labour, and a decline in their wages relative to skilled labour.

Box 3.2 *Sen's Poverty Index (P)*

One method of incorporating the form of a distribution below the poverty line into an index of poverty is to use the Gini coefficient (Sen, 1976). Sen's Poverty Index (P) is as follows:

Poverty Index $(P) = H(I + (1 - I)Gp)$

or (after rearrangement)

$P = HI + H(1 - I)Gp$

Where

    H = Headcount Ratio
    I = Income Gap Ratio
    Gp = Gini coefficient for the population below the poverty line

In effect this transforms the Gini coefficient from a measure of inequality to a measure of poverty. The value of P is between 0 (no one is below the poverty line) and 1 (no one has any income). As the value of I increases, the value of P will become closer to H (when I = 1 then P = H), and as the value of H increases, the value of P will become closer to I (when H = 1 then P = I).

    The calculation of the Sen Poverty Index for the two populations of Figure 3.3 is provided in the tables on pages 79 and 80. The value of the index is lower for population 6 (0.295) compared to population 5 (0.36), reflecting the marked difference in the Gini coefficient between the two.

▶

Population 5

Income category	Individual (i)	Income ($)	(Z − Xi/Z) ($)	Category width Xi	Proportion of total income (Yi)	Cumulative categories σXi	Cumulative income σYi	σXi − σXi − 1	σYi − 1 + σYi	(σXi − σXi − 1)(σYi − 1 + σYi)
Lowest	1	0.10	0.90	0.1	0.023	0.1	0.023	0.1	0.023	0.002
	2	0.15	0.85	0.1	0.035	0.2	0.058	0.1	0.081	0.008
	3	0.20	0.80	0.1	0.047	0.3	0.105	0.1	0.163	0.016
	4	0.25	0.75	0.1	0.058	0.4	0.163	0.1	0.268	0.027
	5	0.30	0.70	0.1	0.070	0.5	0.233	0.1	0.396	0.040
	6	0.40	0.60	0.1	0.093	0.6	0.326	0.1	0.559	0.056
	7	0.50	0.50	0.1	0.116	0.7	0.442	0.1	0.768	0.077
	8	0.70	0.30	0.1	0.163	0.8	0.605	0.1	1.047	0.105
	9	0.80	0.20	0.1	0.186	0.9	0.791	0.1	1.396	0.140
Highest	10	0.90	0.1	0.1	0.209	1.0	1.000	0.1	1.791	0.179
Total		4.30	5.70	1	1.0			1.000	Total	0.650
Average		0.43	0.57						Gini	0.350

Income Gap Ratio 0.570
Headcount Ratio 0.500
Poverty Gap Index 0.285
Sens Poverty Index 0.360

Population 6

Income category	Individual (i)	Income ($)	$(Z - Xi/Z)$ ($)	Category width Xi	Proportion of total income (Yi)	Cumulative categories σXi	Cumulative income σYi	$\sigma Xi - \sigma Xi - 1$	$\sigma Yi - 1 + \sigma Yi$	$(\sigma Xi - \sigma Xi - 1)$ $(\sigma Yi - 1 + \sigma Yi)$
Lowest	1	0.38	0.62	0.1	0.088	0.1	0.088	0.1	0.088	0.009
	2	0.39	0.61	0.1	0.091	0.2	0.179	0.1	0.267	0.027
	3	0.4	0.6	0.1	0.093	0.3	0.272	0.1	0.451	0.045
	4	0.41	0.59	0.1	0.095	0.4	0.367	0.1	0.639	0.064
	5	0.42	0.58	0.1	0.098	0.5	0.465	0.1	0.832	0.083
	6	0.43	0.57	0.1	0.1	0.6	0.565	0.1	1.03	0.103
	7	0.44	0.56	0.1	0.102	0.7	0.667	0.1	1.232	0.123
	8	0.46	0.54	0.1	0.107	0.8	0.774	0.1	1.441	0.144
	9	0.48	0.52	0.1	0.112	0.9	0.886	0.1	1.66	0.166
Highest	10	0.49	0.51	0.1	0.114	1	1	0.1	1.886	0.189
Total		4.30	5.70	1	1.0			1.000	Total 1.886	Total 0.953
Average		0.43	0.57							Gini 0.047

Income Gap Ratio 0.570
Headcount Ratio 0.500
Poverty Gap Index 0.285
Sens Poverty Index 0.295

While the average depth of poverty is the same, the distribution of income for population 5 is less even than that of population 6.

The Sen Poverty Index has been criticized (Shorrocks, 1995). One serious disadvantage is its 'replication invariance'. Merging two or more identical populations will not yield the same value for the index. For example, by merging two sets of population 6, the average income remains the same, as of course do the values of H and I, but the value of P increases from 0.295 to 0.36 (the same value as that of population 5).

There is also a problem with the interpretation of such composite indices in that the same value for an index can be achieved with different contributions from the three components. The following is an example matrix of values for the Income Gap Ratio, Headcount Ratio and Gini coefficient of the poor which all yield values of 0.5 for P.

Income Gap Ratio (I)	Headcount Ratio (H)	Gini coefficient (Gp)	Sen's Poverty Index (P)
1	0.5	1	0.5
1	0.5	0	0.5
0.5	1	0	0.5

But these are very different profiles of poverty! From all of the populations being poor ($H = 1$) to half the population ($H = 0.5$), from the depth of poverty being high ($I = 1$) to medium ($I = 0.5$) and from there being complete equality among the poor ($Gp = 0$) to complete inequality ($Gp = 1$). Sen's Index does not allow us to differentiate between these very different profiles of poverty, and we need to have access to the information for the three components in order to draw conclusions.

SUMMARY

This chapter has discussed three 'poverty line' based indicators of poverty: the Headcount Ratio, the Income Gap Ratio and the Poverty Gap Index. These are quite different in terms of what they measure, but their evolution can be tracked in terms of their failings. The Headcount Ratio does not take into account the depth of poverty, hence the need for the Income Gap Ratio. But the Income Gap Ratio does not take into account the proportion of the population below the poverty line, hence the need for the Poverty Gap Index – the product of the Headcount Ratio and the Income Gap Ratio. However, none of these capture the distribution of the population below the poverty line (ie how uniformly poor they are). Sen's Index of Poverty makes use of the Gini coefficient of the population who are poor to create a composite indicator which also includes the Headcount Ratio and the Income Gap Ratio.

Clearly with something as complex as poverty, even if visualized narrowly in terms of the poverty line, there is a need for a set of indicators to fully capture all of its features. While separate indicators can be combined into a single index, as with Sen's Index of Poverty, we still need to have the disaggregated information in order to best make judgements over what needs to be done to help alleviate the situation. There are parallels here with the suite of economic indicators considered in Chapter 2.

The next chapter will discuss another aggregated index, the HDI. While it has some similarity with the derivation of Sen's Poverty Index – indeed the HDI does draw heavily upon Sen's work with poverty and like P does have three components – the HDI is markedly different. P is an index that has a mathematical basis, with the structure of its equation reflecting an underlying mathematical logic that is set out in an objective and formal language. Beginning with a poverty line, it is logical to consider first the proportion of the population with incomes below it, the average depth of poverty below that line and the distribution of income for those deemed to be in poverty. While it is true that for practical considerations much depends upon the setting of a poverty line, and admittedly there is value judgement involved, P and all of the other poverty indicators discussed do follow from this with a compelling mathematical logic. Alternatives to P can also be rationalized, but again the logic is spelt out in mathematical terms. By way of contrast, the HDI is a composite index put together by a committee of experts, and its components and method of integration are but one choice among a multitude of options that could be equally rationalized.

4 INTEGRATING DEVELOPMENT INDICATORS

INTRODUCTION

The indicators set out in Chapters 2 and 3 are largely one-dimensional. They are designed to capture just one aspect of development, be it economic performance or poverty. While, of course, it is acknowledged that these are complex in themselves, and, as illustrated, the calculation of the GDP can have many elements, nonetheless the indicators presented have been designed to gauge performance (not necessarily progress) in a narrowly defined area of what we today consider as 'development'.

While economic indicators such as the GDP are useful, development is now considered to be a much broader concept and must be more than a focus on economic growth (Carlucci and Pisani, 1995) or even income gaps from a notional poverty line (Othick, 1983). This is certainly not to say that GDP or the Headcount Ratio have diminished in importance, far from it, but there have been numerous calls for a broadening of the concept of development and inevitably this has resulted in demands for more diverse sets of indicators. The problem is which indicators to choose from the many 'social indicators' that are available (Kao and Liu, 1984).

Alongside calls for a broader perspective and matching indicators, there have also been moves to aggregate them into a single index of development, thereby keeping intact the power of a single number as enjoyed, for example, by the GDP (Bayless and Bayless, 1982). There are many examples of composite development indices, and in each case the selection of indicators is rationalized by the authors concerned. Development indicators have often borrowed from much earlier attempts to create social indicators (Sinden, 1982), and Bunge (1981) and Othick (1983) provide early reviews of some issues. Quadrado et al (2001) provide a recent example of a development index for the regions of Hungary based on the following components:

- dwellings supplied with water conduit
- dwellings supplied with public sewerage
- students at primary and secondary school

- doctors (physicians and paediatricians)
- hospital beds
- GDP
- unemployment rate
- investments of the national economy.

This is obviously a diverse group, with GDP as but one component, and their units are quite different. Each of them needs to be made into a 'unit-less' indicator so as to allow aggregation into a single value. For example, Ogwang (1997) and others (see Othick, 1983) have suggested various forms of a Physical Quality of Life Index (PQLI) incorporating a literacy index, a life expectancy at age one index and an infant mortality index. These are combined so that values of the PQLI are between 0 and 100, with higher values implying a better quality of life.

It is obvious that with such indices much depends on what components are included and how they are aggregated (ie combined together into a single numerical value). One method for combining components is to make the index a simple average of the values of a number of separate indicators, but there are other alternatives. While these questions may appear to be somewhat pedantic and mechanical in nature, they do in fact echo deep and value-laden debates that strike at the very heart of the diversity of perspective as to what is considered to be 'development'. As discussed in Chapter 1, the creators of such indices have great power and responsibility.

This chapter will focus on one prominent example of such a call for broader indices of development – the creation of a suite of human development indices by the United Nations Development Programme (UNDP). In fairness to all those who have worked on such indices it should be pointed out that the UNDP development indices are not the only examples, or indeed necessarily the best. Neither are the UNDP indices the first attempt by the UN system to generate aggregated indices of development. The United Nations Research Institute for Social Development (UNRISD), based in Switzerland, had earlier proposed a development index with 18 'core socio-economic indicators' (Khan, 1991).

I have chosen to focus on the UNDP suite of development indices for a number of reasons. First, unlike many other efforts, they have a strong publicity machine behind them given that the Human Development Reports (HDRs) are released every year, usually by each country's UNDP office, to a great fanfare. As we shall see later, the HDRs (and the indices) do get good exposure in national media as a result. Indeed, going back to the students I referred to in Chapter 1, when they are asked for examples of a development index they often name the most prominent of the UNDP suite – the Human Development Index. Second, the HDRs and the associated indices were purposely created to counter the perceived dominance of economic indicators in the World Bank's *World Development Reports*. The UNDP development indices were not modifications of the GDP as was the GPI and its family of indicators.

The chapter will begin with a summary of human development as promoted by the UNDP in the HDRs and the calculation of the HDI. This will be followed by a brief discussion of some of the other UNDP development indices. The chapter will end by setting out some of the criticisms of the HDI and its family.

HUMAN DEVELOPMENT

The HDRs have been called the 'flagship publication not only of the UNDP, but possibly of the entire UN system' (Sagar and Najam, 1999).[1] Their publication, typically in July each year, is an event of note in many countries and is widely reported in the press. Like the World Bank's *World Development Reports* (WDRs), each of the HDRs has a separate theme, and a summary of these is provided in Table 4.1. The first HDR in 1990 put forward the UNDP's vision of human development and explained how this was meant to supplement economic growth rather than replace it. At the time of writing, the latest HDR (2003) focuses on the Millennium Goals to reduce poverty.

Table 4.1 *Themes and main data years for the United Nations Human Development Reports (HDR) and the calculation of the Human Development Index (HDI)*

Year	Theme of the HDR	Data years for the HDI components
1990	Concept and measurement of human development	1985 and 1987
1991	Financing human development	1980/85/85–88
1992	Global dimensions of human development	1989 and 1990
1993	People's participation	1990
1994	New dimensions of human security	1991 and 1992
1995	Gender and human development	1992
1996	Economic growth and human development	1993
1997	Human development to eradicate poverty	1994
1998	Consumption for human development	1995
1999	Globalization with a human face	1997
2000	Human rights and human development	1998
2001	Making new technologies work for human development	1999
2002	Deepening democracy in a fragmented world	2000
2003	Millennium Development Goals: A compact among nations to end human poverty	2001

The reports are similar in style to the WDRs, with which they are sometimes confused, in that each is divided into two parts. The first is a text and diagram based discussion of the main theme of the report, placed into a context of human development and changes in the world. Data tables and graphics are widely used throughout the chapters, and the result is something that is on the whole well-presented and engaging. The second part of each

HDR comprises a dense set of index and data tables that form the basis for the discussion in the first part of the report.

People, rather than money, are the central priority of human development. Economic growth is still regarded as important, but the emphasis is on such growth being one element in an improvement in the well-being of humankind (Anand and Ravallion, 1993; Aturupane et al, 1994; Streeten, 1994). Other vehicles for the dissemination of human development, such as the HDR website, are replete with this message, and even the academic journal established by the UNDP as a parallel endeavour to the HDRs has the telling title *Journal of Human Development. Alternative economics in action*. The man often considered to be the father of the HDRs is Mahbub ul Haq, a Pakistani economist who died in 1998, but the notion of 'human development' as espoused by the UNDP took much from the writings of Amartya Sen, a political economist based at Oxford University in the UK (Anand and Ravallion, 1993). As we have seen from Chapter 3, Sen has been highly influential with his work on poverty, and he also won the Nobel Prize for Economics. One of his central tenets is the importance of 'capability' in development (Sen, 1985), defined as the availability of options and choice open to people to allow them to lead long and healthy lives. When there is less choice ('optionality'), there are fewer opportunities for poor people to adapt and transform, and hence improve, their condition if they so wish.

> *Human development is a process of enlarging people's choices. In principle, these choices can be infinite and change over time. But at all levels of development, the three essential ones are for people to lead a long and healthy life, to acquire knowledge and to have access to resources needed for a decent standard of living. If these essential choices are not available, many other opportunities remain inaccessible.* (UNDP HDR, 1990, p10)

An increase in 'capability' can occur in many ways, for example by an improvement in an educational opportunity or the quality or quantity of a resource base (natural, social or otherwise). Clearly anything which reduces 'capability' is detrimental to human development, and there are obvious overlaps with sustainable development and its emphasis on provision for future generations and increased resilience to shocks (environmental, economic etc) with a more diverse livelihood base. Indeed one of the first steps taken in a livelihood analysis is a consideration of the assets open to an individual, household or a community. The term 'Sustainable Human Development' is sometimes employed to bring out this overlap (Sudhir and Sen, 1994).

The goal of human development is unambiguously stated on numerous occasions throughout the HDRs:

> *The end of development must be human well-being.* (UNDP HDR, 1990, p10)

Economic growth is one important means to this end and not an end in itself.

BIRTH OF THE HUMAN DEVELOPMENT INDEX

A desire to promote a broader vision of human development understandably helped to spawn the need for an alternative index to the GDP and its family of economic indicators. In the first HDR of 1990, the UNDP suggested an alternative index for gauging progress in human development (Kelly, 1991; Anand and Sen, 1994; Dowrick, 1996; Moldan, 1997; Ogwang, 2000). The obvious name to use was the Human Development Index (HDI), but what is most interesting is this perceived need to have a headline index to match the new paradigm. Just as economic development had the GDP, so human development had to have the HDI. The rationale also called for an index that would be transparent (hence relatively simple) and intuitive for the target audience (ie politicians, policy makers, managers and the public; Booysen, 2002). As a part of this strategy, it was decided to present the results of the HDI within a country league table format, a sort of 'naming and shaming' process, akin to the examples shown in Chapter 1. The league table style is combined with a label of 'high', 'medium' or 'low' human development applied by the UNDP depending upon each country's value for the HDI. In effect, countries are encouraged to compare their performance with those of others. As broadly the same HDI methodology is used each year it can be argued that between country comparisons are valid (Ogwang, 2000). However, as we will see later, there has been some year-on-year change. A considerable amount obviously depends on the quality of the data collected within each country, with an assumption that this is more or less comparable across countries.

The HDI has three components encompassing health, education and income. These are measured as:

1   life expectancy (a proxy indicator for health care and living conditions)
2   adult literacy combined with years of schooling or enrolment in primary, secondary and tertiary education
3   real GDP/capita ($ PPP; a proxy indicator for disposable income).

The choice of these three indicators as components for the HDI is not surprising; they can be found in many lists of development indicators (Bunge, 1981), but their selection does pose an immediate problem in that the units by which they are measured are obviously different; life expectancy is measured as years, education typically as a percentage and real GDP/capita in dollars (adjusted for PPP). Whether the HDI includes enough components has often been questioned, but the UNDP has consistently argued that including more elements in the HDI would make it more complex and less transparent, a point that will be discussed further later. The UNDP also expressed a desire to present each of these three components relative to some notional goal in human development.

It has sometimes been said that human development as encapsulated by the HDI seems to have much in common with the notion of 'basic needs' in development championed by the International Labour Organization and others in the 1970s (eg Srinivasan, 1994; Ravallion, 1997). These are different, for while 'basic needs' focus on 'objects', human development should be focused on 'people' (Anand and Ravallion, 1993). Sen himself has discussed the differences between 'basic needs' and 'capabilities' (Sen, 1984, p513–515).

CALCULATING THE HUMAN DEVELOPMENT INDEX

Since the birth of the HDI and its presentation in the first HDR of 1990, its mode of calculation has changed. This is understandable given a desire to learn from experience, and after all, the methods of finding the GDP and GNP have also changed with time. However, there has been some consistency in that the three elements of the HDI have remained the same since the outset. It should be pointed out, however, that the HDI in each of the HDRs is based on data that is at least two years out of date (Table 4.1). Indeed, before 1999 the time lag was three years or more. Therefore, it is possible for politicians and others to conveniently explain a poor performance in the HDI for one year as being due to the data being old, with an implication that matters have since improved.

The first step in the HDI methodology is to express the raw data for the three components in terms of a notional target or goal. For HDRs 1990 to 1993, this was achieved by finding the level of 'deprivation' relative to a maximum value:

$$\text{Standardized value (pre 1994)} = \frac{\text{maximum value} - \text{value for country}}{\text{range (maximum} - \text{minimum)}}$$

In this case, the larger the value for a country, the smaller will be the standardized value (ie smaller values mean less deprivation, and presumably greater development).

From 1994 onwards the process was changed slightly in order to find the level of development relative to a minimum:

$$\text{Standardized value (1994 on)} = \frac{\text{value for country} - \text{minimum value}}{\text{range (maximum} - \text{minimum)}}$$

In this case, larger values for a country will result in larger standardized values (ie presumably signifying greater development). While this change in perspective may be open to philosophical discussion (is development really the inverse of deprivation?) there is no mathematical difference:

$$\text{Standardized value (1994 on)} = 1 - \text{standardized value (pre 1994)}$$

With both approaches the effect is to remove the units (years, percentage and dollars/capita) by scaling the raw data values to between 0 and 1. But where do the maximum and minimum values come from? Who sets them and why? There are two potential answers to this:

1   take them from the list of countries so that standardzation is set relative to the best and worst performing countries respectively
2   employ constant values (ie what would be expected as 'reasonable') that some countries may or may not have attained in practice (or even exceeded).

Both of these have been employed in various HDRs and in various combinations for the three HDI components. The first approach of taking the maximum and minimum values from the data set tends to dominate in the earlier HDRs (1990 to 1993), while the latter approach of setting them as constants predominates from 1994. Each approach has advantages and disadvantages; however, the setting of maximum and minimum values as constants avoids a country being recorded as doing badly or well in the HDI purely because of what other countries had or had not done. If the maximum and minimum values shifted each year with the addition or exclusion of some countries then one country's HDI could go up or down significantly without any change in the performance of their three HDI components. Setting the maximum and minimum values as constants facilitates country comparisons (Noorbakhsh, 1998).

Once standardized, the three partial indices are added and divided by 3 to provide an average. Summing the components in this way, implies replacea bility, that is increases in education can compensate for declines in life expectancy, and it has been criticized (Sagar and Najam, 1998). Nonetheless, it has remained a constant feature of the HDI since its inception. Prior to 1994 the average of the three components yielded an 'average deprivation', and the higher this value the greater the relative deprivation of the country (compared to the maximum). In order to change deprivation to development, the average was subtracted from 1 to give the HDI (ie development seen as the inverse of deprivation). High values of the HDI now relate to 'higher' development or 'low deprivation'. For example, the average deprivation for Kenya in the 1990 HDR is 0.519 and the HDI is $1 - 0.519 = 0.481$. From 1994 onwards the average of the three components directly yielded the HDI.

The third and final stage of the methodology is the presentation of the HDIs for all the countries that year as a league table with labels of 'high', 'medium' or 'low' human development depending upon the value of the HDI. The categories are as follows:

● High human development: HDI between 0.8 and 1.0
● Medium human development: HDI between 0.5 and 0.79
● Low human development: HDI less than 0.49.

There have been other significant changes in the formulation of the HDI in addition to the setting of the maximum and minimum values for the standardization of the three components. For example, between 1991 and 1994 the education component was changed to encompass the adult literacy rate and the number of years in schooling, and the two were weighted as follows:

'Knowledge variable' = 2/3*adult literacy + 1/3*years of schooling

In 1990 this component was based solely on the adult literacy rate. From 1995 on there was a further change with number of years in schooling replaced by combined enrolment ratio (primary, secondary and tertiary levels of education).

Arguably the most significant change in calculating the HDI has been in the handling of GDP/capita. This component is problematic given the substantial inter-country variation in GDP/capita, as it is much larger than for the other two components. In the 2001 HDR, for example, the largest GDP/capita was $42,769 (Luxembourg) while the smallest was $448 (Sierra Leone); a difference of 95 times. As a result, the UNDP have argued consistently for a diminishing return in human development from GDP/capita and hence high values should not be allowed to dominate within the HDI (Sagar and Najam, 1998). Clearly some form of transformation is necessary prior to standardization. In the first HDR of 1990 this was achieved by simply taking the logarithm (base 10) of the GDP/capita. Logarithms compress a scale, as values of 10, 100, 1,000 and 10,000 become 1, 2, 3 and 4. Between 1991 and 1998 the method of transformation was changed so as to employ the more complex Atkinson formula (UNDP HDR, 1991). This approach has the effect of severely penalizing real GDP/capita above a notional target (adjusted GDP/capita more or less levels out beyond this target) whereas logarithms continue to allow a gradual increase without ever levelling off completely. Between 1999 and 2003 there was a return to the logarithm method as it was felt the Atkinson formula was too severe on middle-income countries (UNDP HDR, 1999). A comparison of the two methods is shown as Figure 4.1.

A summary of the changes in HDI methodology from 1990 to 2003 are presented as Table 4.2. This evolution does make year-on-year comparison difficult. After all, how would a country know how much of its league table movement is due to genuine progress in 'development' or due to changes in the way the figures have been calculated? Such shifts as a result of a methodological change can be significant (Morse, 2003b, 2003c). There are islands of stability in the HDI methodology, most notably the periods 1991–1993, 1995–1998 and 1999–2003 (Table 4.3). Within each island of stability, it is possible to make meaningful comparisons over time.

Finally, it should be mentioned that in each year there are a number of assumptions made with regard to missing data, values that exceed the maximum (eg GDP/capita values that exceed the set maximum of $40,000 or enrolment rations that exceed 100 per cent) and so on. Missing data are

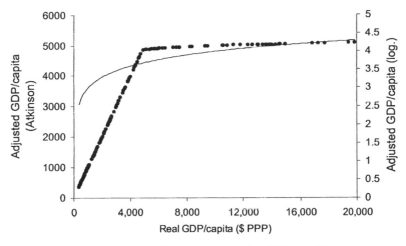

• Adjusted with Atkinson formula   —— Log. (Adjusted with logs)

Logarithm method: adjusted GDP/capita = logarithm (base 10) GDP/capita
Atkinson formula is based on the categorization of real GDP/capita in terms of a multiple of a reference condition
(varies in each year; between 1991 and 1993 = $4,829, in 1994/1995 = $5,120).

Category	Adjusted GDP/capita
< = reference GDP/capita (Y)	same as real GDP/capita (no adjustment)
between Y and 2Y	$= Y + 2(Y)^{1/2}$
between 2Y and 3Y	$= Y + 2(Y)^{1/2} + 3(Y - 2Y)^{1/3}$
between 3Y and 4Y	$= Y + 2(Y)^{1/2} + 3(Y - 2Y)^{1/3} + 4(Y - 3Y)^{1/4}$
etc	

Note how the Atkinson method results in a sharp change once the reference has been reached. In 1991, the
year of the HDR from which the graph was constructed, the levelling occurs once the GDP/capita reaches $4,829.
By way of contrast, the logarithmic transformation allows a continued increase with GDP/capita.

Figure 4.1 *Effects of the two different transformations of GDP/capita employed in the
Human Development Reports*

sometimes found by estimations from neighbouring countries, or simply
'guesstimated'. Excessive values are 'capped' (GDP/capita values greater than
$40,000 are set at $40,000).

In order to provide the reader with a flavour of the HDI values and league
table ranking, Table 4.4 presents the average values taken over the four years
2000–2003 of the three partial indices (life expectancy, education and
GDP/capita) and the HDI. The HDI methodology was relatively consistent
over this period, making it possible to take the average values over the four
year. The lowest HDI in this table is for Sierra Leone (HDI = 0.265), while
the highest is for Norway (HDI = 0.94).

There has been some movement of countries between the UNDP's
classification of high, medium and low human development between 1990

Table 4.2 *Evolution in the calculation of the Human Development Index (HDI)*

Year	Consistent calculation	Health	Education	GDP/capita
1990		Life expectancy (years) Maximum (78.4 years) and minimum (41.8 years) taken from data set	Adult literacy rate (%) Maximum = 100% Minimum = taken from data	Logarithm of GDP/capita Maximum = 3.68 ($4,786/capita PPP) Minimum = taken from data
1991	yes	Life expectancy (years) Maximum (78.6 years) and minimum (42.0 years) taken from data set	Adult literacy rate (%) and years of schooling weighted 2/3 and 1/3 respectively	Adjusted GDP/capita obtained with the Atkinson formula. Minimum for formula set at $4,829/capita Maximum and minimum for adjusted GDP/capita taken from data set
1992		As for 1991	As for 1991	As for 1991
1993		As for 1991	As for 1991	As for 1991
1994		Life expectancy (years) Maximum and minimum set as constants: Maximum = 85 Minimum = 25	Adult literacy rate (%) and years of schooling weighted 2/3 and 1/3 respectively Literacy: maximum = 100% minimum = 0 Schooling: maximum = 15% minimum = 0	As for 1991. Minimum for formula set at $5,120/capita Maximum and minimum for GDP/capita set as constants: Maximum = $40,000/capita Minimum = $200/capita
1995	yes	As for 1994	Adult literacy rate (%) and combined enrolment ratio (primary, secondary and tertiary; %) weighted 2/3 and 1/3 respectively Maximum = 100% Minimum = 0%	As for 1991. Minimum for formula set at $5,120/capita Maximum and minimum for GDP/capita set as constants: Maximum = $40,000/capita Minimum = $100/capita

1996		As for 1994	As for 1995	As for 1991. Minimum for formula set at $5,711/capita Maximum = $40,000; Minimum = $100
1997		As for 1994	As for 1995	As for 1991. Minimum for formula set at $5,835/capita Maximum = $40,000; Minimum = $100
1998		As for 1994	As for 1995	As for 1991. Minimum for formula set at $5,990/capita Maximum = $40,000; Minimum = $100
1999		As for 1994	As for 1995	logarithm of GDP/capita Maximum = $40,000; Minimum = $100
2000	yes	As for 1994	As for 1995 (adult literacy taken from age 15 and above)	As for 1999
2001		As for 1994	As for 1995	As for 1999
2002		As for 994	As for 1995	As for 1999
2003		As for 994	As for 1995	As for 1999

Horizontal lines demarcate periods where the HDI calculation was consistent. Note the relative stability in HDI methodology since the late 1990s.

Table 4.3 *Periods of relative consistency in the calculation of the Human Development Index*

Period	Notes
1991, 1992, 1993	Variable time lag for the data used to calculate the HDI Life expectancy methodology constant Education component methodology constant GDP/capita constant (even the minimum for the Atkinson formula) minimum kept the same at $4,829/capita N = 160 for 1991 and 1992 N = 173 for 1993
1995, 1996, 1997, 1998	A consistent three-year time lag for the data used to calculate the HDI Life expectancy methodology constant Education component methodology kept constant Atkinson formula minimum changed to $5,120, $5,711, $5,835 and $5,990 for 1995 to 1998 respectively N = 174 for 1995, 1996 and 1998 N = 175 for 1997
1999–2003	A consistent two-year time lag for the data used to calculate the HDI Life expectancy methodology constant (indeed same as that of 1994) Education component more or less the same (1999 slightly different from 2000 to 2003) Logarithm GDP/capita adjustment kept constant, with maximum and minimum set at $40,000 and $10,000 respectively. N = 174 for 1999 and 2000 N = 162 for 2001 N = 173 for 2002 N = 175 for 2003

N = number of countries included in the HDI league table.

Table 4.4 *Average values of the HDI and its three components (life expectancy, education and GDP/capita) over the period 2000–2003*

UNDP category	Country	HDI components (averages)			Average HDI
		Life expectancy	Education	GDP/capita	
High Human Development	Norway	0.891	0.984	0.944	0.940
	Canada	0.899	0.983	0.929	0.937
	Sweden	0.908	0.993	0.907	0.936
	Australia	0.896	0.993	0.918	0.936
	US	0.865	0.975	0.965	0.935
	Iceland	0.904	0.958	0.941	0.934
	Belgium	0.885	0.993	0.924	0.934
	Netherlands	0.885	0.992	0.920	0.932
	Japan	0.930	0.937	0.921	0.929
	Finland	0.874	0.993	0.910	0.926
	Switzerland	0.898	0.940	0.937	0.925
	UK	0.877	0.993	0.904	0.925
	France	0.891	0.970	0.908	0.923
	Denmark	0.852	0.981	0.932	0.922

Table 4.4 *Continued*

UNDP category	Country	HDI components (averages)			Average HDI
		Life expectancy	Education	GDP/capita	
	Luxembourg	0.873	0.899	0.993	0.922
	Austria	0.881	0.958	0.924	0.921
	Germany	0.878	0.966	0.915	0.920
	Ireland	0.860	0.963	0.935	0.919
	New Zealand	0.876	0.988	0.875	0.913
	Italy	0.891	0.932	0.906	0.910
	Spain	0.892	0.967	0.871	0.909
	Israel	0.892	0.918	0.875	0.895
	Cyprus	0.883	0.890	0.881	0.885
	Greece	0.886	0.920	0.845	0.883
	Hong Kong	0.905	0.834	0.909	0.882
	Singapore	0.875	0.863	0.906	0.882
	Portugal	0.844	0.938	0.852	0.878
	Slovenia	0.839	0.935	0.849	0.874
	Korea, Rep.	0.823	0.956	0.840	0.873
	Barbados	0.862	0.921	0.828	0.870
	Malta	0.880	0.876	0.841	0.866
	Brunei Darussalam	0.848	0.866	0.863	0.859
	Czech Republic	0.828	0.902	0.819	0.849
	Argentina	0.807	0.926	0.799	0.844
	Slovakia	0.803	0.910	0.782	0.832
	Uruguay	0.824	0.920	0.746	0.830
	Hungary	0.771	0.926	0.793	0.830
	Poland	0.803	0.941	0.744	0.829
	Chile	0.839	0.897	0.751	0.829
	Bahrain	0.805	0.862	0.830	0.829
	Bahamas	0.748	0.885	0.845	0.826
	Kuwait	0.853	0.737	0.875	0.821
	Costa Rica	0.861	0.860	0.734	0.818
	Estonia	0.755	0.948	0.751	0.818
	Seychelles	0.786	0.837	0.814	0.812
	Qatar	0.761	0.794	0.881	0.812
	United Arab Emirates	0.830	0.733	0.872	0.812
	Antigua and Barbuda	0.827	0.838	0.768	0.811
	Saint Kitts and Nevis	0.750	0.879	0.791	0.807
	Lithuania	0.777	0.930	0.712	0.806
	Croatia	0.809	0.881	0.727	0.806
Medium Human Development	Trinidad and Tobago	0.808	0.851	0.740	0.799
	Cuba	0.852	0.894	0.637	0.794
	Latvia	0.749	0.931	0.700	0.793
	Mexico	0.793	0.845	0.739	0.792
	Belarus	0.728	0.930	0.711	0.790
	Panama	0.817	0.858	0.675	0.784
	Dominica	0.816	0.862	0.669	0.782
	Bulgaria	0.766	0.900	0.671	0.779
	Malaysia	0.790	0.806	0.742	0.779
	Belize	0.810	0.866	0.659	0.778
	Russian Federation	0.690	0.924	0.717	0.777

▶

Table 4.4 *Continued*

UNDP category	Country	HDI components (averages)			Average HDI
		Life expectancy	Education	GDP/capita	
	Romania	0.751	0.883	0.683	0.772
	Macedonia	0.803	0.861	0.652	0.772
	Libya	0.764	0.834	0.717	0.772
	Colombia	0.769	0.852	0.690	0.770
	Venezuala	0.799	0.838	0.675	0.770
	Mauritius	0.773	0.778	0.756	0.769
	Suriname	0.759	0.892	0.632	0.761
	Fiji	0.750	0.888	0.640	0.760
	Brazil	0.708	0.853	0.713	0.758
	Thailand	0.741	0.848	0.686	0.758
	Saint Lucia	0.781	0.827	0.665	0.758
	Saudi Arabia	0.777	0.704	0.790	0.757
	Grenada	0.709	0.858	0.701	0.756
	Kazakhstan	0.678	0.916	0.665	0.753
	Lebanon	0.789	0.831	0.631	0.750
	Ukraine	0.727	0.921	0.602	0.750
	Philippines	0.735	0.906	0.607	0.749
	Georgia	0.802	0.894	0.552	0.749
	Oman	0.771	0.667	0.800	0.746
	Peru	0.730	0.867	0.638	0.745
	Jamaica	0.837	0.794	0.597	0.743
	Saint Vincent and Grenadines	0.786	0.782	0.659	0.742
	Paraguay	0.751	0.836	0.638	0.742
	Maldives	0.685	0.900	0.633	0.739
	Armenia	0.785	0.898	0.528	0.737
	Turkey	0.745	0.771	0.694	0.736
	Azerbaijan	0.770	0.886	0.552	0.736
	Sri Lanka	0.790	0.834	0.580	0.735
	Turkmenistan	0.685	0.916	0.592	0.731
	Dominican Republic	0.716	0.797	0.675	0.729
	Ecuador	0.750	0.861	0.574	0.728
	Albania	0.802	0.797	0.582	0.727
	Samoa (Western)	0.747	0.787	0.642	0.726
	Jordan	0.756	0.810	0.606	0.724
	Tunisia	0.760	0.717	0.684	0.720
	China	0.756	0.797	0.601	0.718
	Iran	0.736	0.739	0.673	0.716
	Guyana	0.643	0.892	0.611	0.715
	Kyrgyzstan	0.714	0.884	0.543	0.713
	Uzbekistan	0.728	0.879	0.523	0.710
	Cape Verde	0.742	0.753	0.634	0.710
	El Salvador	0.746	0.735	0.636	0.706
	Moldova	0.706	0.889	0.505	0.700
	South Africa	0.459	0.868	0.759	0.695
	Algeria	0.739	0.683	0.662	0.695
	Syria	0.762	0.697	0.593	0.684
	Viet Nam	0.718	0.837	0.491	0.682

Table 4.4 *Continued*

| UNDP category | Country | HDI components (averages) | | | Average HDI |
		Life expectancy	Education	GDP/capita	
	Indonesia	0.683	0.793	0.560	0.678
	Tajikistan	0.712	0.888	0.400	0.667
	Bolivia	0.623	0.813	0.526	0.654
	Honduras	0.707	0.698	0.538	0.648
	Egypt	0.705	0.618	0.588	0.637
	Nicaragua	0.724	0.662	0.524	0.636
	Guatemala	0.663	0.623	0.609	0.631
	Mongolia	0.645	0.769	0.472	0.629
	Equatorial Guinea	0.421	0.759	0.700	0.627
	Gabon	0.476	0.712	0.687	0.625
	Solomon Islands	0.744	0.642	0.485	0.623
	Namibia	0.363	0.807	0.683	0.618
	Sao Tome and Principe	0.686	0.679	0.453	0.606
	Morocco	0.708	0.494	0.592	0.598
	Swaziland	0.376	0.773	0.622	0.590
	Botswana	0.305	0.754	0.708	0.589
	Vanuatu	0.717	0.448	0.569	0.578
	India	0.635	0.564	0.528	0.576
	Myanmar	0.540	0.741	0.395	0.559
	Ghana	0.548	0.618	0.496	0.553
	Papua New Guinea	0.534	0.556	0.530	0.540
	Lesotho	0.364	0.755	0.497	0.539
	Zimbabwe	0.270	0.803	0.544	0.539
	Cambodia	0.515	0.650	0.448	0.538
	Comoros	0.578	0.508	0.459	0.515
	Cameroon	0.427	0.645	0.403	0.511
	Kenya	0.416	0.717	0.384	0.506
	Congo	0.416	0.742	0.362	0.506
	Pakistan	0.602	0.426	0.486	0.505
Low Human Development	Lao PDR	0.476	0.538	0.462	0.492
	Bhutan	0.613	0.407	0.454	0.491
	Togo	0.428	0.588	0.448	0.488
	Nepal	0.557	0.478	0.422	0.485
	Sudan	0.510	0.497	0.434	0.480
	Bangladesh	0.573	0.408	0.453	0.478
	Madagascar	0.482	0.583	0.348	0.471
	Yemen Arab Republic	0.577	0.474	0.347	0.466
	Haiti	0.450	0.480	0.456	0.462
	Nigeria	0.438	0.570	0.357	0.466
	Djibouti	0.350	0.498	0.502	0.450
	Mauritania	0.452	0.412	0.473	0.446
	Uganda	0.303	0.612	0.418	0.444
	Senegal	0.463	0.367	0.444	0.425
	Tanzania	0.392	0.607	0.271	0.423
	Eritrea	0.448	0.457	0.365	0.423
	Côte d'Ivoire	0.351	0.443	0.462	0.419
	Zambia	0.235	0.677	0.338	0.416
	Gambia	0.388	0.392	0.470	0.416

▶

Table 4.4 *Continued*

UNDP category	Country	HDI components (averages)			Average HDI
		Life expectancy	Education	GDP/capita	
	Benin	0.466	0.407	0.374	0.416
	Congo Dem. Rep. of the	0.392	0.508	0.340	0.413
	Guinea	0.375	0.354	0.493	0.407
	Angola	0.323	0.363	0.520	0.402
	Rwanda	0.245	0.588	0.369	0.401
	Malawi	0.243	0.641	0.291	0.392
	Mali	0.437	0.336	0.338	0.370
	Central African Republic	0.308	0.388	0.413	0.370
	Chad	0.347	0.384	0.368	0.366
	Guinea-Bissau	0.330	0.383	0.335	0.349
	Mozambique	0.259	0.380	0.367	0.335
	Ethiopia	0.321	0.348	0.316	0.328
	Burundi	0.268	0.392	0.301	0.320
	Burkina Faso	0.347	0.232	0.381	0.320
	Niger	0.352	0.158	0.343	0.284
	Sierra Leone	0.207	0.333	0.257	0.265

For each of the years 2000–2003, the HDI is found by averaging the three components, life expectancy, education and GDP/capita. Higher values for the HDI equate to higher levels of human development. In this table the average values for each country of the three partial indices and the HDI are presented for the four years.
Countries which only appeared in one of the HDRs 2000–2003 have not been included.

and 2003. Figure 4.2 is a graph of the percentage of countries classified as high, medium and low. Note the gradual decline in the percentage of countries categorized by the UNDP as 'low' and the relative consistency of the percentage classified as 'high'. Therefore, most of the movement between categories has been from 'low' to 'medium'. Also note some abrupt shifts in percentages from 1990 to 1991 and particularly from 1998 to 1999. This can be explained by a change in the method of calculating the HDI, especially the way in which the GDP/capita component is adjusted.

There are a number of points to make concerning Table 4.4. Admittedly the table is dense, but we do need to present the values of the three components as well as the HDI. As we have seen with Sen's Poverty Index, the same HDI can be obtained with very different balances of the components. However, the density of the table also makes it more likely that we will concentrate on the final HDI, or perhaps only the rank or classification (high, medium or low) in the table, and ignore the components. As a result, people may understandably want to know whether their country has moved up or down the league table year-on-year, and warnings over changes in the technical calculation of the index may not necessarily be heeded. In fairness, the UNDP in its later HDRs does present a table of HDIs calculated on the basis of a uniform methodology, but this may not necessarily be the table that a casual browser of the report will peruse. The

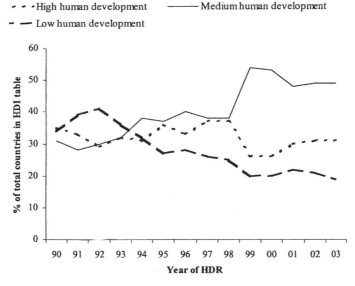

Low human development: HDI between 0 and 0.499
Medium human development: HDI between 0.5 and 0.799
High human development: HDI between 0.8 and 1.0

Figure 4.2 *Percentage of countries included in the human development index tables between 1990 and 2003 categorized as low, medium and high human development by the UNDP*

HDI league table calculated using the methodology of that year is always presented as the first league table in the second part of the HDR.

Before ending this section on methodology, it must be emphasized that the choices regarding the construction of the HDI as well as the methodology are based on judgements made by the UNDP experts. We are entitled to ask:

- Why adult literacy, life expectancy and GDP/capita?
- Why set the maximum and minimum values as constants?
- Why set the constants at the levels chosen?
- Why take the simple average of these three for the HDI?
- Why not 'weight' life expectancy higher than the other two?
- Why transform the GDP/capita with logarithms?
- Why present the results as a league table?
- Why should 'high' human development relate to HDI values between 0.8 and 1?

A multitude of alternatives exist to all of the above questions, but in each case a value judgement was made to use just one.

THE 'HDI FAMILY' OF HUMAN DEVELOPMENT INDICES

While the HDI is the most well known development index produced by the UNDP, there are a number of variants on the same theme. The 'HDI stable' of development indices includes the:

1   Gender-related Development Index (GDI)
2   Gender Empowerment Measure (GEM)
3   Human Poverty Index (HPI)

The GDI was introduced by the UNDP in its HDR of 1995. The aim was to adjust the HDI in order to allow for gender disparity in its three components. For example, women tend to live longer than men but have less income. In effect, the HDI is adjusted downwards by a degree which increases as the disparity between males and females increases (note that it doesn't make any difference to the calculation whether the disparity favours men or women). If there is equality between the sexes, the GDI will equal the HDI. Also note that the GDI cannot be greater than the HDI. Clearly the GDI is more 'data hungry' than the HDI as it requires the same information but disaggregated into male and female.

At the risk of providing the reader with yet another dense data set, Table 4.5 presents the HDIs and GDIs from the HDR 2002, along with the differences between the two indices. Note that not all of the countries in the HDI data set for that year have a GDI. The average decline in the value of the HDI is 1.5 per cent, with a maximum of 10.5 per cent for the Yemen Arab Republic. The negative values (where the GDI is greater than the HDI) are due to rounding, as the lowest value should be zero. Note that the deviations can be significant, of the order of a few percentage points, and indeed are unevenly spread with greater deviations for the lower HDI ranks relative to the higher ranked countries. Also note that at the interface between 'high' and 'medium' human development there are three countries (Latvia, Qatar and Trinidad and Tobago) classified as 'high' using the HDI but 'medium' if we use the GDI.

The GEM differs from the HDI and GDI by focusing specifically on the disparity between men and women in terms of their political and economic power. It has three components:

1   women's political participation and decision-making power
2   women's economic participation and decision-making power
3   women's and men's estimated income (adjusted with PPP).

The first two items are measured in terms of women's and men's share of positions in political, professional and technical bodies.

Table 4.5 *Calculated values for the HDI and GDI (HDR 2002)*

Rank	Country	HDR 2002		% decline
		HDI	GDI	in HDI
1	Norway	0.942	0.941	0.1
2	Sweden	0.941	0.936	0.5
3	Canada	0.940	0.938	0.2
4	Australia	0.939	0.938	0.1
5	Belgium	0.940	0.933	0.7
6	US	0.939	0.937	0.2
7	Iceland	0.937	0.934	0.3
8	Netherlands	0.935	0.931	0.4
9	Japan	0.933	0.926	0.8
10	Finland	0.931	0.928	0.3
11	France	0.928	0.926	0.2
12	Switzerland	0.928	0.923	0.5
13	UK	0.928	0.925	0.3
14	Austria	0.926	0.920	0.7
15	Denmark	0.925	0.924	0.1
16	Germany	0.925	0.920	0.5
17	Ireland	0.925	0.917	0.9
18	Luxembourg	0.924	0.913	1.2
19	New Zealand	0.917	0.914	0.3
20	Italy	0.912	0.907	0.6
21	Spain	0.914	0.906	0.9
22	Israel	0.897	0.892	0.6
23	Hong Kong	0.889	0.886	0.3
24	Greece	0.885	0.879	0.7
25	Singapore	0.883	0.880	0.3
26	Cyprus	0.883	0.078	0.6
27	Korea, Rep.	0.882	0.875	0.8
28	Portugal	0.879	0.876	0.3
29	Slovenia	0.880	0.876	0.5
30	Malta	0.874	0.860	1.6
31	Barbados	0.872		
32	Brunei Darussalam	0.857	0.852	0.6
33	Czech Republic	0.850	0.846	0.5
34	Argentina	0.845	0.835	1.2
35	Hungary	0.835	0.833	0.2
36	Slovakia	0.836	0.833	0.4
37	Poland	0.832	0.831	0.1
38	Bahrain	0.832	0.820	1.4
39	Chile	0.832	0.823	1.1
40	Uruguay	0.831	0.828	0.4
41	Bahamas	0.825	0.825	
42	Estonia	0.825		
43	Costa Rica	0.821	0.813	1.0
44	Saint Kitts and Nevis	0.814		
45	Kuwait	0.814	0.800	1.7
46	United Arab Emirates	0.811	0.798	1.6
47	Seychelles	0.810		
48	Croatia	0.809	0.806	0.4

▶

Table 4.5 *Continued*

Rank	Country	HDR 2002 HDI	GDI	% decline in HDI
49	Lithuania	0.808	0.806	0.3
50	**Trinidad and Tobago**	**0.805**	**0.798**	**0.9**
51	**Qatar**	**0.802**	**0.793**	**1.1**
52	Antigua and Barbuda	0.801		
53	**Latvia**	**0.800**	**0.798**	**0.3**
54	Mexico	0.796	0.789	0.9
55	Cuba	0.795		
56	Belarus	0.788	0.786	0.3
57	Panama	0.787	0.785	0.3
58	Belize	0.784	0.763	2.7
59	Malaysia	0.784	0.776	1.0
60	Russian Federation	0.781	0.781	
61	Bulgaria	0.777	0.778	−0.1
62	Dominica	0.778		
63	Romania	0.775	0.773	0.3
64	Libya	0.773	0.753	2.6
65	Colombia	0.772	0.767	0.7
66	Macedonia	0.772		
67	Mauritius	0.772	0.762	1.3
68	Saint Lucia	0.772		
69	Venezuala	0.771	0.764	0.9
70	Thailand	0.763	0.760	0.4
71	Saudi Arabia	0.759	0.733	3.4
72	Fiji	0.758	0.746	1.6
73	Brazil	0.756	0.750	0.8
74	Suriname	0.756		
75	Lebanon	0.754	0.739	2.0
76	Armenia	0.753	0.751	0.3
77	Philippines	0.753	0.751	0.3
78	Oman	0.752	0.721	4.1
79	Kazakhstan	0.750		
80	Georgia	0.748		
81	Ukraine	0.748	0.744	0.5
82	Grenada	0.746		
83	Peru	0.748	0.729	2.5
84	Maldives	0.743	0.739	0.5
85	Jamaica	0.742	0.740	0.3
86	Turkey	0.743	0.734	1.2
87	Azerbaijan	0.741		
88	Sri Lanka	0.742	0.736	0.8
89	Turkmenistan	0.741		
90	Paraguay	0.739	0.728	1.5
91	Albania	0.733	0.729	0.6
92	Saint Vincent and the Grenadines	0.734		
93	Ecuador	0.733	0.718	2.1
94	Dominican Republic	0.729	0.718	1.5
95	Uzbekistan	0.727	0.725	0.3
96	China	0.725	0.724	0.1

Table 4.5 *Continued*

Rank	Country	HDR 2002 HDI	GDI	% decline in HDI
97	Tunisia	0.722	0.709	1.8
98	Iran	0.721	0.702	2.6
99	Jordan	0.718	0.701	2.4
100	Cape Verde	0.714	0.704	1.4
101	Samoa (Western)	0.714		
102	Kyrgyzstan	0.712		
103	Guyana	0.709	0.698	1.6
104	El Salvador	0.706	0.696	1.4
105	Moldova	0.701	0.698	0.4
106	Algeria	0.698	0.679	2.7
107	South Africa	0.696	0.689	1.0
108	Syria	0.690	0.669	3.0
109	Viet Nam	0.688	0.686	0.3
110	Indonesia	0.684	0.678	0.9
111	Equatorial Guinea	0.679	0.668	1.6
112	Tajikistan	0.667	0.664	0.5
113	Mongolia	0.655	0.652	0.5
114	Bolivia	0.654	0.645	1.4
115	Egypt	0.642	0.628	2.2
116	Honduras	0.639	0.628	1.7
117	Gabon	0.637		
118	Nicaragua	0.636	0.629	1.1
119	San Tome and Principe	0.632		
120	Guatemala	0.632	0.617	2.4
121	Solomon Islands	0.623		
122	Namibia	0.610	0.604	1.0
123	Morocco	0.602	0.585	2.8
124	India	0.576	0.561	2.6
125	Swaziland	0.577	0.565	2.1
126	Botswana	0.572	0.566	1.1
127	Myanmar	0.552	0.547	0.9
128	Zimbabwe	0.551	0.544	1.3
129	Ghana	0.549	0.544	0.9
130	Cambodia	0.543	0.537	1.1
131	Vanuatu	0.542		
132	Lesotho	0.535	0.522	2.4
133	Papua New Guinea	0.535	0.530	0.9
134	Kenya	0.512	0.511	0.2
135	Cameroon	0.513	0.503	2.0
136	Congo	0.514	0.505	1.8
137	Comoros	0.511	0.504	1.2
138	Pakistan	0.499	0.469	6.0
139	Sudan	0.500	0.478	4.4
140	Bhutan	0.494		
141	Togo	0.493	0.475	3.7
142	Nepal	0.491	0.469	4.5
143	Lao PDR	0.485	0.472	2.7
144	Yemen Arab Republic	0.478	0.428	10.5

▶

Table 4.5 *Continued*

Rank	Country	HDR 2002 HDI	HDR 2002 GDI	% decline in HDI
145	Bangladesh	0.478	0.467	2.3
146	Haiti	0.472	0.467	1.1
147	Madagascar	0.470	0.464	1.3
148	Nigeria	0.463	0.448	3.2
149	Djibouti	0.446		
150	Uganda	0.443	0.436	1.6
151	Tanzania	0.439	0.436	0.7
152	Mauritania	0.437	0.429	1.8
153	Zambia	0.433	0.424	2.1
154	Congo Dem. Rep. of the	0.429	0.420	2.1
155	Senegal	0.430	0.421	2.1
156	Côte d'Ivoire	0.429	0.410	4.4
157	Eritrea	0.422	0.410	2.8
158	Benin	0.420	0.405	3.6
159	Guinea	0.413		
160	Gambia	0.406	0.397	2.2
161	Angola	0.403		
162	Rwanda	0.403	0.397	1.5
163	Malawi	0.399	0.389	2.5
164	Mali	0.387	0.377	2.6
165	Central African Republic	0.375	0.365	2.7
166	Chad	0.365	0.353	3.3
167	Guinea-Bissau	0.350	0.325	7.1
168	Ethiopia	0.327	0.314	4.0
169	Burkina Faso	0.326	0.314	3.7
170	Mozambique	0.322	0.306	5.0
171	Burundi	0.312	0.306	1.9
172	Niger	0.277	0.263	5.1
173	Sierra Leone	0.276		
			Average	1.5
			Maximum	10.5
			Minimum	−0.1

The GDI adjusts the HDI downwards to allow for a disparity between males and females in the three components that make up the HDI. It doesn't matter which of the sexes is higher.
There are three countries (in bold) classified as 'high' human development using the HDI but as 'medium' human development if we use the GDI instead.

The final index of the three is the HPI introduced in the HDR 1997. The aim of the HPI was to bring together in a composite index the different features of deprivation in quality of life to arrive at an aggregate judgement on the extent of poverty in a community. In later HDRs the HPI was divided into two versions: HPI-1 (for developing countries) and HPI-2 (for developed countries). The rationale behind this change is the fact that the same measure of poverty cannot be applied to developed and developing countries. The same argument has not been used for the HDI.

In the HDR 2003 there are three elements to HPI-1:

1 survival (percentage of people expected to die before 40; P_1)
2 knowledge (adult literacy rate; P_2)
3 'decent standard of living' (P_3). This is found from two elements:
   – percentage of people without sustainable access to safe water (P_{31})
     percentage of children underweight for their age (P_{32})

These are weighted equally so that:

$$P_3 = \frac{(P_{31} + P_{32})}{2}$$

and

$$HPI - 1 = \left(\frac{P_1^3 + P_2^3 + P_3^3}{3}\right)^3$$

The calculation of HPI-2 has some similarities to HPI-1, but there are notable differences. There are four elements to HPI-2:

1 survival (percentage of people expected to die before 60; P_1)
2 knowledge (adult illiteracy rate; P_2)
3 income (percentage of population below the poverty line; P_3)
4 unemployment (percentage of people who are long-term unemployed; P_4)

and

$$HPI - 2 = \left(\frac{P_1^2 + P_2^3 + P_3^3 + P_4^3}{4}\right)^3$$

Thus it can be seen that the HPI-2 has an income element, even if it is only one of four components, while HPI-1 doesn't. In HPI-2 P_3 is equivalent to the Headcount Ratio described in Chapter 3, with the poverty line set as 50 per cent of the median adjusted household disposable income. The HPI-1 does not have an economic component; it is very much centred on 'material deprivation'.

Even with the growing list of development indicators published by the UNDP, it is interesting to note that the GDP and GNP still receive a significant number of mentions within the text of the reports. Table 4.6 is a list of 'hits' using the search engine provided with the compact disc of the HDR 1999 (which covers the reports from 1990 to 1999). The HDI was introduced in 1990 and the GDI and GEM in 1995, but through all of these years the GDP and GNP receive a healthy airing. The surge of hits for GDP and GNP in 1990 was largely a function of the case being made for the HDI.

Table 4.6 *Number of 'hits' associated with five development indicators listed in the Human Development Reports (1990–1998)*

Development indicators	HDR year								
	1990	1991	1992	1993	1994	1995	1996	1997	1998
Gross Domestic Product (GDP)	23	5	13	12	11	7	16	13	9
Gross National Product (GNP)	23	18	17	3	12	6	7	3	3
Human Development Index (HDI)	10	10	26	11	22	22	23	19	19
Gender related Development Index (GDI)	0	0	0	0	0	26	8	5	10
Gender Empowerment Measure (GEM)	0	0	0	0	0	14	5	4	5

Counts are the number of 'hits' associated with the indicator using the search engine provided with the CD-ROM version of the HDR 1999.

CRITIQUES OF THE HUMAN DEVELOPMENT INDEX

The HDI has been the focus of much debate, particularly in the early years of the HDRs (Kelly, 1991; McGillivray, 1991; Lind, 1992, 1993; Srinivasan, 1994; Sharma, 1997; Noorbakhsh, 1998; Sagar and Najam, 1998, 1999; Lai, 2000, 2003; Lücters and Menkhoff, 2000). Dijkstra (2002) provides a critique of the GDI and GEM. These debates have been wide ranging. Ravallion (1997), for example, has highlighted what he regards as internal inconsistencies and over-simplifications in the HDRs with human development perceived as an 'end' and everything else as a 'means' to that end. He also provides an interesting discussion of the common use of regression analysis in the reports to highlight relationships, or lack of any, between the HDI and economic indicators such as GDP. As with any such analysis intended to simplify a complex set of data, should the focus be on the regression line (the nature of the relationship between human development and economic performance) or on the outliers (countries which appear to lack such a relationship)? The obvious answer would probably be both, but getting the right balance is something of a subjective argument. We will return to this later.

Interestingly, despite being regarded as one of the Father's of human development Amartya Sen initially showed some scepticism towards the HDI given its obvious crudity. In fairness to the UNDP, the HDRs have reflected much of the debate surrounding the HDI and occasionally provided a reasoned defence as to why they feel the HDI should be the way it is. It should also be emphasized that many of the criticisms of the HDI are generic, in the sense that they could equally apply to all aggregated indices of development (social, economic or otherwise; Zerby and Khan, 1984) and indeed measures of 'quality of life' (Bayless and Bayless, 1982; Wish, 1986).

In the following discussion, the criticisms of the HDI are summarized under the following headings:

- data quality
- reduction of between-country variation
- hiding of within-country variation
- method of calculation
- inclusion of other dimensions within the HDI
- alternatives to the HDI.

Data quality

There are understandably a number of critiques of the quality of the data upon which the HDI is based (eg Murray, 1991; Loup et al, 2000). The fundamental dependency on good quality data is all too easily forgotten as one browses the HDI league tables, and indeed the tables (4.4 and 4.5) based on HDR data presented in this chapter. In my opinion this issue has received far too little attention in the literature.

Reduction of between-country variation

Ram (1992) has pointed out that inter-country variation in the HDI is much lower than with GDP/capita, even when the latter has been adjusted for PPP. This may be intuitively obvious as the GDP/capita component of the HDI is adjusted (mostly by taking the logarithm) so as to reduce inter-country variation. However, does this difference matter? It tends to be a matter of opinion. Table 4.7 has been extracted from the HDR 2002.

Table 4.7 *Difference in scale between the Human Development Index (HDI) and GDP/capita for three countries*

	HDI (2002)	Real GDP/capita ($PPP) (2000)
Italy	0.913	23,626
Spain	0.913	19,472
Nigeria	0.462	896

Data taken from the HDR 2002.
Note that Italy and Spain have HDI values approximately double that of Nigeria, while the GDP/capita for Italy is up to 26 times greater than that of Nigeria.

The HDI's for Spain and Italy are roughly twice that of Nigeria but the GDP/capita values are very different (26 and 22 times higher than Nigeria for Italy and Spain respectively). The multipliers are very different, but does this imply that the quality of life (as measured by the HDI) in these 'high' human development countries is only twice as high as that of Nigeria (a 'low' human development country)? Could it not be argued that the much larger gap in GDP/capita is more telling?

Hiding of within-country variation

Allied to the previous point is the hiding of within-country variation in national averages (Indrayan et al, 1999). For example, the use of the GDP/capita component as a proxy for average income can be suspect and some authors have pointed out that this does not allow for perhaps major differences in income distribution within a country (Anand and Sen, 1994; Streeten, 1995; Sagar and Najam, 1999). Given the necessary data, it is possible to produce intra-country HDI's and some countries do just that (Justus, 1995; Thapa, 1995; Indrayan et al, 1999; Lai, 2003). However, it is as well to remember that while the country lists in Tables 4.4 and 4.5 may be compelling, each line of the table hides a complex history and intra-country variation that it is hard to imagine being captured by a single number. Nigeria is a country of approximately 120 million people (no one really knows the figure as there has been no reliable census for many years), comprising many ethnic groups living in urban and rural areas. Its economic development has been complex since independence from Britain in 1960, particularly given the growing dominance of oil, with numerous repercussions in terms of civil strife, crime, corruption and military *coup d'etats*. Is it realistic to capture all of this with only an average life expectancy, education and income/capita for the whole country?

Method of calculation

Beyond the fundamental issues of data quality and the use of national averages, there have been various critiques of the choice of the three components for the HDI, the assumption of equal weighting (Dowrick et al, 2003) and their additivity (Booysen, 2002). Critiques over the means of HDI calculation are usually allied with suggestions for modifying the methodology (Kelly, 1991; Sharma, 1997; Noorbakhsh, 1998; Sagar and Najam, 1998; Lüchters and Menkhoff, 2000) or even for different indices to replace the HDI entirely. Carlucci and Pisani (1995) argue that we should be prepared to consider more components in a multi-attribute measure of human development than the three suggested by the UNDP. The relative weighting of the attributes may also vary. They suggest a more participatory approach to selecting components and weightings that takes into account the opinions of the community.

As noted earlier, while there have been changes, the core of the HDI methodology has remained intact. There are two apparent reasons for this:

1   a desire to keep the methodology transparent and as simple as possible
2   to allow for comparison over time.

Both of these are related to the central purpose of the HDI and indeed the HDRs, namely to influence policy and help improve the human condition. The translation from the raw data sets to the partial indices and the HDI is presented in all of the HDRs. While the detailed steps, for example of the Atkinson formulation, are not presented, one does have a sense of moving from raw data to HDI in stages that are comprehensible and transparent. The methodology employed for each year is explained, with selected examples of the steps involved. One can appreciate the contrast between this desire for transparency and the more technically demanding but perhaps more elegant and logical alternatives put forward by others.

However, while one can understand the fundamental wishes of those framing the HDI to maintain clarity and allow for comparison across years, there are problems. The shifts in methodology, even if the core remains, are significant and do not facilitate year-on-year comparison (Booysen, 2002). Indeed as Lüchters and Menkhoff (2000) point out, the result of trying to follow trends in the HDI can be deterministic chaos. Part of the problem is due to changes in the number of countries included each year (Lai, 2000). A country can move down in the table simply because new countries have been included that happen to come in at a higher rank. Researchers using the HDI for comparisons over time have either used an approach such as principal components analysis (Lai, 2000) or selected the methodology from one HDR and applied it to all years (Crafts, 1998; Morse, 2003b, 2003c). The latter approach has also been taken by the UNDP itself, and tables have been added to later HDRs that show HDI values over time calculated on the basis of a 'consistent methodology and consistent data series' which are at the same time 'not strictly comparable with those in earlier Human Development Reports' (HDR 2002, p156).

Inclusion of other dimensions within the HDI

There have been suggestions that the components of the HDI should be expanded or changed to encompass other important dimensions. There are many possibilities here, and inevitably such suggestions are based on a similar individual perspective as was the original selection of life expectancy, education and GDP/capita. For example, it has been suggested that life expectancy is too simplistic given that poorer societies can be better off than richer ones in terms of a quality of life that takes on board non-material needs (Othick, 1983). One could argue that a better component than 'life expectancy' may be 'happy life expectancy' (HLE; Veenhoven, 1996) defined as:

Happy life expectancy (HLE) = life expectancy × 'happiness score' (0 to 1)

The logic is that 'life expectancy' in itself may not be a good indicator if a long life is an unhappy life! Maybe we are beginning to see the dawn of a new 'science of happiness' (Bond, 2003). Using the HLE instead of life expectancy does make a significant difference to country rankings based on the HDI (Table 4.8), but this difference is only significant for countries at the top of the table. For countries towards the foot of the table there is little difference.

Table 4.8 *Human Development Indices (1993, reported in the HDR 1996) for a sample of countries based on the use of life expectancy and Happy Life Expectancy*

(a) Ranking in terms of original HDI

Country	Life expectancy (years) 1993	Average appreciation of life (scale 0 to 1)	Happy life expectancy (years) 1993	HDI	HDI based on happy life expectancy
Canada	77.5	0.683	52.9	0.951	0.814
US	76.1	0.760	57.8	0.940	0.839
Japan	79.6	0.666	53.0	0.938	0.790
Netherlands	77.5	0.797	61.8	0.938	0.850
Norway	77.0	0.743	57.2	0.937	0.827
Finland	75.8	0.697	52.8	0.935	0.807
France	77.0	0.720	55.4	0.935	0.815
Iceland	78.2	0.793	62.0	0.934	0.845
Spain	77.7	0.680	52.8	0.933	0.795
Sweden	78.3	0.787	61.6	0.933	0.840
Australia	77.8	0.767	59.7	0.929	0.828
Belgium	76.5	0.770	58.9	0.929	0.831
Austria	76.3	0.733	55.9	0.928	0.814
New Zealand	75.6	0.722	54.6	0.927	0.810
Switzerland	78.1	0.767	59.9	0.926	0.826
Denmark	75.3	0.787	59.3	0.924	0.835
UK	76.3	0.760	58.0	0.924	0.823
Germany	76.1	0.680	51.7	0.920	0.784
Ireland	75.4	0.787	59.3	0.919	0.830
Italy	77.6	0.660	51.2	0.914	0.768
Greece	77.7	0.590	45.8	0.909	0.733
Israel	76.6	0.627	48.0	0.908	0.749
Luxembourg	75.8	0.727	55.1	0.895	0.780
Korea, Rep.	71.3	0.620	44.2	0.886	0.735
Argentina	72.2	0.690	49.8	0.885	0.761
Chile	73.9	0.678	50.1	0.882	0.750
Portugal	74.7	0.610	45.6	0.878	0.716
Czech Republic	71.3	0.557	39.7	0.872	0.697
Hungary	69.0	0.573	39.5	0.855	0.692
Mexico	71.0	0.650	46.2	0.845	0.706
Latvia	69.0	0.508	35.1	0.820	0.631
Poland	71.1	0.657	46.7	0.819	0.683
Russian Federation	67.4	0.510	34.4	0.804	0.620
Brazil	66.5	0.647	43.0	0.796	0.667
Belarus	69.7	0.487	33.9	0.787	0.588
Bulgaria	71.2	0.443	31.5	0.773	0.552
Estonia	69.2	0.527	36.5	0.749	0.567
Romania	69.9	0.543	38.0	0.738	0.560
Lithuania	70.3	0.497	34.9	0.719	0.523
Turkey	66.7	0.693	46.2	0.711	0.597
Philippines	66.5	0.693	46.1	0.665	0.551
South Africa	63.2	0.607	38.4	0.649	0.511
China	68.6	0.640	43.9	0.609	0.471
India	60.7	0.603	36.6	0.436	0.302
Nigeria	50.6	0.643	32.5	0.400	0.300

Table 4.8 *Continued*

(b) Ranking in terms of the HDI using happy life expectancy

Rank	Rank with original HDI	Rank with HDI calculated using the happy life expectancy	Difference in ranking (original HDI − HDI with HLE)
1	Canada	Netherlands	+3
2	US	Iceland	+6
3	Japan	Sweden	+7
4	Netherlands	US	−2
5	Norway	Denmark	+11
6	Finland	Belgium	+6
7	France	Ireland	+12
8	Iceland	Australia	+3
9	Spain	Norway	−4
10	Sweden	Switzerland	+5
11	Australia	UK	+6
12	Belgium	France	−5
13	Austria	Canada	−12
14	New Zealand	Austria	−1
15	Switzerland	New Zealand	−1
16	Denmark	Finland	−10
17	UK	Spain	−8
18	Germany	Japan	−15
19	Ireland	Germany	−1
20	Italy	Luxembourg	+4
21	Greece	Italy	−1
22	Israel	Argentina	+3
23	Luxembourg	Chile	+3
24	Korea, Rep.	Israel	−2
25	Argentina	Korea, Rep.	−1
26	Chile	Greece	−5
27	Portugal	Portugal	0
28	Czech Republic	Mexico	+2
29	Hungary	Czech Republic	−1
30	Mexico	Hungary	−1
31	Latvia	Poland	+1
32	Poland	Brazil	+2
33	Russian Federation	Latvia	−2
34	Brazil	Russian Federation	−1
35	Belarus	Turkey	+5
36	Bulgaria	Belarus	−1
37	Estonia	Estonia	0
38	Romania	Romania	0
39	Lithuania	Bulgaria	−3
40	Turkey	Philippines	+1
41	Philippines	Lithuania	−2
42	South Africa	South Africa	0
43	China	China	0
44	India	India	0
45	Nigeria	Nigeria	0

Life expectancy (LE) has been adjusted for 'average appreciation of life' to generate the Happy Life Expectancy (HLE). The higher the 'average appreciation of life', the happier the people. Data have been taken from the HDR 1996 (life expectancy) and Veenhoven (1996; 'average appreciation of life'). Note how the use of the HLE instead of LE does make a difference to the HDI rank.

Given the growing emphasis on sustainable development during the 1990s, is there scope for adapting the HDI to include environmental and natural resource consumption concerns? After all, a link would be expected. Qizilbash (2001), for example, has found relationships between well-being ranking of nations and a range of environmental indicators, such that countries that do well in terms of well-being tend to be the worst performers in environmental terms. Perhaps surprisingly, especially following the high-profile Rio Earth Summit in 1992 organized by the UNEP, there have been relatively few calls to 'green' the HDI along the lines of the GPI being the 'green' version of GDP (Spangenberg and Bonniot, 1998; Neumayer, 2001). Sister UN agencies to the UNDP have called for the HDRs to be enhanced 'to include indicators on progress in attaining sustainable development' (Sustainable Development Networking Programme of the UNDP, September 1992), and some of the HDR data tables do focus on natural resource balance sheets. The terms 'sustainable development' and 'sustainable human development' are liberally sprinkled throughout the HDR's, particularly in 1992 (the year of the Earth Summit) and 1994 (where the theme of the HDR was human security), and in related discussion documents (eg Sudhir and Sen, 1994). The UNDP have also made promises to develop an 'environmentally sensitive HDI' (HDR, 1992, p24), but no such index has emerged. UNDP has financed research into the transformation of the HDI into a 'sustainable' HDI (SHDI) during the mid 1990s, and some ideas appeared in the Armenia HDR of 1996 (Armenia, 1996; Morse, 2003a), although they have not been taken up in the global HDRs. The Armenia pilot study suggested a modification of the HDI by adding an 'integral environmental indicator' (Pe):

$$SHDI = HDI + Pe$$

Pe was the average of two indicators either of which could be positive or negative:

- an indicator of the environmental state of a territory (A)
- an indicator of the environmental evaluation of human activities (B)

such that $Pe = (A + B)/2$. If Pe is negative then the effect will be to reduce the value of the HDI. For example, in the Armenia HDR 1996 the value of Pe for the Republic of Armenia is given as -0.427 and the HDI is 0.831. The value of the SHDI becomes $0.831 - 0.427 = 0.404$.

This is not the only suggestion for modifying the HDI to include a 'sustainability' dimension. Spangenberg and Bonniot (1998) have described what they refer to as a 'Corporate Human Development Index (CHDI), and Hinterberger and Seifert (1997) have made suggestions regarding the potential incorporation of material input into the HDI.

Rather than modify the HDI, a more recent approach suggested by Neumayer (2001) attempts to use additional information on resource use to categorize countries as 'potentially unsustainable'. This method has the advantage that the calculation of the HDI is not changed and neither is there a new index that could create confusion. However, one disadvantage of this approach rests with its convoluted methodology and a high demand for quality data revolving around the financial valuation of resources.

While there has been no shortage of suggestions for modifying the HDI, the UNDP have resisted any changes other than those to do with data transformation (GDP/capita component), the education component and the setting of maximum and minimum values. The reason for this is explained in the HDRs.

> *The ideal would be to reflect all aspects of human experience. The lack of data imposes some limits on this, and more indicators could perhaps be added as the information becomes available. But more indicators would not necessarily be better. Some might overlap with existing indicators: infant mortality, for example, is already reflected in life expectancy. And adding more variables could confuse the picture and detract from the main trends.* (UNDP HDR 1994, p91)

While not closing the door to change, the UNDP see the inclusion of more components in the HDI as potentially confusing and these would not necessarily make the index 'better'. There is a considerable amount of value judgement inherent in this statement, and it would be justifiable to asking why four components would be any more confusing than three.

Alternatives to the HDI

The HDI has helped to generate a range of suggestions for alternative development indices. Only one will be covered here as it helps to reinforce some points of interest. Lind (1993) suggests the use of a Life Product Index (LPI), which unlike the HDI is 'derived mathematically from two fundamental postulates, and its parameter is calibrated to an observed time budget'. Like the HDI, Lind's LPI can also 'serve to rank nations according to social development and help to indicate desirable directions overall for future development'.

$$\text{Life Product Index} = \text{GDP/capita}^w \times \text{life expectancy at birth}$$

where 'w' is a constant which represents the proportion of their lives that people in the countries spend on economic activity. Basically the LPI as defined here is an adjustment of GDP/capita allowing for years spent on economic activity, and follows a similar line of thought to that discussed by Hicks and Streeten (1979). But what value of 'w' is suitable? Lind suggests that a value of 0.1 (ie 10 per cent of one's life spent on economic activity) 'seems appropriate for many contemporary developed societies', but other values could be rationalized.

Table 4.9 presents the results of using the LPI alongside the HDI as a means of ranking countries (in this case it is the same sample of countries used for the Happy Life Index in Table 4.7). While there are some countries that remain at the same ranking no matter what the value for 'w', such as the country at the very bottom of the list, Nigeria, there are also notable differences. Luxemburg for example, has a ranking of 23 using the HDI but a much higher rank of between 2 and 5 with the LPI. Also while the choice of w (0.25, 0.17 or 0.1) may not appear to make a significant difference to ranking with the LPI, shifts of up to three places are relatively common, and remember that this is only a sample of 45 countries. Indeed is it safe to assume that 'w' is constant between all countries even if it can be calibrated for one segment in time?

While it may be mathematically more appealing, the LPI would appear to have exactly the same sort of characteristics as the HDI, given that it is a simplified aggregate index covering a whole country presented in the form of a league table. It is not so much how the numbers are mathematically derived, but assumptions that small differences in value across countries, made more apparent with the league-table style of presentation, actually mean something.

SUMMARY

A small number of examples of aggregated development indices originating from the work of the UNDP and presented in its HDRs have been provided here. There are many others, and two more will be discussed in the next chapter. Composite indices do have a great appeal in that complexity is reduced and made easier to digest, but this very process of simplification carries with it the potential danger of hiding information that may be useful, or at least should be taken into account during interpretation. As we have seen with Sen's Poverty Index, it is necessary to present all of the components so that they can be interpreted properly. The same is true of the HDI and its relatives. Identical values for two or more countries can be obtained with very different balances of the components that comprise the indices. In fairness, the HDRs do contain the disaggregated components of indices such as the HDI as well as notes on the methodology employed, but users may not want to know how an index is calculated and the complexities (and pitfalls) involved. They may simply be seeking the 'big picture' – who has gone up or down the league table? How does the performance of my country compare with its neighbours?

The ease of calculation of the HDI and its relative transparency, given that it only has three equally-weighted components, may have contributed to its broad acceptance (Streeten, 1994). The league table presentation of countries generating a 'name and shame' style has also no doubt played a significant role in enhancing its popularity. As we have seen from Chapter 1, such tables

Table 4.9 *The Life Product Index (LPI) compared with the HDI*

Country	Life expectancy (years) 1993	Real GDP ($/capita) 1993	Values for w (w is proportion of life spent on economic activity)									Reported HDI	HDI Rank
			0.25			0.17			0.1				
				LPI	Rank		LPI	Rank		LPI	Rank		
Canada	77.5	20,950	932.39	0.372	5	406.91	0.976	5	209.51	0.975	3	0.951	1
US	76.1	24,680	953.83	0.995	3	410.62	0.985	4	209.23	0.973	4	0.940	2
Netherlands	77.5	17,340	889.33	0.927	16	394.28	0.946	14	205.69	0.957	12	0.938	3
Japan	79.6	20,660	954.32	0.995	4	416.97	1.000	1	214.99	1.000	1	0.938	4
Norway	77.0	20,370	919.90	0.959	6	402.40	0.965	7	207.68	0.966	9	0.937	5
France	77.0	19,140	905.68	0.945	9	398.24	0.955	10	206.39	0.960	11	0.935	6
Finland	75.8	16,320	856.74	0.893	19	381.76	0.916	19	199.96	0.930	21	0.935	7
Iceland	78.2	18,640	913.73	0.953	7	402.67	0.966	6	209.05	0.972	6	0.934	8
Sweden	78.3	17,900	905.68	0.945	10	400.47	0.960	9	208.47	0.970	7	0.933	9
Spain	77.7	13,660	840.01	0.876	21	379.89	0.911	21	201.36	0.937	18	0.933	10
Belgium	76.5	19,540	904.47	0.943	11	397.02	0.952	12	205.47	0.956	13	0.929	11
Australia	77.8	18,530	907.71	0.947	8	400.21	0.960	8	207.86	0.967	8	0.929	12
Austria	76.3	19,115	897.16	0.936	13	394.54	0.946	13	204.45	0.951	14	0.928	13
New Zealand	75.6	16,720	859.67	0.897	18	382.29	0.917	18	199.92	0.930	20	0.927	14
Switzerland	78.1	22,720	958.86	1.000	1	415.64	0.997	2	212.96	0.991	2	0.926	15
Denmark	75.3	20,200	897.70	0.936	14	392.96	0.942	15	202.92	0.944	16	0.924	16
UK	76.3	17,230	874.17	0.912	17	387.77	0.930	17	202.37	0.941	17	0.924	17
Germany	76.1	18,840	891.57	0.930	15	392.55	0.941	16	203.65	0.947	15	0.920	18
Ireland	75.4	15,120	836.10	0.872	22	374.94	0.899	22	197.39	0.918	22	0.919	19
Italy	77.6	18,160	900.83	0.935	12	397.85	0.954	11	206.91	0.962	10	0.914	20
Greece	77.7	8,950	755.75	0.788	24	354.04	0.849	23	193.02	0.898	23	0.909	21
Israel	76.6	15,130	849.55	0.886	20	380.95	0.914	20	200.55	0.933	19	0.908	22
Luxembourg	75.8	25,390	956.83	0.998	2	410.94	0.986	3	208.99	0.972	5	0.895	23
Korea, Rep.	71.3	9,710	707.77	0.738	26	329.33	0.790	26	178.57	0.831	26	0.886	24
Argentina	72.2	8,350	690.17	0.720	27	325.20	0.780	27	179.12	0.829	27	0.885	25
Chile	73.9	8,900	717.78	0.749	25	336.42	0.807	25	183.48	0.853	25	0.882	26
Portugal	74.7	10,720	760.10	0.793	23	350.77	0.841	24	188.95	0.879	24	0.878	27

▶

Table 4.9 *Continued*

Country	Life expectancy (years) 1993	Real GDP ($/capita) 1993	Values for w (w is proportion of life spent on economic activity)									Reported HDI	HDI Rank
			0.25	LPI	Rank	0.17	LPI	Rank	0.1	LPI	Rank		
Czech Republic	71.3	8,430	683.20	0.713	28	321.66	0.771	28	176.06	0.819	28	0.872	28
Hungary	69.0	6,059	608.76	0.635	30	294.61	0.707	30	164.85	0.767	31	0.855	29
Mexico	71.0	7,010	649.66	0.678	29	310.61	0.745	29	172.12	0.801	29	0.845	30
Latvia	69.0	5,010	580.51	0.605	32	285.42	0.685	33	161.75	0.752	33	0.820	31
Poland	71.1	4,702	588.76	0.614	31	291.02	0.698	31	165.61	0.770	30	0.819	32
Russian Federation	67.4	4,760	559.84	0.584	36	276.44	0.663	36	157.19	0.731	37	0.804	33
Brazil	66.5	5,500	572.68	0.597	34	279.39	0.670	35	157.35	0.732	36	0.796	34
Belarus	69.7	4,244	562.57	0.587	35	280.45	0.673	34	160.70	0.747	34	0.787	35
Bulgaria	71.2	4,320	577.23	0.602	33	287.34	0.689	32	164.45	0.765	32	0.773	36
Estonia	69.2	3,610	536.39	0.559	39	271.03	0.650	38	156.98	0.730	39	0.749	37
Romania	69.9	3,727	546.16	0.570	37	275.24	0.660	37	159.08	0.740	35	0.738	38
Lithuania	70.3	3,110	524.98	0.548	40	268.59	0.644	39	157.12	0.731	38	0.719	39
Turkey	66.7	4,210	537.27	0.560	38	268.02	0.643	40	153.66	0.715	40	0.711	40
Philippines	66.5	2,590	474.40	0.495	42	246.44	0.591	42	145.93	0.679	42	0.665	41
South Africa	63.2	3,127	472.61	0.493	43	241.68	0.580	43	141.33	0.657	43	0.649	42
China	68.6	2,330	476.61	0.497	41	249.78	0.599	41	148.96	0.693	41	0.609	43
India	60.7	1,240	360.20	0.376	44	198.96	0.477	44	123.75	0.576	44	0.436	44
Nigeria	50.6	1,540	316.98	0.331	45	171.95	0.412	45	105.42	0.490	45	0.400	45

The calculation of the Life Product Index (LPI) has been taken from Lind (1993). The LPI is found by:

$$LPI = GDP/capita^w \times \text{life expectancy at birth}$$

where 'w' is the proportion of life expectancy spent on economic activity. The values in bold in the table are the ranks of the countries based on the HDI and on three versions of the LPI using different values for 'w'. Data taken from the HDR 1991 (GDP/capita data from 1985 to 1988).

are becoming increasingly popular as tools for informing policy and even consumer choice in parts of the developed world. It should also be acknowledged that the HDI was not created in an index-free vacuum. Before the advent of the HDRs (and the HDI) in 1990 there were many indices being used to gauge the level of development, and the most dominant of these were the economic indicators. The HDI has helped to shift the reporting agenda away from narrow economic indices, and provided a focus for media reporting as well as debate within practitioner and academic communities. It has also encouraged a host of constructive debates about the nature of human development and how best to gauge progress.

The next chapter will discuss how aggregated indices and league tables have been extended into two specific areas of development: environmental sustainability and good governance (specifically corruption). These examples have a number of similarities to the HDI and its family, such as their basis on value judgements, but they also present some additional dimensions of interest.

5 THE PRECARIOUS ART OF SIMPLIFYING COMPLEXITY

INTRODUCTION

The HDI and its family are by no means the only such aggregated indices of development. However, rather than just catalogue more examples, I have decided to select two indices for further discussion as they attempt to gauge elements that are now considered to be vital for development. They not only reinforce some of the points already covered, but bring out some interesting new ones.

The first index, the Environmental Sustainability Index (ESI), is – as its name suggests – an index designed to gauge the environmental sustainability of countries. The assumption is that for sustainable development to take place there must be no damage to the environment. Like the HDI it utilizes published data sets, but has 20 components rather than just three. Its calculation is also more complex than the HDI, and again there are critical issues over selection of the components and their relative weighting. Indeed, as we will see, this has been the subject of some strong criticism.

The second index, the Corruption Perception Index (CPI), is meant to reflect an important aspect of 'good governance', a feature that is today seen as an important requisite for development. Without good governance, development efforts can be wasted or even be detrimental. The control of corruption is seen as an essential element for this, hence the various efforts to derive indices of corruption, only one of which will be covered here. Like the ESI the methodology of the CPI is more complex than that of the HDI, but unlike these two it is an index of perception. It draws its data from questionnaires completed by business people, mostly based in the developed world, designed to gauge their perceptions of the level of corruption in the countries of which they have experience. As can be appreciated, a reliance on perception of one fairly homogenous group does lead to a host of issues regarding their positionality.

I do realize that by focusing on the ESI and CPI there will be some who will criticize the omission of their own favoured development index. I do not wish to imply that the ESI and CPI are examples of 'best' or 'worst' practice or that they are in some way superior/inferior to other indices. They have been selected for their similarities and differences from the indices discussed so far, and in the case of the ESI, because it opens a door into the realm of sustainable development.

This chapter will begin with a broad discussion of indicators of sustainable development before covering the ESI and CPI in some depth. However, I would repeat here what I have already said in Chapter 1. While the technical calculations behind the ESI and CPI are somewhat involved, the reader is urged to engage with them. It is through these that the reader can gain a better understanding of the assumptions that have been made by the creators of the indices.

INDICATORS OF SUSTAINABLE DEVELOPMENT

The use of indicators and indices as a means of gauging progress towards the attainment of sustainable development, or even as aids within 'learning for sustainability' and sustainable livelihood strategies has gained momentum over the past 20 years (Bell and Morse, 1999, 2003). The history of indicators of sustainable development (ISD) has many parallels with that of development indicators in general, but given that sustainable development also borrows strongly from the ecological and environmental spheres there are also differences. There is a long and rich history of using indicators to gauge environmental quality, for example by the use of indicator species or biodiversity indices.

The GPI (Genuine Progress Indicator), ISEW (Index of Sustainable Economic Welfare) etc are attempts to include elements of consumption and environmental damage within the classic GDP type of economic indicator. While they have their proponents, as we have seen, these indicators also have their problems, not least being the issue of ascribing a monetary valuation to components such as environmental damage. Others have attempted to produce single indices of sustainable development, or to modify existing indices such as the HDI. The logic is similar to that of the HDI, and can be summarized as follows:

> *Not surprisingly, people with good intentions (like myself and all my colleagues in the indicator community) would love to use the immense power of indicators to make the world a better place. If GDP forces the world to run into global disasters, why not produce a replacement for GDP that forces the world to steer 'towards sustainability'?* (Jesinghaus, 2000a)

Another example of a single index of sustainable development that has achieved some popularity is the notion of an 'ecological footprint' (Allenby et al, 1998; Curwell and Cooper, 1998; Haberl et al, 2001). This is commonly expressed as the area of land required to sustain a country or some other unit (county, urban centre etc). The higher the value of the ecological footprint for a country, the more unsustainable it is deemed to be. Morse (2003a) has shown how the ecological footprint can be seen as a 'cost' and related to the HDI as a measure of 'benefit'.

In contrast to the wide publicity accorded the HDI, the acceptance of aggregated indices within sustainable development has been mixed. For example, in April 2001 a paper published by the UN Division for Sustainable Development (DSD, 2001) set out some initial thoughts with regard to the integration of ISDs (DSD, 2001), and the 'HDI' style of integration was discussed as an option. However, the DSD point out that the HDI 'is still viewed with scepticism by some for its lack of sensitivity in some of its components' (DSD, 2001, p20). More popular within sustainable development has been the creation of indicator sets without necessarily attempting to integrate them, except perhaps visually (Morse et al, 2001). The argument is that sustainable development is so broad that if there were an attempt to combine all of the separate indicators into a single index valuable information would be lost, and that this would lead to exactly the same sort of problems discussed for the HDI in Chapter 4. The presentation of such indicator sets in highly visual formats can be quite ingenious, such as the use of a barometer and even a vehicle dashboard (Figure 5.1).[1]

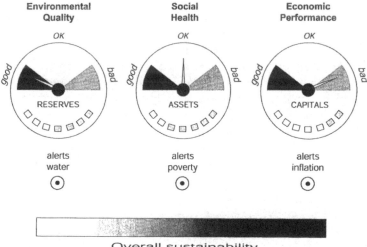

Note the analogy made between sustainable development and a moving vehicle. Each of the three dials covers dimensions seen as important in sustainable development: environmental quality, social health and economic performance. Each dial has three warning lights highlighting problems with water, poverty and inflation. The bar at the foot of the dashboard shows 'overall sustainability' and is an aggregation of all the indicators.
Source: After Hardi (2001)

Figure 5.1 *The dashboard of sustainability*

Given that sustainable development is an all-embracing paradigm, applying at all scales and to all countries, there has also been a deep and prevalent ethos towards the populist and participatory selection of indicators. While there are techno-centric and top-down indices of sustainable development that match those of the HDI and its relatives in style, there are also many efforts to create community indicators of sustainable development to encourage their use at the local level. Indeed, Local Agenda 21 programmes, the commitment of all signatories to the 1992 UNEP facilitated World Summit on Sustainable Development, requires the establishment of local programmes and recommends the use of indicators to help facilitate change. 'Local' in this context can mean anything, and can even be taken to the level of streets and households. Such participatory approaches to indicator creation have in themselves spawned a host of different methodologies, often beginning with a need to establish just what sustainable development means to the actors involved. This book cannot hope to do justice to this diversity, but see Bell and Morse (1999, 2003) for a wider discussion. We will return to this theme in Chapter 7.

ENVIRONMENTAL SUSTAINABILITY INDEX

One example of an aggregated index of sustainable development is the recently created Environmental Sustainability Index (ESI) backed by the powerful World Economic Forum (WEF) in collaboration with Yale and Columbia Universities (WEF, 2000, 2001, 2002; pilot study published in 1999). I will refer to this partnership using the label they have chosen for themselves – the 'Global Leaders of Tomorrow', or simply 'Global Leaders'. The ESI comprises five components deemed desirable by experts within the 'Global Leaders' for environmental sustainability. Within each of these components there is a set of indicators, and each indicator is comprised of a set of variables. The result is a hierarchy of variables (68), indicators (20) and components (5) far more complex than the HDI (a summary breakdown of the indicators and components is given in Table 5.1, while Table 5.2 gives details of the actual components).

Table 5.1 *Summary of indicators and components of the ESI*

Component	Number of indicators	Number of variables
Environmental systems	5	13
Reducing environmental stresses	5	15
Reducing human vulnerability	2	5
Social and institutional capacity	5	22
Global stewardship	3	13
Total	20	68

Table 5.2 *Components of the Environmental Sustainability Index (ESI) for 2002*

Component	Indicator	Variable
Environmental systems	Air quality	Urban SO_2 concentration
		Urban NO_2 concentration
		Urban total suspended particulate concentration
	Water quantity	Internal renewable water per capita
		Per capita water inflow from other countries
	Water quality	Dissolved oxygen concentration
		Phosphorus concentration
		Suspended solids
		Electrical conductivity
	Biodiversity	Percentage of mammals threatened
		Percentage of breeding birds threatened
	Land	Percent of land area having very low anthropogenic impact
		Percent of land area having high anthropogenic impact
Reducing environmental stresses	Reducing air pollution	NO_x emissions per populated land area
		SO_2 emissions per populated land area
		VOCs emissions per populated land area
		Coal consumption per populated land area
		Vehicles per populated land area
	Reducing water stress	Fertilizer consumption per hectare of arable land
		Pesticide use per hectare of crop land
		Industrial organic pollutants per available fresh water
		Percentage of country's territory under severe water stress
	Reducing ecosystem stress	Percentage change in forest cover 1990–95
		Percentage of country with acidification exceedence
	Reducing waste and consumption pressures	Ecological footprint per capita
		Radioactive waste
	Reducing population growth	Total fertility rate
		Percentage change in projected population between 2000 and 2050
Reducing human vulnerability	Basic human sustenance	Proportion of undernourished in total population
		Percent of population with access to improved drinking water supply
	Environmental health	Child death rate from respiratory disease
		Death rate from intestinal infectious disease
		Under-5 mortality rate
Social and institutional capacity	Science/technology	Innovation Index
		Technology Achievement Index
		Mean years of schooling (age 15 and above)
	Capacity for debate	IUCN member organisations per million population
		Civil and political liberties
		Democratic institutions
		Percentage of ESI variables in publicly available data sets

Table 5.2 *Continued*

Component	Indicator	Variable
	Environmental governance	WAF survey questions of environmental governance
		Percentage of land area under protected status
		Number of sectoral EIA guidelines
		FSC accredited forest area as a percent of total forest area
		Reducing corruption
		Ratio of gasoline price to international average
		WEF subsidies survey question
		WWF subsidy measures
	Private sector responsiveness	Number of ISO14001 certified companies per million $ GDP
		Dow Jones sustainability group index
		Average Innovest EcoValue rating of firms
		World Business Council for Sustainable Development members
		WEF survey questions on private sector environmental innovation
	Eco-efficiency	Energy efficiency (total energy consumption per unit GDP)
		Renewable energy production as a percent of total energy consumption
Global stewardship	Participation in international collaborative efforts	Number of memberships in environmental intergovernmental organisations
		Percentage of CITES reporting requirements met
		Levels of participation in the Vienna Convention/ Montreal Protocol
		Levels of participation in the Climate Change Convention
		Montreal Protocol multilateral fund participation
		Global Environmental Facility participation
		Compliance with international agreements
	Reducing greenhouse gas emissions	Carbon lifestyle efficiency (CO_2 emissions per capita)
		Carbon economic efficiency (CO_2 emissions per $ GDP)
	Reducing trans-boundary environmental pressures	CFC consumption (total times per person)
		SO_2 exports
		Total marine fish catch
		Seafood consumption per capita

Source: ESI Report 2002.

Note the 'unevenness' in the number of variables that go to make up each component. For example, 'Social and institutional capacity' is comprised of 22 variables, while 'Reducing human vulnerability' has only five.

Given the need to integrate this diverse hierarchy, it is perhaps of no great surprise that the calculation of the ESI is far more complex than that of the

HDI. This raises several issues of interest. The first is the varied degree of completeness of the data sets for each variable. Given the need for data covering 68 variables and 142 countries, it is only to be expected that there will be substantial gaps. These are filled by a process of 'imputation' based upon regression analysis with another associated variable. For example, for the 'Air Quality' indicator under the 'Environmental systems' component we have the three variables shown in Table 5.3.

Table 5.3 *Variables for the air quality indicator of the environmental systems component of the ESI*

Variable	Observed values	Imputed values	Total
Urban SO_2 concentration	51	91	· 142
Urban NO_2 concentration	50	92	142
Urban total suspended particles (TSP) concentration	49	93	142
Total	150	276	426

Therefore, this indicator has 65 per cent of its data values imputed rather than based on direct measurement, a figure that is high even when it is assumed that the remaining 35 per cent of observed values are of good quality. Twenty-four of the 68 variables have varying degrees of imputed data. We also need to note that for the 'Air Quality' indicator both the SO_2 and NO_2 variables are based on city averages over the period 1990–1996, which were then 'normalized' for the city population in 1995 and scaled-up to give a value for each country. But there is much variation hidden within the single country values, for example, seasonal variation. The allocation of a single figure for these variables to each country does appear to be highly simplistic. Further problems with the choice of variables in the ESI are discussed in the April 2001 edition of the *Ecologist* (p44–47).

The 68 variables all have very different units of measurement, as of course do the three components of the HDI, and the means by which 'Global Leaders' deal with this is much the same. If the data within each variable have a highly skewed distribution (Box 5.1) then the original data are transformed by taking logarithms. This is similar to the logic used to justify the use of logarithms to transform the GDP/capita component of the HDI.

Following transformation (if it was necessary) each variable is 'capped' to remove extreme values, and for the most part this is achieved by employing the 97.5 and 2.5 per cent percentiles. Values greater than the 97.5 per cent percentile are made equal to the value of the 97.5 per cent percentile, while values lower than the 2.5 per cent percentile are made equal to value of the 2.5 per cent percentile. For example, in the SO_2 data set the 97.5 per cent percentile equates to a value of 150.64 micrograms/cubic metre and the 2.5 per cent percentile to 2.9 micrograms/cubic metre. Any value greater than

Box 5.1 *Skewness and the Environmental Sustainability Index (ESI)*

There can significant differences between countries in terms of the 68 variables used to calculate the ESI, a problem also encountered when using GDP/capita in the HDI. As a result it may be necessary to transform the raw data by taking logarithms.

This box illustrates the differences in distribution that can occur between variables. The two examples selected here are the variables urban NO_2 (graph a) and per capita water inflow (graph b). In both graphs the countries have been ranked in terms of their value for the variable, with low values to the left and high values to the right. Unlike the UNDP, which always transforms the GDP/capita component of the HDI and not the others, 'Global Leaders', the creators of the ESI, use a measure of 'skewness' to determine whether the data need to be transformed. They suggest that any variable with a skewness above 4 should be transformed before inclusion in the index.

The two variables presented here have quite different values for skewness, with per capita water inflow being much higher than 4. As a result this variable needs transformation, and the results are shown in graph c.

Urban NO_2

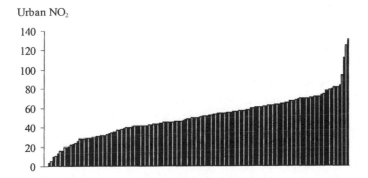

(a) Urban NO_2 (micrograms/cubic metre): skewness $= 0.51$

per capita water inflow

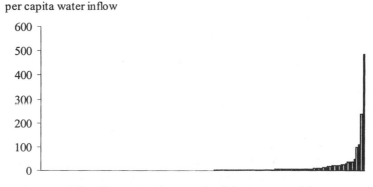

(b) Per capita water inflow (thousand cubic metres/capita): skewness $= 8.4$

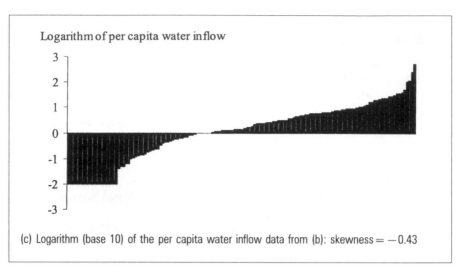

(c) Logarithm (base 10) of the per capita water inflow data from (b): skewness = −0.43

150.64 (such as Iran's figure of 209) is made equal to 150.64, and similarly any value less than 2.9 (0 for example) is made equal to 2.9. In effect the extremes are 'flattened out'. Note that the decision to cap as well as the choice of 97.5 and 2.5 per cent instead of, for example, 95 and 5 per cent or 90 and 10 per cent, have been made by the creators of the index. We have already seen something similar with the HDI, where GDP/capita values greater than $40,000 are capped at $40,000.

Once capped using the percentile, the original data are changed into standardized values (called z-values) by subtracting the mean or subtracting from the mean and dividing by the standard deviation. The format of the standardization depends upon whether higher values of the variable are deemed by the experts to be 'good' or 'bad' for sustainability. If higher values are deemed to be good then the z-value is given by:

$$z\text{-value} = \frac{\text{country value} - \text{mean}}{\text{standard deviation}}$$

The z-value will increase with the country value. A country value less than the mean will yield a negative z-value. However, if high values are deemed to be bad for sustainability then the z-value is given by:

$$z\text{-value} = \frac{\text{mean} - \text{country value}}{\text{standard deviation}}$$

In this case a high value for a country (ie one greater than the mean) will result in a negative z-value.

With the HDI the 'polarity' is only in one direction – higher values of life expectancy, education or income are all deemed to be 'good' for human development. Also, unlike the standardization used in the HDI the z-values of the ESI can be greater than 1 and less than 0. The aim is to standardize the distribution so that the average of all the country z-values for a variable will be 0 and the standard deviation (a measure of variation) between them will be 1.

The next step is to find the average z-value for each country and indicator. Table 5.4 is an example for the two indicators and five variables in the 'Reducing human vulnerability' component of the ESI, the one which has the closest parallel to the HDI and its family. The two indicators are 'Basic human sustenance' and 'Environmental health', comprising two and three variables respectively. In Table 5.4 Nigeria and the UK are used as examples. This process is repeated for the other 18 indicators and 141 countries.

Table 5.4 *Calculation of z-values for two of the indicators used in the Environmental Sustainability Index (2002)*

STEP 1. Data for two countries, Nigeria and the UK are presented here. The raw data are first 'capped' using the 97.5 and 2.5 percentiles. For these countries data no 'capping' was necessary (none of the data exceed the 97.5 percentile or are less than the 2.5 percentile)

Indicator	Variable	Raw data	Adjusted for percentile	z-value
(a) Nigeria				
Basic human sustenance	% of undernourished in total population	7.00	7.00	0.57
	% of population with access to improved drinking water	57.00	57.00	−1.08
			Mean	−0.25
Environmental health	Child death rate from respiratory disease (deaths/100,000 for ages 0–14)	198.83	198.83	−1.67
	Death rate from intestinal infectious disease (deaths/100,000)	33.72	33.72	−1.32
	Under 5 mortality rate (deaths/1000 live births)	187.00	187.00	−1.70
			Mean	−1.56
(b) UK				
Basic human sustenance	% of undernourished in total population	1.00	1.00	0.94
	% of population with access to improved drinking water	100.00	100.00	1.18
			Mean	1.06
Environmental health	Child death rate from respiratory disease (deaths/100,000 for ages 0–14)	1.78	1.78	1.03
	Death rate from intestinal infectious disease (deaths/100,000)	0.75	0.75	1.06
	Under 5 mortality rate (deaths/1000 live births)	6.00	6.00	0.91
			Mean	1.00

▶

Table 5.4 *Continued*

STEP 2. The mean and standard deviations of the variables for all countries after adjustment were then calculated

Indicator	Variable	Mean	Standard deviation	Polarity of variable
Basic human sustenance	% of undernourished in total population	16.52	16.85	LOW
	% of population with access to improved drinking water	77.52	19.22	HIGH
Environmental health	Child death rate from respiratory disease (deaths/100,000 for ages 0–14)	77.00	73.61	LOW
	Death rate from intestinal infectious disease (deaths/100,000)	15.45	13.81	LOW
	Under 5 mortality rate (deaths/1000 live births)	70.04	72.23	LOW

Note: polarity of variable = whether high or low values are considered 'good' for environmental sustainability

STEP 3. z-values for each variable found as follows:
For variables where 'low' values are considered to be good for sustainability

$$z\text{-value} = \frac{\text{mean} - \text{country value}}{\text{standard deviation}}$$

Example (Nigeria; % undernourished in population) $= \dfrac{16.52 - 7}{16.85} = \mathbf{0.57}$

For variables where 'high' values are considered to be good for sustainability:

$$z\text{-value} = \frac{\text{country value} - \text{mean}}{\text{standard deviation}}$$

Example (UK; % of population with access to improved drinking water) $= \dfrac{100 - 77.52}{19.22} = \mathbf{1.18}$

STEP 4. Find the average of the z-values that comprise each indicator
(a) Nigeria

Indicator	Variable		z-value
Basic human sustenance	% of undernourished in total population		0.57
	% of population with access to improved drinking water		−1.08
		Mean	**−0.25**
Environmental health	Child death rate from respiratory disease (deaths/100,000 for ages 0–14)		−0.67
	Death rate from intestinal infectious disease (deaths/100,000)		−1.32
	Under 5 mortality rate (deaths/,000 live births)		−1.70
		Mean	**−1.56**

Table 5.4 *Continued*

(b) UK

Indicator	Variable		z-value
Basic human sustenance	% of undernourished in total population		0.94
	% of population with access to improved drinking water		1.18
		Mean	**1.06**
Environmental health	Child death rate from respiratory disease (deaths/100,000 for ages 0–14)		1.03
	Death rate from intestinal infectious disease (deaths/100,000)		1.06
	Under 5 mortality rate (deaths/1000 live births)		0.91
		Mean	**1.00**

Source of data: ESI Report 2002.

But that is not the end! The average z-values of each indicator are converted to a more intuitively meaningful statistic by calculating the 'standardized normal percentile'. The result is a set of numbers with a theoretical minimum of 0 and a theoretical maximum of 100. In other words, the z-values are converted to numbers that look more like percentages. These are in turn averaged over all the indicators to provide the ESI. The higher the ESI then the better the environmental sustainability of the country, and the results are presented in the by now familiar league table format beloved of the UNDP with its development indices. The ESI values for 2002 are shown in ranked order as Table 5.5.

Table 5.5 *Values of the Environmental Sustainability Index for 2002*

Country	ESI	Country	ESI
Finland	73.9	Guatemala	49.6
Norway	73.0	Malaysia	49.5
Sweden	72.6	Zambia	49.5
Canada	70.6	Algeria	49.4
Switzerland	66.5	Bulgaria	49.3
Uruguay	66.0	Morocco	49.1
Austria	64.2	Russia	49.1
Iceland	63.9	Egypt	48.8
Costa Rica	63.2	El Salvador	48.7
Latvia	63.0	South Africa	48.7
Hungary	62.7	Uganda	48.7
Croatia	62.5	Japan	48.6
Botswana	61.8	Dominican Republic	48.4
Slovakia	61.6	Tanzania	48.1
Argentina	61.5	Senegal	47.6
Australia	60.3	Malawi	47.3
Estonia	60.0	Italy	47.2

▶

Table 5.5 *Continued*

Country	ESI	Country	ESI
Panama	60.0	Macedonia	47.2
New Zealand	**59.9**	Mali	47.1
Brazil	59.6	Bangladesh	46.9
Bolivia	59.4	**Poland**	**46.7**
Colombia	59.1	Kazakhstan	46.5
Slovenia	58.8	Kenya	46.3
Albania	57.9	Myanmar	46.2
Paraguay	57.8	**UK**	**46.1**
Namibia	57.4	Cameroon	45.9
Lithuania	57.2	**Mexico**	**45.9**
Portugal	**57.1**	Benin	45.7
Peru	56.5	Chad	45.7
Bhutan	56.3	Vietnam	45.7
Denmark	**56.2**	Cambodia	45.6
Laos	56.2	Guinea	45.3
France	**55.5**	Nepal	45.2
Netherlands	**55.4**	Indonesia	45.1
Chile	55.1	Burkina Faso	45.0
Gabon	54.9	Gambia	44.7
Armenia	54.8	Sudan	44.7
Ireland	**54.8**	Iran	44.5
Moldova	54.5	Togo	44.3
Congo	54.3	Lebanon	43.8
Ecuador	54.3	Syria	43.6
Mongolia	54.2	Ivory Coast	43.4
Central African Republic	54.1	Zaire	43.3
Spain	**54.1**	Angola	42.4
US	**53.2**	Tajikistan	42.4
Zimbabwe	53.2	Pakistan	42.1
Honduras	53.1	Azerbaijan	41.8
Venezuela	53.0	Ethiopia	41.8
Belarus	52.8	Burundi	41.6
Germany	**52.5**	India	41.6
Nicaragua	51.8	Philippines	41.6
Papua New Guinea	51.8	Uzbekistan	41.3
Jordan	51.7	Rwanda	40.6
Thailand	51.6	Oman	40.2
Bosnia and Herzegovina	51.3	Jamaica	40.1
Kyrgyzstan	51.3	Trinidad and Tobago	40.1
Sri Lanka	51.3	Niger	39.4
Cuba	51.2	Libya	39.3
Mozambique	51.1	**Belgium**	**39.1**
Greece	**50.9**	Mauritania	38.9
Tunisia	50.8	Guinea-Bissau	38.8
Turkey	**50.8**	Madagascar	38.8
Israel	50.4	China	38.5
Czech Republic	**50.2**	Liberia	37.7
Ghana	50.2	Turkmenistan	37.3
Romania	50.0	Somalia	37.1

Table 5.5 *Continued*

Country	ESI	Country	ESI
		Nigeria	36.7
		Sierra Leone	36.5
		Korea, Republic	**35.9**
		Ukraine	35.0
		Haiti	34.8
		Saudi Arabia	34.2
		Iraq	33.2
		Korea, Dem. Rep.	32.3
		United Arab Emirates	25.7
		Kuwait	23.9

Bold countries are members of the Organization for Economic Cooperation and Development (OECD). One member of the OECD, Luxembourg, was not included in the ESI report.
Source of data: ESI Report 2002.

As can be seen from the foregoing discussion, Box 5.1 and Table 5.4 the ESI methodology is clearly quite involved, but at the heart of the calculation is the need for a reliable date set with a good coverage across countries. The need for imputed data is a concern, especially as the imputed values are derived from a regression analysis of variables that are assumed to be associated. Ideally, each of these should include an error term thereby providing a range rather than a single value for each of the imputed data, but that would perhaps complicate the methodology so much as to make it unusable.

The ESI has had some exposure within the popular press, although as we shall see this has not been as extensive as the HDI. Jesinghaus (2000a) makes the following observation:

> *The WEF Environmental Sustainability Index was, compared to many other indicators initiatives, particularly successful in getting the attention of the media: it was even published in the Economist of January 29th – February 4th 2000. Actually, it occupied approximately 32% of the space of page 138, 0.23% of the whole journal, and 0.004% of the annual information produced by The Economist, one of the most important journals world-wide.* (Jesinghaus, 2000a)

However, the ESI has been criticized for reasons other than the quality of the data used as its foundation. For example, the selection of components was claimed to be biased towards the richer countries at the expense of the poorer (Jesinghaus, 2000a; *Ecologist*, 2001). In Table 5.5 the countries that are members of the OECD (ie the richer countries of the world) are in bold. Of the 29 members of the OECD included in the table (Luxembourg is not included) 22 of them have an ESI of 50 or above, the better performers in terms of environmental sustainability. Indeed the five best performers are

OECD countries. Of the 76 countries with an ESI of less than 50, the poorer performers in terms of environmental sustainability, only seven are members of the OECD. But does this seem like a realistic representation, or are we seeing a bias towards the richer countries which overachieve in terms of the 'Social and institutional capacity' component that comprises nearly a third of the ESI? In an elegant presentation of this structural criticism, the *Ecologist* in cooperation with the *Friends of the Earth* produced their own version of the ESI by downplaying the contribution from the 'Social and institutional capacity' component and in effect were able to almost reverse any conclusions that could be derived from the 'Global Leaders' version of the ESI.

> *if we are going to label nations 'good' or 'bad' in environmental terms, we must get our measurements right. Studies like the ESI, based on misleading data, which fail to take into account the true environmental costs that rich countries impose on the world, are designed to make dirty nations look clean. (The Ecologist, 2001, p47)*

Worryingly, could we not say the same for the HDI and labels of human development?

CORRUPTION AND HUMAN DEVELOPMENT

Corruption has long been highlighted as an important element in development, and today is part of the wider 'good governance' agenda promoted by aid agencies worldwide. In 1996, the World Bank President, James Wolfensohn, highlighted corruption as a major inhibitor of development, and this organization has implemented more than 600 anti-corruption programmes in nearly 100 borrowing countries. As Hisamatsu (2003, p1) states 'it is difficult to overstate the economic and social significance of corruption':

> *Studies have shown a clear negative correlation between the level of corruption (as perceived by businesspeople) and both investment and economic growth. . . . Yet it is not just a cost of doing business. Other surveys and anecdotal evidence suggest that the greatest victims of petty corruption are usually the poor.[2]*

The assumption of a damaging impact on development is straightforward. Corruption can result in resources being diverted from the public good to private consumption with the result that impacts intended to be of wider benefit are lost. As can be imagined from the above quotation, such a hindrance to business is likely to deter investment and hamper economic growth (Mauro, 1995).

Yet corruption is a notoriously difficult and complex element to gauge because its very nature makes it opaque (Lambsdorff, 1999; Hisamatsu, 2003).

Those benefiting from corruption are unlikely to say so and even more unlikely to say how much they receive. Those on the 'giving' end (ie the payers) are less reticent to talk about the extent of corruption, but there may be a danger of them exaggerating their problems by confounding difficult bureaucracies and different ways of doing business with 'corruption'.

The Corruption Perception Index (CPI), created by the Berlin-based Transparency International (TI) is another complex index. However, what distinguishes it from both the HDI and ESI is that it is based on the perception that givers of bribes have towards various countries. In the ESI there are measures of water quality not people's perceptions of water quality. Similarly the HDI includes measures of GDP/capita and is not founded on perceptions of wealth. While there is subjective judgement regarding different ways of measuring water quality (and indeed GDP), as well as the decision to include them in the indices, the CPI embraces such judgement to its heart.

The CPI is an index of indices. It is found by combining data from a variety of sources (Lambsdorff, 2002), including (in the 2002 CPI):

- the World Economic Forum (WEF) corruption reports (GCR = global; ACR = African)
- the Institute for Management Development, Lausanne (IMD)
- PricewaterhouseCoopers (PwC)
- the World Bank's World Business Environment Survey (WBES)
- The Economist Intelligence Unit (EIU)
- Freedom House, Nations in Transit (FH)
- the Political and Economic Risk Consultancy, Hong Kong (PERC)
- Gallop International on behalf of Transparency International (TI/GI)
- the State Capacity Survey by Columbia University (CU).

Most of these sources have their own index of corruption and a ranking of nations based on that index. Methodologies do vary between them, including the group sampled and the questions asked about corruption. Some of them only have the results for one year (TI/GI, WBES, PwC), while others have several years of data (PERC, WEF, IMD). The sources of data, number of respondents and countries, are shown in Table 5.6. For each county there is also a summary of the number of surveys of corruption for that country, and the number of different institutions involved in those surveys. A single institution may have implemented a number of corruption surveys. For example, the World Economic Forum (the organization involved in the ESI) has implemented four surveys used for the compilation of the CPI for 2002.

All of the surveys in Table 5.6 were used in the calculation of the CPI in 2002 'to reduce abrupt variations in scoring that might arise due to random effects' (Lambsdorff, 2002). This mixture of data sets over a number of years is different to the approach taken with the HDI where new data, albeit time-lagged typically by two years, are used in the annual league table. Some countries have been covered by relatively few surveys (as few as three) while

Table 5.6 Countries and sources of data for the 2002 Corruption Perception Index (CPI)

Country	Surveys	Institutions	IMD 2000	IMD 2001	IMD 2002	PERC 2000	PERC 2001	World economic forum GCR 2000	GCR 2001	GCR 2002	ACR 2000	WBES 2001	EIU 2002	PwC 2001	FH 2002	TI/GI 2002	CU 2001
Albania	3	3										*			*		*
Angola	3	3									*						*
Argentina	10	6	*	*	*			*	*	*		*	*	*			*
Australia	11	6	*	*	*	*	*	*	*	*			*			*	*
Austria	8	4	*	*	*			*	*	*		*	*			*	*
Azerbaijan	4	4										*	*				
Bangladesh	5	4						*	*	*		*	*		*		*
Belarus	3	3										*	*				*
Belgium	8	4	*	*	*			*	*	*		*	*		*	*	*
Bolivia	6	4						*	*	*		*	*				*
Botswana	5	4						*				*	*				*
Brazil	10	6	*	*	*			*	*	*	*	*	*	*	*		*
Bulgaria	7	5		*				*	*	*		*	*				*
Cameroon	4	4						*			*	*	*				*
Canada	10	6	*	*	*			*	*	*		*	*	*		*	*
Chile	10	6	*	*	*			*	*	*		*	*	*		*	*
China	11	6	*	*	*	*	*	*	*	*	*	*	*	*			*
Colombia	10	6	*	*				*	*	*		*	*	*			*
Costa Rica	6	4						*	*	*		*	*				*
Côte d'Ivoire	4	4										*	*				*
Croatia	4	4										*	*				
Czech Republic	10	6	*	*	*			*	*	*		*	*	*	*	*	*
Denmark	8	4	*	*	*			*	*	*		*	*		*		
Dominican Rep.	4	3										*	*				*
Ecuador	7	5						*	*	*	*	*	*	*			*
Egypt	7	5						*	*	*		*	*	*			*
El Salvador	6	4								*		*	*				*

	Estonia	Ethiopia	Finland	France	Georgia	Germany	Ghana	Greece	Guatemala	Haiti	Honduras	Hong Kong	Hungary	Iceland	India	Indonesia	Ireland	Israel	Italy	Jamaica	Japan	Jordan	Kazakhstan	Kenya	Latvia	Lithuania	Luxembourg	Madagascar	Malawi	Malaysia	Mauritius	Mexico	Moldova
	6	3	4	6	3	6	4	4	5	3	4	6	7	2	7	7	4	5	7	2	7	3	4	5	3	6	2	3	4	6	3	6	4
	8	3	8	0	3	10	4	8	5	3	5	11	11	6	12	12	8	9	11	3	12	5	4	5	4	7	5	3	4	11	6	10	4

Table 5.6 *Continued*

Country	Surveys	Institutions	IMD 2000	IMD 2001	IMD 2002	PERC 2000	PERC 2001	World economic forum GCR 2000	GCR 2001	GCR 2002	ACR 2000	WBES 2001	EIU 2002	PwC 2001	FH 2002	TI/GI 2002	CU 2001
Morocco	4	3						*			*		*				*
Namibia	5	4						*			*	*	*				*
Netherlands	9	5	*	*	*			*	*	*			*			*	*
New Zealand	8	4	*	*	*			*	*	*			*				*
Nicaragua	5	4						*	*	*			*				*
Nigeria	6	4						*	*	*	*		*				*
Norway	8	4	*	*	*			*	*	*			*				*
Pakistan	3	3							*			*		*			
Panama	5	4						*	*	*			*				*
Paraguay	3	2						*				*	*				
Peru	7	5						*	*	*		*	*	*			*
Philippines	11	6	*	*	*	*	*	*	*	*			*			*	*
Poland	11	7	*	*	*			*	*	*			*	*	*	*	*
Portugal	9	5	*	*	*			*	*	*		*	*				*
Romania	7	6		*	*			*	*	*		*	*	*			
Russia	12	8	*	*	*			*	*	*		*	*	*	*	*	*
Senegal	4	4									*	*	*				*
Singapore	13	8	*	*	*	*	*	*	*	*		*	*	*		*	*
Slovak Republic	8	5	*	*	*			*	*	*			*				*
Slovenia	9	6	*	*	*			*	*	*			*		*		*
South Africa	11	6	*	*	*			*	*	*	*	*	*			*	*
South Korea	12	7	*	*	*	*	*	*	*	*			*	*		*	*
Spain	10	6	*	*	*			*	*	*		*	*			*	*
Sri Lanka	4	3							*			*	*				*
Sweden	10	6	*	*	*			*	*	*		*	*			*	*
Switzerland	9	5	*	*	*			*	*	*			*			*	*
Taiwan	12	7	*	*	*	*	*	*	*	*			*	*		*	*

Morocco	4	3						*		*	*				*
Tanzania	4	4						*		*	*				*
Thailand	11	6	*	*	*	*		*	*	*	*	*	*		*
Trinidad & Tobago	4	3							*	*	*				
Tunisia	5	4						*		*	*		*		*
Turkey	10	6	*	*	*	*		*	*	*	*	*	*		*
Uganda	4	4						*		*	*				
Ukraine	6	4						*		*	*	*		*	
UK	11	7	*	*	*	*		*	*	*	*	*	*		*
Uruguay	5	4						*		*	*		*		*
US	12	7	*	*	*	*		*	*	*	*	*	*	*	*
Uzbekistan	2	4						*		*	*				
Venezuela	10	6	*	*	*	*		*	*	*	*	*	*		*
Vietnam	7	4			*			*	*	*	*				*
Zambia	4	4					*	*	*	*	*				
Zimbabwe	6	3					*	*	*	*	*				
Number of respond.			4,160	3,678	3,532	1,027	1,000	4,022	4,600	4,700	10,090	NA	1,357	NA	835	251
Number of countries for which data were included			47	49	49	14	14	59	76	80	79	115	34	27	21	121

IMD = Institute for Management Development; PERC = Political and Economic Risk Consultancy; WBES = World Bank's World Business Environment Survey; EIU = Economist Intelligence Unit; PwC = PricewaterhouseCoopers; FH = Freedom House, Nations in Transit; TI/GI = Gallop International on behalf of Transparency International; CU = State Capacity Survey by Columbia University.

Source: Transparency International Report of 2002. NA = Information not available.

others have up to 12. The respondents for the surveys are predominantly western businesspeople, and this has resulted in some criticism. Transparency International are aware of this and do attempt to provide a counter within their publications. For example, the TI/GI survey listed above includes respondents from less developed countries.

> *TI/GI now surveys respondents from less developed countries, asking them to assess the performance of industrial countries. This balances the sample; yet . . . it does not bring about noteworthy different results. Thus the comparative assessments gathered in the CPI do not disproportionately reflect the perceptions of western businesspeople.* (Lambsdorff, 2002)

However, the TI/GI survey is only 1 out of the 15 surveys and is not extensive in terms of country coverage (only 21 countries) and respondents (835 out of a total of nearly 40,000 in Table 5.6). While Transparency International may be correct in its conclusions that 'In sum, it seems that residents tend to have a consistent ethical standard with regard to assessments of corruption, while expatriates do not tend to impose an inappropriate ethical standard or to lack cultural insights' (Lambsdorff, 2002), it is nonetheless a nagging concern.

The calculation of the CPI has something in common with the ESI in appearing to be quite laboured with various steps in the process. The steps basically entail a standardization of the country ranks in the league tables (for the 2002 CPI) rather than a focus upon the values of the corruption indices reported in the various surveys. The value of the previous year's CPI for a particular rank (irrespective of country) is assigned to the equivalent rank the following year. For example, in 2001 the 'top' three and 'bottom' four countries in the CPI league table had the values shown in Table 5.7.

Higher values for the CPI imply lower levels of corruption, so in this list Finland is perceived to be the least corrupt and Bangladesh the most corrupt. Note that as two countries share the '88th' spot (Indonesia and Uganda) there

Table 5.7 *The highest and lowest scoring countries in the 2001 CPI league table*

Rank	Country	CPI (2001)
1	Finland	9.9
2	Denmark	9.5
3	New Zealand	9.4
. . .		
88	Indonesia	1.9
88	Uganda	1.9
90	Nigeria	1.0
91	Bangladesh	0.4

is no '89th' rank. The 2002 version of the CPI would include the ranks from a number of new surveys. For each survey, whichever country is ranked '1' would be allocated a score of 9.9 (Finland's value for 2001), the country ranked '2' a score of 9.5 (Denmark's value in 2001), the country ranked '3' a score of 9.4 etc. For example, assume a survey in 2002 ranks New Zealand as the 'best' country in terms of corruption (ie New Zealand is the least corrupt), for the calculation of the CPI it would be given a score of 9.9. A different survey in 2002 may have Denmark as the least corrupt – for this survey it would then receive the top score of 9.9. This process is continued until all of the new sources of data have been included.

This method is referred to as 'matching percentiles', and has the advantage that all resulting scores must be between 0 and 10, as the CPI values for 2001 used as the source of the scores are between 0 and 10. A further key advantage is that it does not matter how the values in the source surveys were distributed. We have come across the importance of distribution in previous chapters as well as with the ESI. Figure 5.2, for example, shows the hypothetical distributions in corruption score arising from three separate surveys. Even though the maximum and minimum scores have been set at 10 and 0 respectively (same as for the CPI) it is obvious that the three surveys have very different distributions. Survey 1 has an even distribution of scores over all of the countries included, while survey 2 has some 'bunching' of countries at low and high scores. In survey 3, while the same number of

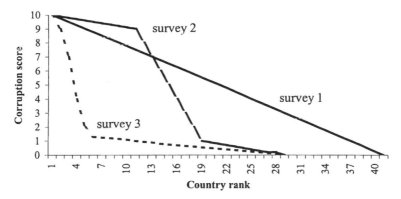

The 40 hypothetical countries have been ranked in terms of their corruption indices, with the least corrupt to the left and the most corrupt to the right of the graph.

The maximum and minimum values of the three surveys have been kept the same as those for the CPI (10 and 0 respectively).

Sample size for survey 1 is larger than that of surveys 2 and 3.

Note the very different distributions of countries over corruption scores (vertical axis). Survey 1 generates an even distribution over all corruption scores. Survey 2 has a 'Z' shaped distribution with a number of countries having similar scores at the high and low end of the scale. Survey 3 has few countries with high corruption scores, most countries have a corruption score less than 2.

Figure 5.2 *Hypothetical distributions of a corruption score found by three separate surveys*

countries has been included as in survey 2, there is bunching at the lower end of the scale with only a quarter of the sample having scores above 1.0. The use of matching percentiles for the CPI would hide these different distributions as all countries ranked at the same level would get the same score. This does mean that information is lost. After all, it may be useful to know why the distributions of corruption indices are so different.

Once all of the new scores have been allocated to the countries in the sample it would seem at first glance that the simplest way of proceeding would be to take the average as the CPI. Unfortunately it is not a simple process, as it is necessary to have CPIs that will be the basis for allocating scores in following years using the 'matching percentile' process. As more data sets are included in successive years and scores are allocated on the basis of the previous year's CPI, the diversity between ranks will steadily decline. The problem of diminishing variation is illustrated in Box 5.2. In order to avoid this the country averages require a transformation, and the method selected by Transparency International is the rather complex sounding 'beta-transformation'. Box 5.2 illustrates the effects of applying the beta-transformation, and what would happen if it were not used. It 'stretches' out the values of the CPI (ie putting some variation back in) while ensuring that the maximum and minimum values remain at 0 and 10 respectively.

The resultant CPI scores (and the league table) for 2002 are presented as Table 5.8. Finland comes top (least corrupt) and Bangladesh is at the bottom (most corrupt). Unlike the HDI and ESI tables, this one does include a measure of 'confidence' (ie allowing for an element of statistical uncertainty in the calculation of the CPI based upon the various surveys that were used). Most of the countries in the table have a CPI less than 5.0.

Despite the assumptions and mathematical contortions involved in the underlying methodology of the CPI (for example Box 5.2) the league table presentation is compelling in its simplicity. We can immediately 'see' how the different countries fare in much the same 'name and shame' mode as we saw for the ESI and the HDI. If anything, the results are more emotive as the CPI has an intriguing and captivating allure of a link to a country's 'culture' (whatever that may be!). Countries that perform badly in the corruption stakes are sometimes said to do so because of their 'culture' that facilitates or tolerates such corruption. Discussions can rapidly become heated. After all, it is one thing to admit to one's own country being 'poor' in terms of development (low HDI) or even 'dirty' in terms of environmental sustainability (low ESI), but to accept a label of being 'corrupt' may be deeply insulting, especially as the label is apparently being applied to all of the people in that country and not to a minority. Link this label to decisions over aid allocation (who would want to give funds to a corrupt country?) and the ramifications can be severe. However, it would be advisable to remember where these statistics came from – the CPI is an index of perception, and the respondents are primarily *western businesspeople*.

Box 5.2 *The beta-transformation employed in the calculation of Transparency International's Corruption Perception Index (CPI)*

The original value of the CPI (ie that obtained from applying the 'matching percentile' method to the country ranks in the source surveys) are transformed using the beta-transformation.

| | CPI | |
Original value	Transformed value	Difference
0.000	0.0000	0.0000
0.500	0.3538	−0.1462
1.000	0.7950	−0.2050
1.500	1.2736	−0.2264
2.000	1.7763	−0.2237
2.500	2.2958	−0.2042
3.000	2.8276	−0.1724
3.500	3.3681	−0.1319
4.000	3.9148	−0.0852
4.500	4.4652	−0.0348
5.000	5.0174	0.0174
5.500	5.5692	0.0692
6.000	6.1187	0.1187
6.500	6.6638	0.1638
7.000	7.2021	0.2021
7.500	7.7310	0.2310
8.000	8.2469	0.2469
8.500	8.7452	0.2452
9.000	9.2187	0.2187
9.557	9.6997	0.1427
10.000	10.0000	0.0000

The mechanics of this are straightforward and beta-transformed values can easily be found with an EXCEL spreadsheet using the function:

BETADIST(original CPI, alpha, beta, 0, 10)

The terms 'alpha' and 'beta' are constants. Transparency International use the values 1.1756 and 1.1812 for these respectively. The other constants '0' and '10' set the minimum and maximum values for the transformation.

The differences in the above table are given by the raw value minus the transformed value, and this is plotted (against the original value of the CPI) in graph (d). Note that at the extremes of 0 and 10 (and indeed at a CPI value just under 5) the original CPI is not altered, but there is some stretching of values between those extremes. The stretching is most pronounced for CPI values between 1 and 2 and between 8 and 9.

▶

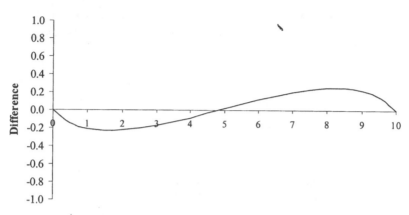

Original value of the CPI

But why is the beta-transformation necessary? After all, it would appear to be a very laboured and complicated way of transforming the original CPI values.

The 'matching percentile' methodology of the CPI is problematic as values will tend to converge (standard deviation becomes less) over time as CPI values from the previous year are awarded to the ranked countries the following year. This problem is illustrated with a theoretical example using Singapore, the UK, Malaysia, Argentina and Venezuela. The starting CPIs in the first part of the table are real values from the 2001 report for five countries, but the data for subsequent years are theoretical. Using these values, Singapore is ranked first as the least corrupt (CPI = 9.2) and Venezuela the most corrupt (CPI = 2.8).

In each year we have two new sets of results, sources A and B, that rank the same group of countries between 1 (least corrupt) and 5 (most corrupt). Each rank is allocated the score of the CPI from the previous year. In 2002, for example, the country that ranks '1' is given 9.2 (the value for Singapore) while the country that ranks '5' is given 2.8 (the value for Venezuela). Note that the two sources (A and B) do not provide identical rankings – there is variation between them. The average scores from the two sources for each country are provided at the right, and the average and standard deviation of these averages is also given.

Assuming that the average CPI for each country is used as the matching figure for the following year, the table shows a progression from 2002 to 2006. Note how the average of all the country scores remains constant at 5.76 but the standard deviation between country scores declines from 2.86 for 2002 to 2.07 for 2006. Given that the variation in scores between sources for the same countries is inevitable, the average scores for the countries will become more uniform. Given more time, this convergence would continue.

	CPI 2001	Ranks Source A		Ranks Source B		2002 Average
Singapore	9.20	1	9.20	1	9.20	9.20
UK	8.30	2	8.30	2	8.30	8.30
Malaysia	5.00	3	5.00	3	5.00	5.00

Continued

Argentina	*3.50*	*4*	*3.50*	*4*	*3.50*	**3.50**
Venezuela	2.80	5	2.80	5	2.80	**2.80**
					Mean	**5.76**
					SD	**2.86**

	CPI *2002*	*Ranks* *Source A*		*Ranks* *Source B*		*2003* *Average*
Singapore	9.20	1	9.20	1	9.20	**9.20**
UK	8.30	2	8.30	2	8.30	**8.30**
Malaysia	5.00	4	3.50	3	5.00	**4.25**
Argentina	3.50	3	5.00	5	2.80	**3.90**
Venezuela	2.80	5	2.80	5	3.50	**3.15**
					Mean	**5.76**
					SD	**2.78**

	CPI *2003*	*Ranks* *Source A*		*Ranks* *Source B*		*2004* *Average*
Singapore	9.20	1	8.30	2	9.20	**8.75**
UK	8.30	2	8.30	3	4.25	**6.28**
Malaysia	4.25	1	4.25	3	9.20	**6.73**
Argentina	3.90	5	3.15	5	3.10	**3.15**
Venezuela	3.15	4	3.90	4	3.90	**3.90**
					Mean	**5.76**
					SD	**2.26**

	CPI *2004*	*Ranks* *Source A*		*Ranks* *Source B*		*2005* *Average*
Singapore	8.75	1	8.75	3	6.28	**7.52**
Malaysia	6.73	3	6.28	2	6.73	**6.51**
UK	6.28	2	6.73	1	8.75	**7.74**
Venezuela	3.90	5	3.15	5	3.15	**3.15**
Argentina	3.15	4	3.90	4	3.90	**3.90**
					Mean	**5.76**
					SD	**2.11**

	CPI *2005*	*Ranks* *Source A*		*Ranks* *Source B*		*2006* *Average*
UK	7.74	2	7.52	1	7.74	**7.63**
Singapore	7.52	1	7.74	3	6.51	**7.13**
Malaysia	6.51	3	6.51	2	7.52	**7.02**

▶

Continued

	CPI 2005	Ranks Source A		Ranks Source B		2006 Average
Argentina	3.90	4	3.90	4	3.90	3.90
Venezuela	3.15	5	3.15	5	3.15	3.15
					Mean	5.76
					SD	2.07

The use of the beta-transformation stretches out the extremes of the range, thereby keeping variation intact from year to year. The following example illustrates the effects of this with the same starting point and ranks from sources A and B. The only difference is that the average scores for each country are beta-transformed and it is the transformed values that are used as the matching scores for the following year. Note that in this case the standard deviations fluctuate but, unlike the previous example, they do not show a gradual decline over time.

	CPI 2001	Ranks Source A		Ranks Source B		2002 Average	Beta-transform
Singapore	9.20	1	9.20	1	9.20	9.20	9.40
UK	8.30	2	8.30	2	8.30	8.30	8.55
Malaysia	5.00	3	5.00	3	5.00	5.00	5.02
Argentina	3.50	4	3.50	4	3.50	3.50	3.37
Venezuela	2.80	5	2.80	5	2.80	2.80	2.61
						Mean	5.79
						SD	3.05

	CPI 2002	Ranks Source A		Ranks Source B		2003 Average	Beta-transform
Singapore	9.40	1	9.40	1	9.40	9.40	9.57
UK	8.55	2	8.55	2	8.55	8.55	8.79
Malaysia	5.02	4	3.37	3	5.02	4.20	4.13
Argentina	3.37	3	5.02	5	2.61	3.82	3.71
Venezuela	2.61	5	2.61	4	3.37	2.99	2.82
						Mean	5.80
						SD	3.13

	CPI 2003	Ranks Source A		Ranks Source B		2004 Average	Beta-transform
Singapore	9.57	1	9.57	2	8.79	9.18	9.38
UK	8.79	2	8.79	3	4.13	6.46	6.62
Malaysia	4.13	3	4.13	1	9.57	6.85	7.04

Continued

Argentina	*3.71*	*5*	*2.82*	*5*	*2.82*	*2.82*	**2.63**
Venezuela	2.82	4	3.71	4	3.71	3.71	**3.60**
						Mean	**5.85**
						SD	**2.73**

	CPI 2004	*Ranks Source A*		*Ranks Source B*		*2005 Average*	*Beta-transform*
Singapore	9.38	1	9.38	3	6.62	8.00	**8.25**
Malaysia	7.04	3	6.62	2	7.04	6.83	**7.02**
UK	6.62	2	7.04	1	9.38	8.21	**8.46**
Venezuela	3.60	5	2.63	5	2.63	2.63	**2.43**
Argentina	2.63	4	3.60	4	3.60	3.60	**3.48**
						Mean	**5.93**
						SD	**2.79**

	CPI 2005	*Ranks Source A*		*Ranks Source B*		*2006 Average*	*Beta-transform*
UK	8.46	2	8.25	1	8.46	8.36	**8.60**
Singapore	8.25	1	8.46	3	7.02	7.74	**7.98**
Malaysia	7.02	3	7.02	2	8.25	7.64	**7.87**
Argentina	3.48	4	3.48	4	3.48	3.48	**3.35**
Venezuela	2.43	5	2.43	5	2.43	2.43	**2.22**
						Mean	**6.00**
						SD	**2.98**

Graph (e) is a plot of the standard deviations using the untransformed and transformed CPIs from the examples. The decline in the standard deviation between 2002 and 2006 using the untransformed CPI is obvious. The beta-transformation prevents such a loss of variation, and by 2006 the variation between the transformed CPI scores for each country is markedly higher than for the unstransformed scores.

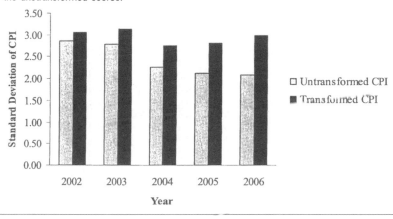

Table 5.8 *Values of the Corruption Perception Index reported by Transparency International in 2002*

Rank	Country	Final CPI	90% confidence range
1	Finland	9.7	9.5–9.9
2	Denmark	9.5	9.3–9.7
2	New Zealand	9.5	9.3–9.6
4	Iceland	9.4	9.2–9.7
5	Singapore	9.3	9.2–9.4
5	Sweden	9.3	9.2–9.4
7	Canada	9.0	8.9–9.2
7	Luxembourg	9.0	8.7–9.5
7	Netherlands	9.0	8.8–9.1
10	UK	8.7	8.4–8.9
11	Australia	8.6	8.0–9.0
12	Norway	8.5	8.0–8.9
12	Switzerland	8.5	7.9–8.9
14	Hong Kong	8.2	7.8–8.6
15	Austria	7.8	7.6–8.1
16	US	7.7	7.2–8.0
17	Chile	7.5	7.0–7.9
18	Germany	7.3	6.7–7.7
18	Israel	7.3	6.7–7.7
20	Belgium	7.1	6.6–7.6
20	Japan	7.1	6.6–7.4
20	Spain	7.1	6.5–7.6
23	Ireland	6.9	6.4–7.4
24	Botswana	6.4	5.6–7.6
25	France	6.3	5.9–6.8
25	Portugal	6.3	5.8–6.9
27	Slovenia	6.0	5.3–6.9
28	Namibia	5.7	4.3–7.3
29	Estonia	5.6	5.4–6.0
29	Taiwan	5.6	5.2–6.0
31	Italy	5.2	4.6–5.7
32	Uruguay	5.1	4.6–5.6
33	Hungary	4.9	4.6–5.2
33	Malaysia	4.9	4.6–5.2
33	Trinidad & Tobago	4.9	3.8–5.9
36	Belarus	4.8	3.3–5.4
36	Lithuania	4.8	3.7–5.9
36	South Africa	4.8	4.5–5.0
36	Tunisia	4.8	4.1–5.3
40	Costa Rica	4.5	4.0–5.1
40	Jordan	4.5	4.0–4.9
40	Mauritius	4.5	4.0–4.9
40	South Korea	4.5	3.9–5.1
44	Greece	4.2	3.8–4.6
45	Brazil	4.0	3.8–4.2
45	Bulgaria	4.0	3.5–4.6
45	Jamaica	4.0	3.6–4.2
45	Peru	4.0	3.7–4.4

Table 5.8 *Continued*

Rank	Country	Final CPI	90% confidence range
45	Poland	4.0	3.4–4.5
50	Ghana	3.9	3.1–5.1
51	Croatia	3.8	3.6–3.9
52	Czech Republic	3.7	3.3–4.2
52	Latvia	3.7	3.5–3.9
52	Morocco	3.7	2.2–4.8
52	Slovak Republic	3.7	3.3–4.0
52	Sri Lanka	3.7	3.4–4.0
57	Colombia	3.6	3.3–4.0
57	Mexico	3.6	3.3–3.9
59	China	3.5	3.1–4.1
59	Dominican Republic	3.5	3.2–3.7
59	Ethiopia	3.5	3.0–3.8
62	Egypt	3.4	2.6–4.2
62	El Salvador	3.4	2.8–3.8
64	Thailand	3.2	2.8–3.6
64	Turkey	3.2	2.7–3.7
66	Senegal	3.1	2.0–4.5
67	Panama	3.0	2.3–3.4
68	Malawi	2.9	2.4–3.7
68	Uzbekistan	2.9	2.0–3.5
70	Argentina	2.8	2.5–3.1
71	Côte d'Ivoire	2.7	2.0–3.1
71	Honduras	2.7	2.3–3.2
71	India	2.7	2.5–2.9
71	Russia	2.7	2.3–3.3
71	Tanzania	2.7	2.0–3.3
71	Zimbabwe	2.7	2.4–3.0
77	Pakistan	2.6	1.7–3.3
77	Philippines	2.6	2.4–2.9
77	Romania	2.6	2.2–3.1
77	Zambia	2.6	2.2–3.0
81	Albania	2.5	1.7–3.0
81	Guatemala	2.5	2.1–2.9
81	Nicaragua	2.5	2.0–3.0
81	Venezuela	2.5	2.2–2.7
85	Georgia	2.4	1.7–2.8
85	Ukraine	2.4	2.0–3.0
85	Vietnam	2.4	2.0–2.9
88	Kazakhstan	2.3	1.8–3.4
89	Bolivia	2.2	1.9–2.5
89	Cameroon	2.2	1.8–2.6
89	Ecuador	2.2	2.0–2.4
89	Haiti	2.2	0.8–3.3
93	Moldova	2.1	1.7–2.7
93	Uganda	2.1	1.9–2.3
95	Azerbaijan	2.0	1.7–2.2
96	Indonesia	1.9	1.7–2.2
96	Kenya	1.9	1.8–2.2

▶

Table 5.8 *Continued*

Rank	Country	Final CPI	90% confidence range
98	Angola	1.7	1.6–1.9
98	Madagascar	1.7	1.3–2.1
98	Paraguay	1.7	1.5–1.8
101	Nigeria	1.6	1.2–1.9
102	Bangladesh	1.2	0.7–1.6

Higher values of the CPI (maximum value obtainable is 10) indicate lower perceptions of the incidence of corruption and vice versa. Hence countries at the top of the table are those perceived to have the least corruption and those towards the foot of the table are those perceived to have the highest levels of corruption.

The table presents the CPI for each country along with a 90 per cent confidence range.

SUMMARY

The ESI and CPI are not intended to capture the wholeness of development in the same way that the HDI was meant to do for the UNDP's vision of human development. The ESI is meant to proxy a environmental performance and the CPI is meant to proxy corruption. These two indices span two important dimensions of development – environmental sustainability and 'good governance'.

All three indices, the HDI, ESI and CPI, are similar in that they aim to simplify complexity. It must be stressed again that this is not an unfortunate side-effect of such indices – it is their very raison d'etre. They exist to simplify.

With the HDI, the degree of simplification is perhaps hidden by the fact that it has only three components – life expectancy, education and income. The methodology is also relatively straightforward, with but a few steps between the raw data and the final index. All of the steps are presented in the HDRs and a reader can recreate the process of calculation for themselves.

In the case of the ESI the reduction process is far more severe. The starting point is not three data sets but 68, and one can begin to get a sense of the extensive data sets required and how gaps have to be filled. Taking these quite disparate data sets and combining them into a single index requires a more involved methodology than the HDI, and the transparency, for all of the detail provided in the ESI reports (2000–2002) is not as good. For example, while the raw data for the 68 variables are provided there is no detail regarding the imputation process.

The data sets are more uniform (all of the surveys used focus on corruption) in the construction of the CPI and the steps involved in getting to the index are not as complex as those for the ESI. The major difference between them is that the CPI is an 'index of indices' and is founded on 'perceptions' of a particular state rather than being a direct measure of that state. Measuring the SO_2 or NO_2 concentration in an urban atmosphere may not be straightforward, but asking people's perception of the quality of the atmosphere is something entirely different. With the former there are issues such as where do we measure, when and how, while with the latter there is the fundamental question of who do we ask and how? The answer to this question is open to value judgements, and will be influenced partly by the resources available.

However, despite the differences, the ESI and CPI do share the same underlying 'league table' style as the HDI. It is not just the calculations involved in getting to an end value for a country that matter, but how these results are presented. As discussed in Chapter 4, given the mathematics and assumptions involved in the creation of these indices, it appears to be most likely that consumers will tend to focus on the league table position of a country. But can these indices be properly interpreted and 'used' without an understanding of the assumptions and steps that were involved? The next chapter will explore some of the dangers associated with the use of development indices.

6 TAKING CARE WITH DEVELOPMENT INDICATORS

INTRODUCTION

Chapters 4 and 5 have explained in some detail the methodology and central assumptions that rest behind the creation of three indices that apply to development. The first of these, the Human Development Index (HDI), has only three components (life expectancy, education and income), and was envisioned by its designers – the UNDP – to be a general index of human development . The other two indices, the Environmental Sustainability Index (ESI) and the Corruption Perception Index (CPI) are more specialized than the HDI, but at the same time are more complex. The ESI comprises a diverse set of 20 indicators, and 68 variables, while the CPI is an 'index of indices'. The ESI illustrates how the choice of components is critical, with some pointing out that very different values for the index and accompanying interpretation can be gleaned by changing the nature of the index components. The CPI is a perception index, predominantly the perception of those living in the developed world, of corruption. With all three indices there are issues surrounding the league table style of presentation.

This chapter will concentrate more on the use of development indices rather than their derivation. It is divided into two parts. The first will focus on the HDI as one of the most widely used development indices, and provide examples of how it is reported in the popular press. The second part of the chapter will take quite a different approach and instead focus on how the indices are typically used in academic and technical circles. I will describe some of the approaches taken, and illustrate the potential dangers that are inherent within them. It is assumed that the reader has a basic knowledge of the statistical tools of correlation and regression. A brief explanation of factor analysis is provided as Appendix 1. The final part of the chapter will explore the use of development indices to guide policy, and will specifically focus on the European Union.

IS THE HUMAN DEVELOPMENT INDEX USED
BY ANYONE?

Having a vision of human development or an elegant methodology for calculating the HDI can be wasted unless the message is first promoted and then acted upon, but what evidence is there that the HDI does influence policy? After all, the very rationale for the HDI is that there should be 'considerable political appeal in a simple indicator that identifies important objectives and contrasts them with other indicators' (Streeten, 1994, p236). Certainly some have questioned whether the HDI is of any use in terms of influencing policy (Srinivasan, 1994), although Jahan (undated) argues that it 'has started a desirable healthy competition among countries to surpass its neighbours or favourable competitors in rankings'. Whether such a focus on league table position is 'healthy' is no doubt debatable, but it is probably true that 'inter-country comparisons of socio-economic development are virtually inevitable' (Zerby and Khan, 1984, p49). It should also be mentioned that concerns over the use of such development indices is not new. Bayless and Bayless (1982, p422) in a much earlier review of quality of life indicators point out that 'there is no evidence to indicate that policymakers have employed these indices in any way', largely because of a lack of faith that the indices do measure anything 'useful or meaningful'!

However, perhaps as a first step towards a consideration of 'use', we can examine the press coverage that the HDI receives. While, of course, reporting in the popular press is no guarantee of an impact on policy, it is a reasonable question to ask whether an index such as the HDI that has been designed to appeal should be picked up by those in a position to publicize.

> *Governments do not take the decisions that really informed voters would expect, but instead concentrate their efforts, willingly or not, on the small fragment of reality that is represented in the limited set of indicators that the media use to report on politics.* (Jesinghaus, 1999)

The good news for the proponents of the HDI is that there is certainly evidence of healthy coverage in the press of many countries. The following are but a few examples from a number of continents in recent years.

Europe

> *The UNDP's Human Development Report is the best measure we have of quality of life, and its publication each year is eagerly awaited throughout the world. . . . Human Development Index (is) the main indicator of quality of life around the world. (The Irish Times, 10 July 2001)*

> *African states occupy the bottom 22 places in the most widely accepted ranking of civilization, the human development index of the United Nations Development Programme. (The Irish Times, letters; 26 January 2000)*

Ireland ranks 18th out of 173 countries on the [Human Development] report's main measure of quality of life, the Human Development Index. This is the same as last year. (Paul Cullen, *The Irish Times*, 18 November 2003)

Africa

Mauritius is the best African country to live in according to this year's human development report of the United Nations Development Programme (UNDP). (African National Congress Daily News Briefing, 22 August 1995)

Norway, best country in the world. Norway ranks first and United States (U.S.) is in sixth place as the best country in which to live in the world. (*Daily Champion*, Nigeria, 11 July 2001)

Asia

The United Nations' latest so-called Human Development Index – a ranking some diplomats call the 'misery table' – places Afghanistan 170th of 174 countries. (*Turkish Daily News*, August 1997)

In the Human Development Index (HDI), India stands at a low 138th (of the total 175 countries). But the fact is that for the first time, India has done better than Pakistan. HDI of Pakistan is only 139, and this does bring a small measure of solace. (*Indian Express Newspaper*, India, 12 June 1997)

Pak beat India, both lose! The United Nations Development Programme report for 1998, released on Wednesday, shows that India and Pakistan continue to be somewhere at the bottom of the ladder of human development. . . . Had the 'human development' contest between the two been for the top positions, there may still have been something in it for either side to crow about. . . . The UNDP has given Canada the top rank on the human development scale for the fifth consecutive year. India should study and adapt the Canadian model for moving up the human development ladder. (*The Tribune*, India, 14 September 1998)

There is a spiral of underdevelopment. That this is at work in Pakistan is evident from the fact that on the United Nations Development Programme's aggregated measure of the quality of people's lives in different countries, the Human Development Index, Pakistan has slipped from number 120 in 1992, to 128 in 1995 and now is ranked 134. (Article by Zia Mian, 29 May 1998, Himan South Asia)

Korea is placed 30th in a set of rankings based on the HDI, while Canada retained the top spot out of 174 countries assessed. The elevation of Korea's position from 32nd in 1997 may be an indication that our development efforts are paying off. Yet any complacency would be counter-productive. (The Korea Times, 16 July 1999)

Nepal has made marginal progress on the human development ladder but remains 144th out of 174 nations, the United Nations Development Programme (UNDP) said on Thursday. This year's Human Development Report (HDR) assigns Nepal a Human Development Index value of 0.474 (out of a maximum achievable 1.0). Nepal's HDI in 1999 was 0.463. Among Nepal's closest neighbours Thailand betters all ranking 76th on the HDI ladder with Sri Lanka standing 84th. The Maldives is at 86th position, China 99th, Myanmar 125th, India 128th, Pakistan 135th and Bhutan 146th. Only Bangladesh has a lower ranking (146th) than Nepal. This year's HDI 'topper' is Canada, with a HDI score of 0.935. (Nepalnews.com, 3 July 2000)

Kudos for India in Human Development Report. . . . India has 'moved up four notches' giving enough reason for satisfaction. (The Hindu, India, 30 June 2000)

Burma has moved up from low human development to medium human development in four years and ranked 118th on the Human Development Index of the United Nations Development Programme (UNDP) out of 162 countries. . . . Burma, which is near the bottom of the Medium Human Development, is above some of its Asian partners. Pakistan, Nepal and Bhutan, which fall into the low human development category, are slotted at 127, 129 and 130 respectively. However, Burma is far below that of other South East Asian countries. Thailand is ranked at 66, Malaysia at 56, Philippines at 70, Indonesia at 102 and Viet Nam at 101. (Burmanet News, Burma, 13 July 2001)

I think our most significant achievement is the improvements in the quality of life enjoyed by the people. It is our success in this area that gives the highest ranking in South Asia in UNDP's human development index. (Interview with President Maumoon Abdul Gayoom of the Maldives, reported in the *Sunday Times,* Sri-Lanka,11 November, 2001)

Norway is now ranked first in the world in terms of HDI followed by Australia. Both moved narrowly ahead of Canada, the leader in the previous six years. India jumped 13 places to rank 115 on the HDI due to consistent progress in poverty reduction. (Article by J. Niti, *Daily Excelsior,* India, 22 July 2001)

The U.N. Human Development Index (HDI) is a good indicator of broad social development in a country and includes social indicators as well as economic ones. In the HDI ranking of 1991, Pakistan was placed higher (better) than India and Bangladesh. In 2003, India is ranked far higher than Pakistan, as is Bangladesh. More importantly, Pakistan's rank fell from 138 to 114 in just one year, 2002–03, and Nepal and Pakistan are the only

two non-African countries to be classified in the low human development group.
(S. Akbar Zaidi, *The Hindu*, 23 October 2003)

Madhya Pradesh, Kerala and west Bengal have received considerable appreciation in the 2003 Human Development Report (HDR) of the United Nations Development Programme (UNDP) even as India was pushed down three rungs on the Human Development Index (HDI) to the 127th position in the comity of 175 nations. . . . As for India slipping down the list, the explanation was that it was a consequence of Bosnia and Herzegovina and Occupied Palestinian Territories joining the list, and Botswana moving up the order. (*The Hindu*, 9 July 2003)

Nepal has slipped down to the rank of 143 in the UN's Human Development Index (HDI). . . . This one point slip in the HDI in itself does not hold much importance since it reflects relative, not absolute, progress of the member countries. (*The Kathmandu Post*, 24 July 2003)

On Wednesday Filipinos saw another demonstration of the decline in the national quality of life and discovered for themselves why the Philippines has slipped anew in the global human development index. A poor housewife gave birth to quadruplets, all of whom died. The woman and her husband suffered indignities at the hands of hospital authorities while their babies died one after the other because most of the hospitals did not have the necessary means – the basic incubator – that could have saved lives. (*The Manila Times*, 19 July 2003)

The dramatic failure of the [President] Arroyo administration has been confirmed by our deep slide from No. 77 to No. 85 in the 2003 Human Development Index of the United Nations. (Malaya, 10 July 2003)

I have read the 2002 Human Development Report. Reading through the comparative data of more than 130 countries in the Report's Human Development Index, I cannot but feel disgusted. . . . The Philippines is No. 77 in HDI. This could mean the country belongs to the world's middle class in terms of quality of life. But compared with its neighbours in Asia, the Philippines is the region's economic laggard. (Tony Lopez, *The Manila Times*, 7 March 2003)

The Human Development Index (HDI) ranking shows that Bangladesh has improved slightly as it reached 139th position among 175 countries for the year 2001. In 2000, Bangladesh held the 145th position. This improvement puts Bangladesh in the Medium Human Development category of the United Nations Development Programme (UNDP). . . . The UNDP Human Development report released yesterday shows that Bangladesh along with China, Laos, Malaysia, Nepal and Thailand are moving up among the developing countries in terms of HDI. (*The Daily Star*, 9 July 2003)

North America

Canada, the World's Best Country to Live In. . . . For the sixth year in a row, Canada ranks first among 175 countries in the United Nations quality of life survey. . . . Canada has the best educated people and the highest literacy rate in the world. Canadians live longer than anyone on the planet, except people in Japan and Iceland. (Vancouver English Centre, 1997)

We're not No. 1! Canada drops in UN rankings. Seven-year reign at top is coming to an end. . . . Prime Minister Jean Chretien often refers to the report in public statements and speeches. . . . And veteran Chretien Cabinet minister John Manley has used the UN report card as a shield when the opposition attacked him in the House of Commons over Canada's lagging productivity. 'Canada topped the United Nation's human development index,' Manley said. 'That is where we measure the quality of life in this country.' (*The National Post,* 3 July 2001)

Just when Canadians started feeling good about themselves over winning the race to play host to the 2010 Winter Olympics, the United Nations has pulled Canada down a few notches on its annual quality-of-life ranking. . . . Canada had owned the No. 1 spot throughout most of the 1990s but fell behind Norway in 2001. Last year Sweden squeezed by, pushing Canada down to third place. . . . However the [UNDP] official, who asked to remain anonymous, said Canada is penalized under the approach adopted by the UN agency for being a more open and heterogeneous country. . . . The official also cautioned against reading too much into Canada's sinking status in the world 'The difference between eight place and first place is really quite small', he said, 'It could be attributed to statistical fluctuations. They are so close together . . . it does not really mean anything'. 'If you looked at the difference between Canada and Sierra Leone (which is at the bottom of the list), you would really see some major differences', he said. (Robert Matas National, 5 July 2003).

South America

In the international arena Belize made a strong showing on the UNDP Report for 2003 in Human Development Index. Out of the 175 nations reviewed Belize was in the top third. In relation to our 15 member Caricom countries we ranked an impressive sixth. And among our Central America neighbours we ranked considerably higher than Guatemala, El Salvador, Honduras and Nicaragua in human development. At age 22 Belize is full of vim and vigour. (*The Belize Times,* 17 September 2003)

I have no desire to labour the point, and the interested reader is invited to make their own search, but the above quotations do raise a number of points for discussion. First, and perhaps most importantly, the sample does suggest that the HDI is picked up by the popular press, even if only at the time of the HDR publication for that year. It should also be stressed that even this coverage is no doubt far behind that received by the leading economic indicators and such socially-sensitive indicators as the unemployment rate (Jesinghaus, 1999). Even so, it is a good start. Second there are the numerous references to the HDI as a measure of 'quality of life' rather than human development, and the tendency for comparisons to be made over time and between neighbours. We have references to a 'race', 'best country to live in' and 'laggard'. The reporting can border on light jingoism at times. Whether that is good or bad is left for the reader to judge, but it is an almost inevitable repercussion of using such an index in conjunction with a league table ('winners and losers') style of presentation.

Note also how, for the most part, even very minor shifts of but a few places in the table are seen as worthy of mention and discussion. Sometimes this is put into context with a caveat that other countries have entered the table for that year or perhaps because other countries have done better. There is also a quote from a 'UNDP official' that 'The difference between eight place and first place is really quite small. . . . It could be attributed to statistical fluctuations. They are so close together . . . it does not really mean anything.' The same UNDP official, who interestingly is mentioned as wanting to be anonymous, goes on to make the rather extraordinary statement that 'If you looked at the difference between Canada and Sierra Leone (which is at the bottom of the list), you would really see some major differences'. Yes, no doubt, but this does not fill us with confidence that the HDI is of any great benefit if it only helps to pick up the extremes. What is the point of the HDI league table in between those extremes?

One advantage of the HDI is its clear, unambiguous and undiluted focus on people, and the three components of the HDI resonate loudly with the major concerns of many: education, health and income. Many of the press extracts above go on to discuss why a country has done well or badly in terms that all of us can appreciate, such as the sad case reported in the *Manila Times* (19 July 2003) when a set of quadruplets died 'because most of the hospitals did not have the necessary means – the basic incubator – that could have saved lives'. The 'people centred' nature of the HDI allows an extension of its meaning into all of our lives. The league table style also helps with a propagation of the message by inviting year-on-year and across country comparisons. Some have criticized what they see as a routine reporting and perhaps even stagnation within the 'human development' message (Sagar and Najam, 1999), but the continued press interest would not appear to back that up.

INTERPRETING INDICES: OVER-REDUCTION?

The generation of indices of development almost inevitably leads to inter-country comparison, and it is also inevitable that such comparisons generate questions as to why some countries are ranked higher than others. What are the driving forces at play (Konrad and Wahl, 1990; Basu, 2001)? With composite indices, we can study the individual components and again ask why there are inter-country differences? There is a wealth of potential analyses, and the literature is not short of examples. A small number of simple examples are presented in Box 6.1, employing the HDI, ESI and CPI, and I am confident that the comparisons in Box 6.1 would have come to the mind of the reader having read the previous two chapters. It seems reasonable to ask whether there is a link between the environmental sustainability of a country (as represented by the ESI) and human development (as represented by the HDI). Are more developed countries better at limiting environmental damage or vice versa? Similarly, we can glean the obvious conclusion that perceptions of corruption differ across nations, and does this relate to human development or perhaps income/capita? Surely, as average incomes fall, is it not likely that corruption as a means of supplementing income will rise? But the regressions in Box 6.1 also tell us that there are residuals – countries which do not sit on the regression line. Indeed, while the regressions in Box 6.1 are significant, the coefficients of determination are not especially high. Are we really looking at universal relationships between the variables or can the nature of the relationship, if there is one, vary from country to country? Even for countries that do sit on the best-fit regression line, the interpretation is more complex than a simple cause–effect implied by the allocation of dependent and independent variables. Is there a danger of deception? For example, with the CPI and GDP/capita relationship it may be that the bulk of the corruption resides with those having higher incomes, especially as these are more likely to have the power to take decisions and provide 'favours'. Does the use of an average income for a whole country in our regression make sense?

The very existence of simplifying indices cries out for such fundamental and important questions to be answered. In fairness, those involved in creating the indices do stress that they are only meant to help with an initial analysis of the phenomenon being studied, but, as can be seen in Box 6.1, even here the answers may not always be clear.

Another method often employed to analyse development indices such as the HDI is factor analysis, one form of which, Principal Component Analysis (PCA), is especially popular (Appendix 1). PCA is a convenient technique for separating out groups of countries and testing linkages between HDI components (Cahill, 2002; Morse, 2003a) over space (Thapa, 1995; Justus, 1995, Lai, 2003) and time (Indrayan et al, 1999; Lai, 2000). It allows an exploration of underlying relationships between variables to see whether a small number of explanatory factors can be elucidated (Hardi and Semple, 2000). The interpretation of such a factor analysis with the three components of the HDI (as in Appendix 1) may suggest that we only need to report one of them – all three are not needed. Indeed this point has been made by Ogwang (1994, 1997) who suggests using only the life expectancy component

Box 6.1 *Some regressions with the HDI*

The existence of national development indicators, such as the Human Development Index (HDI), encourages a host of analyses to see how these indices relate to each other and how they progress with time. Here I have only provided two simple examples using the HDI, Environmental Sustainability Index (ESI) and the Corruption Perception Index (CPI). The hypotheses (assumptions) are as follows:

1   that the level of human development for a country will be related to its environmental sustainability
2   that the level of corruption in a country will be related to the level of human development in that country.

The data taken for the analyses shown here are the ESI and CPI data sets presented in Chapter 4, and the HDI values from the HDR 2002 (based on data collected in 1998). The time periods for the data collection may not be entirely compatible, and the reader needs to bear in mind the assumptions that underpin all three indices. Also, only regression has been applied here. While this is, of course, a limited analysis, it could be argued that indices designed to simplify complexity would encourage simple comparisons, at least as a first step!

Human development and environmental sustainability

The first analysis presented here is a linear regression with the ESI 2002 as the dependent variable and the HDI 2002 as the independent variable. The assumption is that as the level of human development (HDI) increases so will environmental sustainability (ESI).

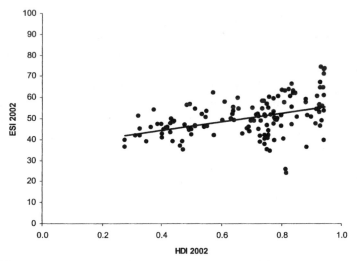

Graph (a)

Graph (a) suggests that a relationship does exist (it is statistically significant), with the best fit equation as follows:

   ESI $2002 = 35.93 + 20.44 \times$ HDI 2002

The analysis suggests that countries with a higher level of human development are better achievers in terms of environmental sustainability, a point made in Chapter 5 in relation to a critique of the ESI provided in *The Ecologist* magazine. However, even if we ignore the concerns raised over the ESI, this graph is still somewhat worrying. Note that the R^2 for this regression is only 18 per cent, hardly convincing. The scatter around the line is not evenly spaced, and as the HDI increases, so does the degree of scatter. A more detailed analysis is clearly required to prise apart these indices and explore why the residuals are so large (or small) for come countries.

Corruption and human development

Our second analysis assumes that corruption will be greater for countries with lower levels of human development. There are two graphs presented here. Graph (b) is a plot of CPI 2002 as the dependent variable and HDI 2002 as the independent variable. Again there is a lot of scatter, but the data do suggest that corruption is worse (low values of the CPI) at lower levels of the HDI.

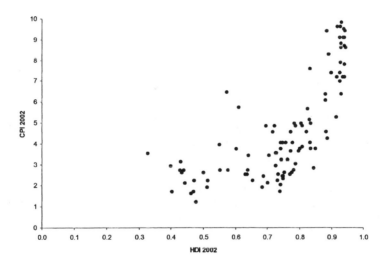

Graph (b)

In fact most of this apparent relationship can be explained by a regression analysis of CPI 2002 on just one of the components of the HDI, income (measured as GDP/capita). Graph (c) illustrates this linkage (note that the logarithm of GDP/capita has been taken to allow a linear model to be fitted).

Again, as with the ESI model, this regression is statistically significant and the R^2 is also much better (69 per cent). The model is as follows:

CPI 2002 = $-11.36 + 4.18 \times$ logarithm GDP/capita

While the R^2 is reasonable, and indeed the underlying assumption of there being greater corruption with lower income seems logical, there is still a lot of scatter. Some countries have higher levels of corruption than predicted by income while others have lower levels of corruption

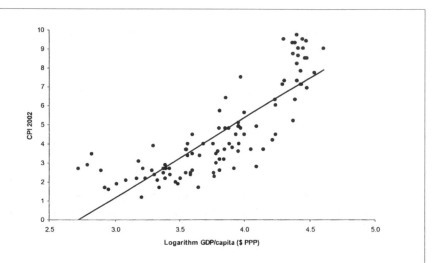

Graph (c)

than predicted. Not many of the countries actually sit on the fitted regression line. What is causing this? Are there cultural differences at play (Lambsdorff, 1999)? Is there more effective enforcement in some countries than others with a comparable income? These are interesting and important questions, and it could be suggested that we can learn far more about corruption and its causes by exploring the residuals in this graph than by our simplifying regression. Ignoring the residuals and focusing on just the line could encourage a very one-dimensional vision of corruption that fails to take into account the diversity that rests behind each of the points in the graph. We also need to question assumptions of cause–effect. Is corruption a cause of low income or does corruption inhibit economic growth and hence result in low income (Mauro, 1995)?

Finally we need to keep reminding ourselves that each of the 'points' on the graphs is one country. Does it appear reasonable to present the richness of human development, environmental quality and corruption as single points on two-dimensional graphs such as these, even if the regressions appear to be compelling?

as a measure of human development. While a direct linkage between an economic indicator such as GDP/capita and life expectancy or mortality may not be anticipated, indirect correlations via quality of nutrition, housing, water and health care are obvious (Preston, 1975). However, some (eg McGranahan, 1972; McGranahan et al, 1985) have opposed the use of dimension-reducing techniques like factor analysis, as development indicators tend to correlate highly with each other, making it difficult if not impossible to establish which is 'dependent' and which is 'independent'? With the examples in Box 6.1, is corruption a cause of low average income or does low average income cause corruption? While the simple analysis may be indicative of a link, the usefulness of proving a relationship between the two would appear to be limited unless we know how they are related and the underlying pressures involved.

There is one example which I feel illustrates the dangers of oversimplification only too well. In 2002 Richard Lynn and Tatu Vanhanen published a book entitled *IQ and the Wealth of Nations* and prior to that (2001) a paper entitled 'National IQ and economic development: A study of eighty-one nations' in the journal *Mankind Quarterly*. In their book they begin by exploring the various explanations why some countries are poorer than others. The explanations, such as Dependency Theory, are rejected. For example:

> *Most economists do not accept that the economically developed West has been responsible for the poverty of third world countries.* (Lynn and Vanhanen, 2002, p12)

Having summarized, and largely rejected, other explanations, Lynn and Vanhanen set out to provide an alternative hypothesis for unequal economic development between countries. Put simply, their contention is that the level of national economic development is partly a function of the innate ability of the population in that country. Therefore, as national 'ability' increases, so should the GDP/capita as an indicator of economic development. They use national intelligence scores as proxy indicators of 'ability'. They also suggest that differences in national intelligence scores between countries are largely genetic (ie racial) in origin, although they may be improved by 'nurture' such as good nutrition. In effect this is a genetic deterministic theory of development quite different from any other, and if true it is of major importance. As one reviewer of their book suggested:

> *This is a book that social scientists, policy experts and global investment analysts cannot afford to ignore. It is one of the most brilliantly clarifying books this reviewer has ever read.*
>
> *The final conclusion of IQ and the Wealth of Nations is that national differences are here to stay, as is the gap between rich and poor nations. Hitherto, theories of economic development have been based on the presumption that the gaps between rich and poor countries are only temporary, and that they are due to various environmental conditions that could be changed by aid from rich countries to poor countries, and by poor countries adopting appropriate institutions and policies.*
>
> *It has been assumed that all human populations have equal mental abilities to adopt modern technologies and to achieve equal levels of economic development. The authors call for the recognition of the existence of the evolved diversity of human populations.* (Rushton, 2003, p367 and 372)

Racial differences in 'ability' would imply that efforts to bridge the gap in development with aid will be seriously limited.

> *aid to the third world should be targeted on attempting to improve the intelligence of the populations by improving the quality of nutrition.*

> *Nevertheless, we believe that the conclusion to be drawn from our study is that it will never be possible to achieve an economic equality between nations. The poor will always be with us.* (Lynn and Vanhanen, 2001, p432–433)

> *The two most important implications of our study are these. First, the world needs a new international moral code based on the recognition of significant national differences in human mental abilities and consequent economic inequalities. The populations of the rich countries may have to accept that they have an ethical obligation to provide financial assistance to the peoples of the poor countries for the indefinite future. . . . Second, the rich countries' economic aid programs for the poor countries should be continued and some of these should be directed at attempting to increase the intelligence levels of the populations of the poorer countries by improvements in nutrition and the like.* (Lynn and Vanhanen, 2002, p196)

Therefore poor countries 'will always be with us' because the people (races) within them have less innate ability, and the best that rich countries can do is to come to terms with this with a new moral code and perhaps try to alleviate the consequences as best as they can.

But how do Lynn and Vanhanen arrive at such a momentous and earth-shattering conclusion?

At the heart of their theory is a set of regression tests similar in style to those of Box 6.1 but with economic indicators as the dependent variable and the results of national intelligence tests spanning 70 years as the independent. For example, one of the tests is a regression between the GDP/capita data set from the HDR 2000 (data collected in 1998 and adjusted for PPP) and national intelligence tests. The reader is referred to the earlier discussion in Chapter 2 regarding the use of GDP/capita as an indicator of economic performance. The national intelligence test results have been collected from a variety of sources, and have been adjusted relative to a value for Britain of '100' and a standard deviation of 15. As the results of human intelligence tests have been showing a gradual increase ('IQ inflation', or the Flynn Effect) of approximately 2.5 points a decade since the 1930s, Lynn and Vanhanen also took this inflation into account. They tested the 'validity' of their national intelligence values by correlating them with national scores in mathematics and science that are available.

In their paper they include 81 countries for which they are able to generate national intelligence scores, and the data are presented in Table 6.1. The authors claim that this is 'a representative sample of the world's nations'. However, it should be noted that not all of them (Puerto Rico, Marshall Islands, Tonga and Taiwan) can be found in the HDR 2000 data set.

To arrive at a single value for 'national intelligence', Lynn and Vanhanen averaged the results of what tests were available. For example, the following two sources were used to produce data for Argentina, the first country listed in Table 6.1:

1   The results of Progressive Matrices applied to a sample of 1,680 9–15 year olds between 1942 and 1946. The mean of these when standardized to a British 1979 sample was 86.
2   The results of Coloured Progressive Matrices from 1993 applied to a sample of 420 5–11 years olds. The mean of these when standardized to a British 1979 sample was 101.

Progressive Matrices is a non-reading visual test designed to measure a person's ability to form perceptual relations and to reason by analogy. The test is independent of language and it is also claimed to be independent of formal schooling. Coloured Progressive Matrices are a variant on the theme that are designed specifically for young children (ages 5–11) and the elderly. Each test comprises a series of diagrammatic puzzles with a missing piece that the person being tested is expected to find from a series of options. Higher scores relate to higher levels of intelligence.

The first set of tests used for the Argentina score had a gap of 35 years between the time of the tests (assumed to be 1944) and the British standard in 1979. Allowing for an approximate inflation of 7 points over the three decades, results in an increase of the mean from 86 to 93. Similarly the results of the second test had to be reduced from 101 to 98 to allow for the 14 year difference. The average of 93 and 98 is 95.5, and this is rounded up to 96 (four points lower than the UK figure of '100'). However, are these samples 'representative' of the population in Argentina at the time? Can we really extrapolate from these tests applied to a total of just over 2,000 children to arrive at a figure for Argentina's 'national intelligence'?

In their book Lynn and Vanhanen (2002) take this analysis further by expanding their 'sample' to 185 countries by a process of 'neighbour extrapolation'. For example, the national intelligence score for Afghanistan (83) was found by averaging the values for India (81) and Iran (84) and rounding up. India does not share a border with Afghanistan, but primary national intelligence scores data for other neighbours, Pakistan, Turkmenistan and Tajikistan, were not available. While this increases sample size, the process is a self-reinforcing one as existing data are duplicated. In the book they also calculated regression between national intelligence and other indicators of economic performance such as GNP and economic growth rate. However, this adds little to the discussion, given that GDP tends to be highly correlated with GNP and economic growth rate. Therefore, only Lynn and Verhanen's 81 country analysis with GDP/capita will be used here.

A graph and regression equation of GDP/capita as a function of national intelligence tests is shown as Figure 6.1. The regression is statistically significant, and would appear to suggest that GDP/capita can be explained by national intelligence. But at the same time there are many outliers in the graph, and the residuals (observed–predicted values) are presented in Table 6.1. The largest positive and negative residuals (ie those larger than ±$5,000/capita) are presented in Table 6.2. Lynn and Vanhanen claim that

Table 6.1 *Data employed in the analysis of the relationship between real GDP/capita and national intelligence*

Country	Real GDP ($/capita) 1998	Logarithm of GDP/capita 1998	National IQ	Real GDP/capita (US$ PPP) Fitted GDP/capita	Residual GDP/capita	Logarithm GDP/capita Fitted GDP/capita	Residual GDP/capita
Argentina	12,013	4.0797	96	14,107	−2,094	11,363	650
Australia	22,452	4.3513	98	15,145	7,307	13,301	9,151
Austria	23,166	4.3649	102	17,221	5,945	18,227	4,939
Barbados	12,001	4.0792	78	4,765	7,236	2,753	9,248
Belgium	23,223	4.3659	100	16,183	7,040	15,571	7,652
Brazil	6,625	3.8212	87	9,436	−2,811	5,593	1,032
Bulgaria	4,809	3.6821	93	12,550	−7,741	8,972	−4,163
Canada	23,582	4.3726	97	14,626	8,956	12,294	11,288
China	3,105	3.4921	100	16,183	−13,078	15,571	−12,466
Colombia	6,006	3.7786	89	10,474	−4,468	6,547	−541
Congo	995	2.9978	73	2,170	−1,175	1,857	−862
Congo Dem. Rep. of the	822	2.9149	65	−1,982	2,804	989	−167
Croatia	6,749	3.8292	90	10,993	−4,244	7,084	−335
Cuba	3,967	3.5985	85	8,398	−4,431	4,778	−811
Czech Republic	12,362	4.0921	97	14,626	−2,264	12,294	68
Denmark	24,218	4.3841	98	15,145	9,073	13,301	10,917
Ecuador	3,003	3.4776	80	5,803	−2,800	3,223	−220
Egypt	3,041	3.4830	83	7,360	−4,319	4,082	−1,041
Equatorial Guinea	1,817	3.2594	59	−5,096	6,913	617	1,200
Ethiopia	574	2.7589	63	−3,020	3,594	845	−271
Fiji	4,231	3.6264	84	7,879	−3,648	4,416	−185
Finland	20,847	4.3190	97	14,626	6,221	12,294	8,553
France	21,175	4.3258	98	15,145	6,030	13,301	7,874
Germany	22,169	4.3457	102	17,221	4,948	18,227	3,942
Ghana	1,735	3.2393	71	1,132	603	1,586	149
Greece	13,943	4.1444	92	12,031	1,912	8,292	5,651
Guatemala	3,505	3.5447	79	5,284	−1,779	2,979	526

Guinea	1,782	3.2509	66	−1,463	3,245	1,070	712
Hong Kong	20,763	4.3173	107	19,816	947	27,023	−6,260
Hungary	10,232	4.0100	99	15,664	−5,432	14,391	−4,159
India	2,077	3.3174	81	6,322	−4,245	3,487	−1,410
Indonesia	2,651	3.4234	89	10,474	−7,823	6,547	−3,896
Iran	5,121	3.7094	84	7,879	−2,758	4,416	705
Iraq	3,197	3.5047	87	9,436	−5,239	5,593	−2,396
Ireland	21,482	4.3321	93	12,550	8,932	8,972	12,510
Israel	17,301	4.2381	94	13,069	4,232	9,707	7,594
Italy	20,585	4.3136	102	17,221	3,364	18,227	2,358
Jamaica	3,389	3.5301	72	1,651	1,738	1,716	1,673
Japan	23,257	4.3666	105	18,778	4,479	23,084	173
Kenya	980	2.9912	72	1,651	−671	1,716	−736
Korea, Rep.	13,478	4.1296	106	19,297	−5,819	24,976	−11,498
Lebanon	4,326	3.6361	86	8,917	−4,591	5,170	−844
Malaysia	8,137	3.9105	92	12,031	−3,894	8,292	−155
Marshall Islands	3,000	3.4771	84	7,879	−4,979	4,416	−1,416
Mexico	7,704	3.8867	87	9,436	−1,732	5,593	2,111
Morocco	3,305	3.5192	85	8,398	−5,093	4,778	−1,473
Nepal	1,157	3.0633	78	4,765	−3,608	2,753	−1,596
Netherlands	22,176	4.3459	102	17,221	4,955	18,227	3,949
New Zealand	17,288	4.2377	100	16,183	1,105	15,571	1,717
Nigeria	795	2.9004	67	−944	1,739	1,158	−363
Norway	26,342	4.4206	98	15,145	11,137	13,301	13,041
Peru	4,282	3.6316	90	10,993	−6,711	7,084	−2,802
Philippines	3,555	3.5508	86	8,917	−5,362	5,170	−1,615
Poland	7,619	3.8819	99	15,664	−8,045	14,391	−6,772
Portugal	14,701	4.1673	95	13,588	1,113	10,502	4,199
Puerto Rico	8,000	3.9031	84	7,879	121	4,416	3,584
Qatar	20,987	4.3220	78	4,765	16,222	2,753	18,234
Romania	5,648	3.7519	94	13,069	−7,421	9,707	−4,059
Russian Federation	6,460	3.8102	96	14,107	−7,647	11,363	−4,903
Samoa (Western)	3,832	3.5834	87	9,436	−5,604	5,593	−1,761

Table 6.1 Continued

Country	Real GDP ($/capita) 1998	Logarithm of GDP/capita 1998	National IQ	Real GDP/capita (US$ PPP)		Logarithm GDP/capita	
				Fitted GDP/capita	Residual GDP/capita	Fitted GDP/capita	Residual GDP/capita
Sierra Leone	458	2.6609	64	-2,501	2,959	914	-456
Singapore	24,210	4.3840	103	17,740	6,470	19,720	4,490
Slovakia	9,699	3.9867	96	14,107	-4,408	11,363	-1,664
Slovenia	14,293	4.1551	95	13,588	705	10,502	3,791
South Africa	8,488	3.9288	72	1,651	6,837	1,716	6,772
Spain	16,212	4.2098	97	14,626	1,586	12,294	3,918
Sudan	1,394	3.1443	72	1,651	-257	1,716	-322
Suriname	5,161	3.7127	89	10,474	-5,313	6,547	-1,386
Sweden	20,659	4.3151	101	16,702	3,957	16,846	3,813
Switzerland	25,512	4.4067	101	16,702	8,810	16,846	8,666
Taiwan	13,000	4.1139	104	18,259	-5,259	21,336	-8,336
Tanzania	480	2.6812	72	1,651	-1,171	1,716	-1,236
Thailand	5,456	3.7369	91	11,512	-6,056	7,664	-2,208
Tonga	3,000	3.4771	87	9,436	-6,436	5,593	-2,593
Turkey	6,422	3.8077	90	10,993	-4,571	7,084	-662
Uganda	1,074	3.0310	73	2,170	-1,096	1,857	-783
UK	20,336	4.3083	100	16,183	4,153	15,571	4,765
Uruguay	8,623	3.9357	96	14,107	-5,484	11,363	-2,740
US	29,605	4.4714	98	15,145	14,460	13,301	16,304
Zambia	719	2.8567	77	4,246	-3,527	2,545	-1,826
Zimbabwe	2,669	3.4263	66	-1,463	4,132	1,070	1,599

Sources: Real GDP/capita as presented in the UNDP Human Development Report of 2000. National intelligence scores from Lynn and Vanhanen (2001, 2002).

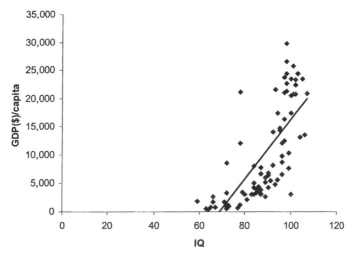

$R^2 = 54\%$
GDP/capita $= -35,717 + 519 \times$ national intelligence
$F = 91.53$; df $= 1$, 79; $P < 0.001$
Sources: National intelligence data from Table 6.1 (Lynn and Vanhanen, 2001, 2002). GDP/capita data from the Human Development Report (2000).

Figure 6.1 *GDP/capita ($) as a function of national intelligence*

the countries with the largest negative residuals in their list, representing an 'underperformance' in GDP/capita compared to that predicted by national intelligence, can be explained at least in part by their being 'impaired by socialism and communism' (a third of the countries with such a high negative residual are present or former socialist countries). The remaining 12 are explained in various ways, including civil strife for Peru, Suriname and the Philippines. Explanations provided by the authors for the large positive residuals revolve around the countries having free-market economies, large oil reserves (Qatar), large EU subsidies (Ireland), or because their 'economies have been largely run by fairly small minorities of whites' (South Africa and Barbados).

While an R^2 of 54 per cent may look impressive, it is possible to improve on this by using the logarithm (base 10) of GDP/capita as the dependent variable. The results of such a transformation are shown in Figure 6.2, and the R^2 is increased to 70 per cent. The residuals using the logarithm of GDP/capita are also presented in Table 6.1 and, using a residual of $\pm \$4,000$/capita instead of $\pm \$5,000$/capita (to compensate for the better R^2), the countries with the largest positive and negative residuals are shown in Table 6.2. While this list has some similarity with the 'high' residual countries from the original analysis there are also notable differences, particularly in the 'negative' group which now includes Hong Kong and the Republic of Korea, and does not include Peru, Suriname or the Philippines (the three countries

Table 6.2 *Countries with the largest residuals following a regression analysis between GDP/capita and national intelligence scores*

Original analysis ($R^2 = 54\%$) Residuals larger than $\pm\$5,000$/capita		Analysis with logarithm GDP/capita ($R^2 = 70\%$) Residuals larger than $\pm\$4,000$/capita	
Large positive residuals	Large negative residuals	Large positive residuals	Large negative residuals
Australia	Bulgaria	Australia	Bulgaria
Austria	China	Austria	China
Barbados	Hungary	Barbados	Hong Kong
Belgium	Indonesia	Belgium	Hungary
Canada	Iraq	Canada	Korea, Rep.
Denmark	Korea, Rep.	Denmark	Poland
Equatorial Guinea	Morocco	Finland	Romania
Finland	Peru	France	Russian Federation
France	Philippines	Greece	Taiwan
Ireland	Poland	Ireland	
Norway	Romania	Israel	
Qatar	Russia	Norway	
Singapore	Suriname	Portugal	
South Africa	Taiwan	Qatar	
Switzerland	Thailand	Singapore	
US	Tonga	South Africa	
	Uruguay	Switzerland	
	Western Samoa	UK	
		US	

These residuals have been found from two regression analyses. The first uses GDP/capita ($ PPP) and national intelligence scores, while the second uses the logarithmic transformation of GDP/capita.

with the 'civil strife' explanation). No doubt there are different explanations for these residuals, but it does become rather worrying when a different (and arguably more valid analysis) requires a significant re-think for explaining the larger residuals.

The reader can probably see many problems with this analysis for many of the same reasons as were discussed in Box 6.1, particularly the relative crudity of the cause–effect assumption. Added to these must be a concern over data quality, given the reliance on intelligence tests performed over 70 years. After all, what if national intelligence as assessed for this study is also a function of 'environment' within a country? What if there are feedback processes whereby the quality/quantity of education in a country influences the scores achieved in the various tests used to find the 'national intelligence'? As seen earlier, GDP/capita is highly correlated with the other two components of the HDI, one of which is participation rates in education. As a result national intelligence is also significantly correlated with these components (proof not provided here), but what are the 'causes' and what are the 'effects'? Economic growth can generate better public services (education and health care are but two), the 'capability expansion through social services' of Anand and Ravallion (1993), and better education could impact positively on intelligence test performance.

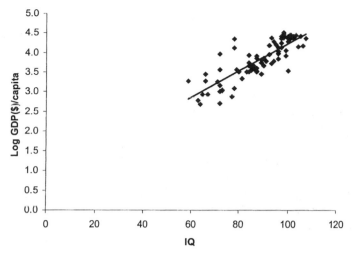

$R^2 = 70\%$
Log GDP/capita $= 0.772 + 0.0342 \times$ national intelligence
$F = 182.8$; df $= 1, 79$; $P < 0.001$
Sources: National intelligence data from Table 6.1 (Lynn and Vanhanen, 2001, 2002). GDP/capita data from the Human Development Report (2000).

Figure 6.2 *Logarithm (Base 10) of GDP/capita ($) as a function of national intelligence*

In fairness it should be pointed out that Lynn and Vanhanen do not end their thesis with the regressions outlined earlier. Their thesis is in fact an extension of much earlier work exploring the genetic basis of intelligence. The story begins at the turn of the century with the psychologist and mathematician Charles Spearman, inventor of the 'Spearman Rank Correlation Coefficient' and one of the inventors of factor analysis outlined in Appendix 1. Spearman observed that individuals who do well on one type of intelligence test also tend to do well on others (Spearman, 1904, 1927). While this may seem intuitively obvious it does pose a question: is it possible to take the results of a series of intelligence tests and look for an underlying structure? Spearman invented factor analysis to do just that, and it has been consistently shown that approximately 40 per cent of the variation in the results of such tests can be explained by a vector (usually referred to as general intelligence or 'g'). This may not sound a large percentage, the example in Appendix 1 explained 86 per cent of the variation between the three components of the HDI, but 40 per cent is significant nonetheless. Given a range of intelligence tests, it is possible to asses their loading with 'g', with some being higher than others (Jensen, 1998). Progressive Matrices, the tests used by Lynn and Vanhanen to arrive at the national intelligence score for Argentina, are said to be highly loaded with 'g'.

It has been argued that 'g' stays more constant after childhood than other behavioural traits, and that it can be used to predict later educational level of attainment far better than other measures. But is this intelligence or just 'ability'? The current consensus is that 'g' has a biological basis (Brody, 1998, 1999), with some even pointing to a specific site within the brain (Duncan et al, 2000). Results over many years suggest that intelligence does have some genetic basis although there are complications. For example, it appears that 'intelligence' is not fixed throughout the lifetime of an individual, as it should be if solely determined by genes, but is malleable and influenced to some extent by environment (Brody, 1998, 1999; Garlick, 2002). For example, learning (eg quality and quantity of schooling) may influence performance on intelligence tests (eg Jensen, 1980; Garlick, 2002) and this may partly explain the gradual increase in intelligence test scores over time (Flynn, 1987). Nevertheless, a genetic basis to intelligence has been used by some to promote policy regarding immigration and education provision to name but two applications (Gould, 1996). Schönemann (1997, p314) paraphrases those promoting changes to the education policy in the US based on a genetic basis for 'g': 'Federally funded compensatory education programs cannot "boost IQ and scholastic achievements" because "intelligence", g, is largely innate and "the disadvantaged" are deficient in g-genes'. Therefore why not target the limited resources at those with better 'g' genes? Assuming a genetic basis for 'g', if only in part, and hence what could be called intellectual 'ability' (or 'appetite' as some prefer; Plomkin, 2001) has also been used to explore assumed linkages between intelligence and other factors such as income, crime and poverty (Jensen, 1998).

Given evidence for some genetic influence on intelligence it is but a small step to look for differences between races. Spearman (1927) and Miele (2003) provide two examples spanning 70 years. While within race variation in intelligence is acknowledged to be much greater than variation between races (Spearman, 1927; Brody, 1998), results have consistently implied a hierarchy: Asians perform best, followed by Europeans with those of African origin performing the worst (Lynn, 1996; Rushton, 1997, 2001). However, it has been disputed whether these racial differences really exist or are mere methodological artefacts (Rutter, 2003). Intelligence tests can bias against certain groups and individuals and may not provide the 'indifferent indicators' of intelligence that some think (Sternberg, 1987). However, from here to the initial hypotheses of Lynn and Vanhanen that national economic performance is positively related to national intelligence is but a small step. Their conclusion would appear to be that Africa is poor because Africans (particularly the blacks) are, to use Schönemann's (1997) term, "deficient in g-genes", and because this is 'nature' there is little that can be done about it. Yet remember that at the heart of this conclusion is the evidence of Figure 6.1 with all of its simplification.

DEVELOPMENT INDICES AND POLICY

While there is some media reporting of development indices and researchers have used them to explore spatial and temporal differences, what evidence is there that such indices are used to directly influence policy? A direct linkage between a policy and an indicator, even one as common as the GDP, can be surprisingly difficult to prove (Jesinghaus, 2000b). However, as the UN, World Bank and others have promoted the use of indicators in general, it would seem logical to think that they also use them (Gill and Hall, 1997). But what about other major development agencies?

Whether the HDI and its relatives have had any impact in policy terms is debatable (Srinivasan, 1994). Surprisingly, as least to this author, while there have been numerous attempts to provide modifications or alternatives to the HDI, there has been little if any empirical research on its policy impact. There is certainly evidence that development indices are used by agencies other than the Bretton Woods and UN institutions. The 'First Workshop on Composite Indicators of Country Performance' organized by the Joint Research Centre of the European Commission and the OECD was held in Ispra, Italy, 12 May 2003. The summary made the point that 'composite indicators are increasingly being used by national and international organizations, such as the OECD, the United Nations and the EC, for cross-country comparisons'.

The example I wish to focus on here is the European Development Fund (EDF) of the European Union (EU).[1] The EDF is the main development organization of the EU, although its funding does not come from the general Community budget. Instead it is funded directly by EU member states and has its own financial rules and management structure. The current budget for the EDF is set at EUR 13.5 billion over a period of five years (2000–2005). Since 1959 there have been nine EDFs, each one lasting typically for five years (Table 6.3).

In addition, each of the individual members states also has their own bilateral development programmes. On a global basis the EDF is certainly a significant provider of development funding.

Table 6.3 *European development funds, 1959–2005*

EDF	Years
1	1959–64
2	1964–70
3	1970–75
4	1975–80
5	1980–85
6	1985–90
7	1990–95
8	1995–2000
9	2000–2005

The broad aim of the EU's development policy is to reduce and eventually eliminate poverty, and it works in partnership with other agencies towards a common set of development goals (The Millennium Development Goals), namely:

- achieve universal primary education
- promote gender equality and empower women
- reduce child mortality
- improve maternal health
- combat HIV/AIDS, malaria and other diseases
- eradicate extreme poverty and hunger
- ensure environmental sustainability.

The HDI and other indices are liberally referred to in EU development documentation, and are often employed to justify individual country programmes. Even so there has been some criticism of the 'policy patchwork' that marks the EU's engagement with the developing world (Holland, 2003).

> *It should be noted, however, that the definition of LDC in the Cotonou Agreement does not perfectly match that used by other agencies or follow the UN's HDI (Human Development Index) exactly.* (Holland, 2003, p170)

Perhaps even worse than this apparent mismatch, is a recent study of aid allocation by the EU which noted that:

> *In our analysis we found that EU aid p.c. [per capita] towards ACP [African, Caribbean and Pacific] countries is not correlated with GDP p.c. to a significant extent and it is positively correlated to the Human Development Index (HDI), which is a combined index of income, health and education indicators. . . . That means that currently aid is not given according to needs. Partly this result is driven by the fact that small islands (that often have a higher HDI rank) receive relatively big amounts of aid because there is a minimum amount needed to have a reasonable relation between aid and administrative costs for the EU. In fact there is a negative correlation between the total population of an ACP country and the EU aid p.c. it receives.* (Wolf and Spoden, 2000, p12)

A positive correlation between the HDI and the amount of aid coming from the EU would appear quite worrying, but the EU does use other indicators for gauging progress towards the Millennium Development Goals. Some of these are components of indices covered in this book such as the HPI and ESI. In the 2003 annual report from the European Commission to the Council and European Parliament, the list of indicators shown in Table 6.4 is provided (p38).

Table 6.4 *European Commission indicators towards Millennium Development Goals*

Indicator	Component of other indices
Headcount Ratio. Proportion of population below $1 per day (using national poverty line)	HPI-2
Prevalence of underweight children (under-5 years of age)	HPI-1
Under-5 mortality rate (per 1000 live births)	ESI
Enrolment ratio in primary education	HDI
Ratio of girls to boys in primary, secondary and tertiary education	GDI
Proportion of pupils beginning the first year in the primary education and completing the fifth year	
Proportion of births attended by skilled health personnel	
Proportion of 1-year old children immunized against measles	
HIV prevalence among 15–24 year old pregnant women	
Proportion of population with sustainable access to an improved water source	HPI-1, ESI
GDP/capita and GDP growth	HDI

Source: Annual Report from the European Commission to the Council and European Parliament (2003).

Even with this relatively small set of indicators (compared to the demands of the ESI for example) there are problems:

> *Although the availability of data is improving, there are still gaps that limit the number of countries where it is possible to measure the evolution over the last five or ten years. The quality of data also varies between indicators. It is especially insufficient on the lead poverty indicator of 'proportion of population below $1 per day' (so the proxy of GDP per capita was used instead) and 'primary school completion rate'.* (European Commission, 2003, p40)

As we have seen in Chapter 3, the Headcount Ratio is just about the simplest of the poverty-line based indicators, but the EU is having to proxy even this with GDP/capita. The concern over data quality just does not seem to go away.

SUMMARY

This chapter has sought to illustrate how development indices are reported in the press and used by those wishing to explore spatial and temporal differences in development. The first part of the chapter showed how the HDI in particular receives much coverage in the popular press, with a particular theme of inter-country comparison (usually with neighbours) and changes over time. Assuming that press coverage can have an influence on national policy, then for those wishing to promote the HDI as a counter to the dominance of economic indicators, this can only be good news. What is surprising is that there has been so little, if any, research in this area.

The second part of the chapter explored how development indices are used as data sets to explore difference and change. The danger is that the widespread popularity of simple measures can be driven by a human desire to simplify in order to understand and intervene, and hence ironically the indices can begin to define what they were intended only to proxy. The HDI becomes 'human development' just as GDP/capita becomes 'economic development'. Statistical techniques, such as regression and factor analysis, designed to reduce data sets, are used to simplify what are already highly simplified indices. Problems of defining cause–effect begin to emerge, as, for example, with the corruption and economic development analysis of Box 6.1, and this can become so oversimplified as to be dangerous. For example, the use of intelligence tests on relatively small samples taken over 70 years have been used to create national scores of intelligence hypothesized as a 'cause' of inter-country variation in economic development. Assuming that differ-ence in national intelligence is largely due to the genetic makeup of the populations, then the best the rich countries can do is to come to terms with it and try to alleviate the worst consequences with a bit of 'nurture'. There are so many simplifying assumptions in here that we can but wonder whether so much has ever been built from so little.

It is important to remember that development indices are constructs of human beings. The HDI is a reflection of what UNDP and its advisors see as important in human development and, while they make a good case for their position, others may not necessarily agree (Chowdhury, 1991; Jahan, undated). The UNDP selected the three components and decided upon an equal weighting. It was also the UNDP that chose the league table style of presentation. Indeed the HDI was purposely created as a feed into policy; organizations are meant to use it to help them prioritize their interventions and measure success. It is an aid to management and was not created to help people understand the nature of human development. Evidence as to whether development agencies use such indices is mixed, but they are often referred to in reports and as justifications for specific projects. The EU, for example, does use indicators to check for progress towards meeting the Millennium Development Goals, although there do seem to be worryingly persistent gaps in the availability of quality data upon which these indicators are based. It would certainly be good to know more about the extent and ways in which such indices influence policy.

Intelligence tests were created with a mixture of motives, to understand intelligence and also as a basis for various interventions such as immigration, selection for the military and education, and 'g' has gradually emerged out of these studies (Gould, 1996). Suggestions that intelligence tests should be used to guide policy have created many dispute and allegations of racism have been fired at some researchers, with at least one book being 'de-published' as a result (Brand, 1996). Much of this debate was based on charge and countercharge of gross oversimplification in the face of complexity and the damage that could result if presumed and contended genetic differences in intelligence began to influence government policy.

By comparison to this intense maelstrom, debates surrounding the HDI, ESI and CPI (desirability, methodology and implications of use in policy) have been tame. While there have been critiques of the HDI, these have been more related to technical issues such as method of calculation (eg Sharma, 1997; Noorbakhsh, 1998; Sagar and Najam, 1998, 1999; Lüchters and Menkhoff, 2000) and to a lesser extent issues over data quality (Murray, 1991; Loup et al, 2000). It does appear that development indices could benefit from the vigorous debate and questioning we have seen with the measurement of human intelligence.

7 A COMPARATIVE INDICATOROLOGY

SOME MEETINGS IN ITALY

Development indices have been with us for some time, and over the years there have been numerous national and international meetings, consultations and workshops designed to generate recommendations for the creation and use of development indices. For example, a meeting funded by the Rockefeller Foundation in 1996 generated what are now known as the Bellagio Principles for Sustainable Development (the meeting took place in the town of Bellagio, in the north of Italy). One of the recommendations of the meeting was a call for indicators as an essential tool for measuring progress towards the attainment of sustainable development. More specifically the meeting called for:

- Progress towards sustainable development to be based on the measurement of a limited number of indicators based on standardized measurement.
- Methods and data employed for assessment of progress (ie the indicators) to be open and accessible to all and not the preserve of a select few.
- Allowance to be made for repeated measurement of the indicators in order to determine trends and incorporate the results of experience.
- Indicators to be effectively communicated to all of those with a stake in sustainable development.
- Broad participation from stakeholders in the setting of indicators.

The Bellagio recommendations have been influential in sustainable development (Bell and Morse, 2003), and the 'Italian influence' on indicators came into play seven years later in May 2003, when a workshop was held in the small but scenic town of Ispra, also in north of the country, to help set out recommendations for the use of development indices to gauge country performance. The workshop was organized by the Joint Research Centre (JRC) of the European Commission and the OECD,[1] an organization with an enviable location close to Ispra. The Ispra workshop identified areas 'where guidelines or best practices are needed for the construction of composite indicators', and seven of them will be discussed here as they concern points of interest from previous chapters in this book. The seven I have selected are presented in Table 7.1 (the titles are those of the Ispra Summary document), and these have arisen in this or a similar form in Chapters 1 to 6.

Table 7.1 *Some issues regarding development indices designed for inter-country comparison*

Issue	Notes
Theoretical framework	A theoretical framework and rationale should be provided for the components that make up the index. This includes how components are to be weighted and how the index feeds into policy.
Data selection	Variables should be selected on the basis of: • soundness • measurability • country coverage • relevance • inter-relationship with other variables.
Correlation analysis of data	Encourage use of factor analysis to gain insights into the relationships between the variables and an understanding of the 'phenomenon to be measured'.
Standardization methods	Components of the index have to be standardized or normalized to make them comparable.
Weighting approaches	Components need to be weighted in accord with the theoretical framework. Weights may be assigned through 'expert opinion, techniques such as principal components analysis or factor analysis, or through correlations with dependent variables such as economic growth rates'.
Transparency/accessibility	Indices should be presented alongside detailed explanations of: • underlying data sets • standardization techniques • weighting methods • alternative approaches.
Visualization	Presentation of indices should include an acknowledgement of their limitations as well as a 'confidence limit'. 'Composite indicators should be acknowledged as simplistic presentations and comparisons of country performance in given areas to be used as starting points for further analysis.'

Table adapted from the summary of a workshop organized by the Joint Research Centre of the European Commission and the OECD, in Ispra, Italy, May 2003.

The first item listed in Table 7.1 relates to the 'theoretical framework' for the index. The theoretical framework is presented by the creators of the three indices – the HDI (UNDP), ESI ('World Leaders') and CPI (Transparency International). This is perhaps the easiest issue to address given that, within reason, it is possible to rationalize any index and choice of components. We have seen how one can rationalize the inclusion of 'happy life expectancy' instead of 'life expectancy' in the HDI, and how Lind (1992), to take but one example, rationalizes the Life Product Index (LPI) as an alternative to the HDI. There are hundreds of examples of composite indices, and no doubt the creators of every one of them would argue that their choices have been logical. Note that, for the most part, these have not been mathematical formulations in tune with the rationalization of Sen's Poverty Index. Instead we are usually dealing with value judgements.

Perhaps a more thorny issue listed in Table 7.1 is the weighting of the components of an index. A common option, as we have seen with the HDI and ESI, is to weight the components equally. In the thirteen years of the HDI's existence and the substantial literature surrounding its calculation, the three components have maintained their equal weight. But while it is easy to rationalize a choice of education, life expectancy (health) and income as important components of human development, it must be almost impossible to convincingly argue that any one should be weighted more than the others. One can only suspect that in the end this will still be a subjective judgement.

With regard to transparency and accessibility all three of the indices – HDI, ESI and CPI – are presented alongside the data sets and steps of calculation that have been used, and for the ESI and CPI it is possible to download some of the information in electronic format. However, the degree of detail provided does vary. As the HDI only has three components, it is possible to present all of the necessary information in one table. As may be expected given the greater complexity of the ESI, presenting the raw data and the steps in the calculations are much more involved. The ESI reports (WEF, 2001, 2002) are substantial documents, with detailed data sets for all of the 64 variables, although details of the imputation of missing data are not provided. Presentation of raw data for the CPI is not as good, and presumably part of the problem here is due to it being an 'index of indices'. While it is possible to go to some of the sources of the indices used in the CPI, this is a more cumbersome process.

Each of the three indices are accompanied by warnings which reiterate the fact that they are but simplified representations of the phenomenon (human development, environmental sustainability and corruption) being measured. The HDRs are replete with warnings of this sort concerning the HDI and its relatives. Whether, of course, those consuming the indices note them is an entirely different issue.

The issue of 'correlation analysis of data' has been covered in Chapter 6, where we explored the potential dangers of oversimplification. As discussed earlier, while such indices should only be seen as an initial foray into understanding the complex and diverse nature of the phenomenon, they can be deceptive. The use of data reducing techniques may provide some clues, but great care does need to be taken. A cavalier approach could be detrimental.

Perhaps the most significant issue outlined at the Ispra workshop is that of the data which underpin the indices. This has arisen on numerous occasions throughout this book, and has been the subject of various studies. Even the International Comparison Programme (ICP) that helps generate Purchasing Power Parity (PPP) values has been the subject of criticism over data quality, and here we are dealing with something that should be far more straightforward than, say, the complex matrix of 64 variables in the ESI. I find it surprising that more has not been done to deal with this issue, and it is worrying to find major development donors such as the EU still decrying the quantity, and perhaps more importantly, the quality of data that are essential to create meaningful development indices. Maybe this is due to a number of reasons:

- processes of data collection are less glamorous than creating headline-grabbing indicators
- data collection in the field is a far more involved, time-consuming, uncomfortable, repetitive and expensive task than sitting at a computer to create an index or indeed to write a book about indices!
- because of the expense, data collection may be seen as a lower priority by national governments.

While the UN and others do continue to reiterate that improving data collection is seen by them as a priority, one wonders whether the effort is enough. The production of indices using data that may be of marginal quality could be harmful.

> *Human development is too important to monitor and evaluate to allow data limitations to wholly prevent attempts at measurement. . . . As currently formulated, the human development index risks to be counterproductive. Instead of highlighting the tremendous importance of improvements in mortality and education for human development, it gives the false impression that we know the levels of these important activities in all developing countries. In some sense, it devalues a host of efforts that are needed to get real and timely information on mortality and education in developing countries.* (Murray, 1991, p19)

> *Human development and related measures such as GDI (Gender-related Development Index), GEM (Gender Empowerment Measure) and HPI (Human Poverty Index) are necessarily more frail, the result of having to use imperfect data, often out of date by three or four years, and of needing to use indicators available for the majority of countries, even the poorest.* (Richard Jolly, SEF News, no. 1, October 1998)

PEOPLE'S INDICATORS

Comparing the two sets of recommendations from the Bellagio (for sustainable development) and Ispra meetings, there is one obvious difference. The Bellagio meeting recommended a degree of stakeholder involvement in the process of setting indicators and indeed with regard to their use. The flavour is more 'bottom up', with a strong sub-theme of 'participation' and neopopulism. By way of contrast, we see nothing like this 'populist' theme from the Ispra meeting, but perhaps we should not be surprised given that this workshop was more concerned with inter-country comparisons. The flavour here is unashamedly 'top down'. Nevertheless, there is something of a conundrum. Highly aggregated indices are designed to hide valuable information about their underlying components and data sets (Rennings and Wiggering, 1997; Hardi and Semple, 2000). While the disaggregated information may be provided alongside the index, the very people being targeted as users may be those who are least likely to want to disaggregate, and if the index has to be disaggregated to be truly informative why aggregate in the first place?

The dilemma can be illustrated using a favourite visual device of the OECD and others – the 'pyramid of indicator sets' (Braat, 1991; see also Figure 7.1). In Figure 7.1a the integration from raw data to indices is presented as a equilateral triangle, with the highly aggregated indices at the apex. Different 'users' (scientists, policy makers/managers and the public) will be interested in different levels of aggregation, with the public wanting the most highly aggregated indices at the apex and scientists being interested in the raw data sets at the foot of the triangle. Each layer of the OECD-triangle is a reduction of the layers beneath, and the result is an attenuation of the information. Perhaps what is not so intuitively obvious is that even at the base of the triangle we have only a representation of the 'real world' given that it has been collected by scientists who in part have to meet the demands of those providing the funding for the collection process. As a result, there will be a focus on relatively few issues to the detriment of others.

Assuming that the base of Figure 7.1a does align with 'reality', the symmetrical triangle implies that the apex sits towards the centre of the total information available and hence is a good representation of 'reality'. The visual representation implies an 'ideal', but the reality may be closer to some of the triangles in Figure 7.1b. Here the apices of two triangles (corresponding to indices 'X' and 'Y') are not over the centre of the base but to one side of it. The triangle from Figure 7.1a, with apex at 'Z', has also been included for comparison. While the information upon which the triangles have been built is the same, the attenuation has been different. The result is that indices 'X', 'Y' and 'Z' summarize the same information in different ways, but the users towards the top of each triangle have only the vision of reality given to them by those creating the indices. In all triangles one can get closer to

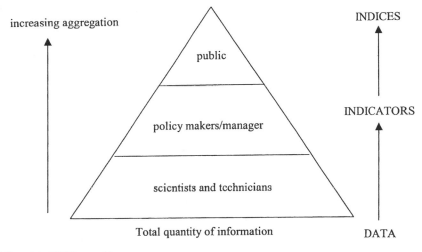

(a) The original OECD pyramid

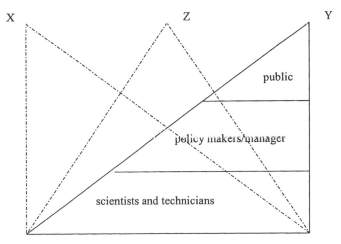

Total quantity of information

(b) A distorted pyramid with the apex away from the centre point of the 'total quality of information' available
Source: Both diagrams are based on the OECD 'pyramid of indicator sets' (after Braat, 1991).

Figure 7.1 *Relationships between indicators, data and information*

'reality' by disaggregation (the bases of the triangles are in the same place), but this may not be an easy process for those groups towards the top of the triangle for whom the indicators and indices were designed. In our examples, the HDI and even the ESI are based on a small part of the total information available and the decisions about what to include and why have been made by experts. They decide where the apex lies, and in effect the triangles are representations of power.

It could be argued, of course, that those towards the top of the triangles in Figure 7.1 should also be involved in setting the indicators and indices. After all, they know what they want to use the indices for and should be able to provide an input into the process of information attenuation. This brings us closer in style to the commonly espoused use of indicators in sustainable development (Bell and Morse, 2001, 2003), and there have been efforts to use participatory techniques to generate indicators of basic need (Brinkerhoff et al, 1997). Even so, participation is not a panacea. For example, Participatory Poverty Analysis (PPA) promoted by the World Bank is founded on the assumption that poverty alleviation will more likely succeed if the poor have a voice in how poverty is assessed and addressed (Narayan, 1997; Rob, 1998). Many examples of PPA exist (Holland and Blackburn, 1998), and indicators developed via participatory techniques are an important element (IDS, 1998). With expert facilitation, such indicators have a richness that goes well beyond the one-dimensional 'poverty line' examples of Chapter 3 or even the HPI of Chapter 4. However the results have been mixed (Rob, 1998; Norton, 1998), and it is not particularly useful to help people identify what they mean by poverty and the reasons why they are poor if they are unable to do anything about it (Bevan, 2000). Without the power to make change, indicators can be nothing more than a source of frustration and generate an even greater sense of helplessness.

Perhaps one compromise may be to continue the devolution of indicator and index creation to the national level. For example, K. C. Plant, the deputy chairman of the Planning Commission in India, has said of the HDI:

> *For our purposes, therefore, we need to develop indices which are relevant to our specific conditions. This would require reconsideration not only of the exact variables contained in the HDI but also of the weights accorded to each of them.* (*Indian Express* Newspapers, Bombay, 14 July 1997)

But this has to go hand in hand with a greater emphasis on the collection of quality data, and maybe this is where the UNDP, World Bank, and others could provide greater assistance.

SENSE, FONDNESS OR OBSESSION?

The attraction of simple explanations in development has been very persistent, although the success of the simplifying process can depend largely upon who is doing it and how. 'Postist' (post-modern, post-structural) critiques of development abound, and challenge the development visions of the development industry, exemplified by the likes of the UN, World Bank and International Monetary Fund (Estreva, 1992; Escobar, 1995). The world cannot be made into a simpler place even if we wish it to be, but given the need to 'do something' people have to do the best they can without being overwhelmed with data. The Millennium Development Goals are crucial to helping us address the inequities we see in the world today, and, despite all of the problems outlined in this book, development indicators and indices can play a vital role in helping us to achieve them. However, it is important that indices are handled as but one feed into policy and not the only one (Justus, 1995; Streeten, 1995; Jahan, undated).

We tend to see development indicators and indices as devices for 'good', but they do reflect narrow visions of reality and there is a strong and perhaps dangerously hidden power axis at the heart of their creation and presentation to potential users. Making the index methodology transparent, while relatively easy to achieve, may not necessarily help to address this power differential. The problem is that it is all too easy to create development indices, and we can become blind to their limitations as they pander to a desire for quick fixes to complex problems. The world is complex and the human race faces many challenges. Of course we all want to 'do something' to help, but moving a country up the HDI table, while being good politics, may not necessarily benefit most of the people who live there.

Culture is smitten with counting and measuring; it feels out of place and uncomfortable with the innumerable; its efforts tend, on the contrary, to limit the numbers in all domains; it tries to count on its fingers. (Jean Dubuffet, 1901–1985) 'Asphyxiating Culture', *Asphyxiating Culture and Other Writings*, 1986.

Notes

Chapter 1

1   These can be found at the BBC News website (www.news.bbc.co.uk/1/hi/education/3289279.stm). Accessed in October, 2003. The presentation of the story includes a set of links to allow the reader to access the league tables for their town.
2   www.trumanlibrary.org/educ/inaug.htm
3   www.nathanielturner.com/ujamaanyerere.htm and at www.blackstate.com/nyerere.html

Chapter 2

1   Cited from *GDP: One of the Greatest Inventions of the 20th Century*, www.mines.edu/Academic/courses/econbus/ebgn412/readings/GDP. html
2   Ibid
3   Website www.rprogress.org/projects/gpi/

Chapter 4

1   UNDP 1990 to 2003. There is an excellent Human Development Report website at www.hdr.undp.org.

Chapter 5

1   See also the 'do it yourself' sustainability dashboard site at www.esl.irc.it/envind/dashbrds.htm
2   Source: World Development Report (1997). The State in a Changing World. World Bank: Washington, pp102 and 103. For a selection of documents and resources on corruption and governance see the World Bank Institute website (www.worldbank.org/wbi/governance/).

Chapter 6

1   www.europa.eu.int/comm/development

Chapter 7

1   Publications and background papers available at www.jrc.cec.eu.int/uasa/evt-oecd-jrc.asp

REFERENCES

Acton, C (2000) *Community Indicators for Sustainability: A European Overview*, Environ Trust, Leicester

Allenby, B; Yasui, I; Lehni, M; Züst, R and Hunkeler, D (1998) 'Ecometrics' Stakeholder Subjectivity: Values, issues and effects', *Environmental Quality Management*, vol 8, no 1, pp1–18

Anand, S and Ravallion, M (1993) 'Human Development in Poor Countries: On the role of private incomes and public services', *Journal of Economic Perspectives*, vol 7, no 1, pp133–150

Anand, S and Sen, A K (1994) *Human Development Index: Methodology and Measurement*, Human Development Report Office Occasional Paper, UNDP, New York

Armenia Human Development Report (1996) UNDP Yerevan. Available at www.arminco.com/Armenia/HDR/,accessed on 17 April 2002

Asheim, G B (1994) 'Net National Product as an Indicator of Sustainability', *Scandinavian Journal of Economics*, vol 96, no 2, pp257–265

Atkinson, A N (1970) 'On the Measurement of Inequality', *Journal of Economic Theory*, vol 2, pp244–263

Atkinson, A B and Bourguignon, F (1982) 'The Comparison of Multi-dimensional Distributions of Economic Status', *Review of Economic Studies*, vol 49, no 2, pp183–201

Aturupane, H; Glewwe, P and Isenman, P (1994) 'Poverty, Human Development and Growth: An emerging consensus?', *The American Economic Review*, vol 84, no 2, pp244–249

Bartelmus, P (1997) 'Greening the National Accounts', in Moldan, B; Billharz, S and Matravers, R (eds), *Sustainability Indicators: A Report on the Project on Indicators of Sustainable Development*, John Wiley and Sons, Chichester, pp198–205

Basu, A (2001) 'A Comparative Analysis of India and Other Asian Countries Based on Science, Technology and Development Indicators', *Research Evaluation*, vol 10, no 1, pp19–32

Bayless, M and Bayless, S (1982) 'Current Quality of Life Indicators: Some theoretical and methodological concerns', *American Journal of Economics and Sociology*, vol 41, no 4, pp421–437

Bell, S and Morse, S (1999) *Sustainability Indicators: Measuring the Immeasurable*, Earthscan, London

Bell, S and Morse, S (2003) *Measuring Sustainability. Learning by Doing*, Earthscan, London

Bevan, P (2000) 'Who's a Goody? Demythologizing the PRA agenda', *Journal of International Development*, vol 12, pp751–759

Blaikie, P (2000) 'Development, Post-, Ant-, and Populist: A critical review', *Environment and Planning A*, vol 32, pp1033–1050

Blomstrom M and Hettne, B (1984) *Development Theory in Transition*, Zed Books, London

Bond, M (2003) 'The Pursuit of Happiness', *New Scientist*, 4 October 2003, pp40–43

Booysen, F (2002) 'An Overview and Evaluation of Composite Indices of Development', *Social Indicators Research*, vol 59, no 2, pp115–151

Boyd, D and Smith, R (1999) 'Testing for Purchasing Power Parity: Econometric issues and an application to developing countries', *The Manchester School*, vol 67, no 3, pp287–303

Braat, L (1991) 'The Predictive Meaning of Sustainability Indicators', in Kuik, O and Verbruggen, H (eds) *In Search of Indicators of Sustainable Development*, Kluwer Academic Publishers, Dordrecht, pp57–70

Brand, C (1996) *The g Factor*. Originally published by John Willey and Sons, Chichester but withdrawn. The book can be found at www.ed.ac.uk/crb/book and www.webcom.com/zurcher/thegfactor/index.htm

Brinkerhoff, M B; Fredell, K A and Frideres, J S (1997) 'Basic Minimum Needs, Quality of Life and Selected Correlates: Explorations in villages in Northern India', *Social Indicators Research*, vol 42, pp245–281

Brody, N (1998) 'Jensen and Intelligence', *Intelligence*, vol 26, no 3, pp243–247

Brody, N (1999) 'What is Intelligence?', *International Review of Psychiatry*, vol 11, pp19–25.

Buhler, W; Morse, S; Arthur, E; Bolton, S and Mann, J (2002) *Science, Agriculture and Research. A Compromised Participation?*, Earthscan, London

Bunge, M (1981) 'Development indicators', *Social Indicators Research*, vol 9, pp369–385.

Cahill, M B (2002) 'Diminishing Returns to GDP and the Human Development Index', *Applied Economics Letters*, vol 9, no 13, pp885–887

Caldwell, J C (1986) 'Routes to Low Mortality in Poor Countries', *Population and Development Review*, vol 12, no 2, pp171–220

Carlucci, F and Pisani, S (1995) 'A Multivariate Measure of Human Development', *Social Indicators Research*, vol 36, pp145–176

Chowdhury, O H (1991) 'Human Development Index: A critique', *The Bangladesh Development Studies*, vol 19, no 3, pp125–127

Cohen, E (2000) 'Multidimensional Analysis of International Social Indicators. Education, economy, media and demography', *Social Indicators Research*, vol 50, pp83–106

Cowen, M P and Shenton, R W (1996) *Doctrines of Development*, Routledge, London

Crafts, N (1998) 'Forging Ahead and Falling Behind: The rise and relative decline of the first industrial nation', *Journal of Economic Performance*, vol 12, no 2, pp193–210

Curwell, S and Cooper, I (1998) 'The Implications of Urban Sustainability', *Building Research and Information*, vol 26, no 1, pp17–28

de Greene, K B (1994) 'The Rocky Path to Complex-systems Indicators', *Technological Forecasting and Social Change*, vol 47, pp171–188

Davidson, B (1992) *The Black Man's Burden. Africa and the Curse of the Nation-State*, James Currey, London

Dijkstra, A G (2002) 'Revisiting UNDP's GDI and GEM: Towards an alternative', *Social Indicators Research*, vol 57, pp 301–338

Division of Sustainable Development (DSD) (2001) *Report on the Aggregation of Indicators of Sustainable Development*, Background paper for the 9th session of the Commission on Sustainable Development. United Nations Department of Economic and Social Affairs, Geneva

Dowrick, S (1996) 'Swedish Economic Performance and Swedish Economic Debate: A view from outside', *Economic Journal*, vol 106, no 439, pp1772–1779

Dowrick, S and Quiggin, J (1997) 'True Measures of GDP and Convergence', *The American Economic Review*, vol 87, no 1, pp41–64

Dowrick, S; Dunlop, Y and Quiggin, J (2003) 'Social Indicators and Comparisons of Living Standards', *Journal of Development Economics*, vol 70, pp501–529

Duncan, J; Seitz, R J; Kolodny, J; Bor, D; Herzog; H, Ahmed; A, Newell; F N and Emslie, H (2000) 'A Neural Basis for General Intelligence', *Science*, vol 289, no 5478, pp457–460

Ecologist (2001) 'Keeping Score', *Ecologist*, vol 31, no 3, pp44–47

Escobar, A (1991) 'Anthropology and the Development Encounter: The making and marketing of development anthropology', *American Ethnologist*, vol 18, no 4, pp658–682

Escobar, A Q (1992) 'Reflections on 'Development'. Grassroots approaches and alternative politics in the Third World', *Futures*, June, pp411–436

Escobar, A (1995) *Encountering Development: The Making and Unmaking of the Third World*, Princeton University Press, Princeton

Estreva, C (1992) 'Development', in Sahs, W (ed), *The Development Dictionary: A Guide to Knowledge and Power*, Zed Books, New York, pp6–25

European Commission (2003) *Annual Report 2003 from the Commission to the Council and the European Parliament on the EC Development Policy and the Implementation of External Assistance in 2002*, European Commission, Brussels

Fagan, H (1999) 'Cultural Politics and (Post) Development Paradigm(s)', in Munck, R and O'Hearn, D (eds), *Critical Development Theory: Contributions to a New Paradigm*, Zed Books, London, pp178–195

Flynn, J (1987) 'Race and IQ: Jensen's case refuted', in Modgil, S and Modgil, C (eds), *Arthur Jensen. Consensus and Controversy*, The Falmer Press, New York, Philadelphia and London, pp 221–235

Gallopin, G C (1997) 'Indicators and their Use: Information for decision-making', in Moldan, B; Billharz, S and Matravers, R (eds), *Sustainability Indicators: A Report on the Project on Indicators of Sustainable Development*, John Wiley and Sons, Chichester, pp13–27

Garlick, D (2002) 'Understanding the Nature of the General Factor of Intelligence: The role of individual differences in neural plasticity as an explanatory mechanism', *Psychological Review*, vol 109, no 1, pp116–136

George, R F (1937) 'A New Calculation of the Poverty Line', *Journal of the Royal Statistical Society*, vol 100, no 1, pp74–95

Gill, P and Hall, P (1997) 'Playing Numbers or Politics? Approaches to the prioritisation of development needs in South Africa', *Social Indicators Research*, vol 41, pp251–278

Gould, S J (1996) *The Mismeasure of Man*, 2nd edn, Norton, New York

Haberl, H; Erb K-H and Krausmann, F (2001) 'How to Calculate and Interpret Ecological Footprints for Long Periods of Time: The case of Austria 1926–1995', *Ecological Economics*, vol 38, pp25–45

Hamilton, C (1999) 'The Genuine Progress Indicator Methodological Developments and Results from Australia', *Ecological Economics*, vol 30, pp13–18

Hardi, P (2001) 'The Dashboard of Sustainability', paper presented at a conference entitled *Measure and Communicate Sustainable Development. A Science and Policy Dialogue*. Stockholm 3-4 April

Hardi, P and Semple, P (2000) 'The Dashboard of Sustainability. From a metaphor to an operational set of indices', paper presented at the Fifth International Conference on Social Science Methodology, Cologne Germany, 3–6 October

Hardi, P; Barg, S; Hodge, T and Pinter, L (1997) *Measuring Sustainable Development: Review of Current Practice*, Occasional Paper no. 17, Industry Canada, Ottawa

Hicks, N and Streeten, P (1979) 'Indicators of Development: The search for a basic needs yardstick', *World Development*, vol 7, pp567–580

Hinterberger, F and Seifert, E K (1997) 'Reducing material throughput: A contribution to the measurement of dematerialization and sustainable human development', in Tylecote, A and van der Straaten, J (eds), *Environment, Technology and Economic Growth*, Edward Elgar, Cheltenham, pp75–92

Hisamatsu, Y (2003) 'Does Foreign Demand Affect Corruption?', *Applied Economics Letters*, vol 10, pp1–2

Holland, M (2003) '20/20 Vision? The EU's Cotonou Partnership Agreement', *The Brown Journal of World Affairs*, vol 9, no 2, pp161–175

Holland, J and Blackburn, J (1998) *Whose Voice? Participatory Research and Policy Change*, IT Publications, London

Holmes, M J (2000) 'Does Purchasing Power Parity Hold in African Less Developed Countries? Evidence from a panel data unit root test', *Journal of African Economies*, vol 9, no 1, pp63–78

Hueting, R and Bosch, P (1991) 'Note on the Correction of National Income for Environmental Losses', in Kuik, O and Verbruggen, H (eds) *In Search of Indicators of Sustainable Development*, Kluwer Academic Publishers, Dordrecht, pp29–38

IDS (1998) *Participatory Monitoring and Evaluation: Learning from Change*, Policy Briefing Issue 12, Brighton, Institute of Development Studies

Indrayan, A; Wysocki, M J; Chawla, A; Kumar, R and Singh, N (1999) '3-Decade Trend in Human Development Index in India and its Major States', *Social Indicators Research*, vol 46, pp91–120

Jahan S (undated) Measuring Living Standard and Poverty: Human Development Index as an alternate measure. Available at www.umass.edu/peri/pdfs/glw_jahan.pdf

Jensen, A R (1980) *Bias in Mental Testing*, Methuen, London

Jensen, A R (1998) *The g Factor. The Science of Mental Ability*, Praeger, London

Jesinghaus, J (1999) 'Indicators for Decision-Making', draft paper of 12 December 1999, European Commission, Brussels

Jesinghaus, J (2000a) 'The World Economic Forum's Environmental Sustainability Index: Strong and weak points'. European Commission Joint Research Centre, Ispra, Italy. Review posted on the web, 9 April

Jesinghaus, J (2000b) 'On the Art of Aggregating Apples and Oranges', Foundazione Eni Enrico Mattei, Milan, Italy

Joint Research Centre (JRC) of the Eueropean Comission and the Organization for Economic Cooperation and Development (OECD) (2003) 'Summary. First workshop on composite indicators of country performance', 12 May, Ispra, Italy.

Justus, M (1995) 'Towards a Provincial Human Development Index', *Monthly Economic Review*, vol 14, no 9, pp5–8

Kao, C H C and Liu, B-C (1984) 'Socio-economic Advance in the Republic of China (Taiwan): An intertemporal analysis of its quality of life indicators', *American Journal of Economics and Sociology*, vol 43, no 4, pp399–412

Kelly A C (1991) 'The Human Development Index: "Handle with care"', *Population and Development Review*, vol 17, no 2, pp315–324

Khan, H (1991) 'Measurement and Determinants of Socio-economic Development. A critical conspectus', *Social Indicators Research*, vol 24, pp153–175

Konrad, N and Wahl, D (1990) 'Science, Technology and Development Indicators for Third World Countries – Possibilities for analysis and grouping', *Scientometrics*, vol 19, no 3–4, pp245–270.

Lai, D (2000) 'Temporal Analysis of Human Development Indicators: Principal component approach', *Social Indicators Research*, vol 51, no 3, pp331–366

Lai, D (2003) 'Principal Component Analysis on Human Development Indicators of China', *Social Indicators Research*, vol 61, pp319–330

Lambsdorff, J G (1999) 'Corruption in Empirical Research – A review'. Transparency International Working Paper, Berlin, Germany

Lambsdorff, J G (2002) Background Paper to the 2002 Corruption Perceptions Index. Framework Document 2002. Transparency International and Göttingen University, Germany

Lawn, P A (2003) 'A Theoretical Foundation to Support the Index of Sustainable Economic Welfare (ISEW), Genuine Progress Indicator (GPI), and other related indexes', *Ecological Economics*, vol 44, pp105–118

Lind, N C (1992) 'Some Thoughts on the Human Development Index', *Social Indicators Research*, vol 27, pp89–101

Lind, N C (1993) 'A Compound Index of National Development', *Social Indicators Research*, vol 28, pp267–284

Liverman, D M; Hanson, M E; Brown, B J and Merideth, R W (1988) 'Global Sustainability: Toward measurement', *Environmental Management*, vol 12, no 2, pp133–143

Long, N and Long A (1992) *Battlefields of Knowledge*, Routledge, London

Loup, J; Naudet, D and Développment et insertion internationale (DIAL) (2000) The State of Human Development Data and Statistical Capacity Building in Developing Countries, Human Development Report Office Occasional Paper, New York, UNDP

Lüchters, G and Menkhoff, L (2000) 'Chaotic Signals from HDI Measurement', *Applied Economics Letters*, vol 7, pp267–270

Lynn, R (1996) 'Racial and Ethnic Differences in Intelligence in the United States on the Differential Ability Scale', *Personality and Individual Differences*, vol 20, pp271–273

Lynn, R and Vanhanen, T (2001) 'National IQ and Economic Development: A study of eighty-one nations', *Mankind Quarterly*, vol XLI, no 4, pp415–435

Lynn, R and Vanhanen, T (2002) *IQ and the Wealth of Nations*, Westport CT, Praeger

Maasoumi, E (1986) 'The Measurement and Decomposition of Multi-dimensional Inequality', *Econometrica*, vol 54, no 4, pp991–997

Maasoumi, E and Jeong, JH (1985) 'The Trend and the Measurement of World Inequality over Extended Periods of Accounting', *Economic Letters*, vol 19, pp295–301

Maddison, A (1983) 'A Comparison of Levels of GDP per Capita in Developed and Developing Countries, 1700–1980', *The Journal of Economic History*, vol 43, no 1, pp2741

Mauro, P (1995) 'Corruption and Growth', *The Quarterly Journal of Economics*, vol 10, no 3, pp681–712.

Mayo, E; MacGilvray, A and McLaren, D (1997) 'The Index of Sustainable Economic Welfare for the United Kingdom', in Moldan, B; Billharz, S and Matravers, R (eds) *Sustainability Indicators: A Report on the Project on Indicators of Sustainable Development*, John Wiley and Sons, Chichester, pp293–298

McGillivray, M (1991) 'The Human Development Index: Yet another redundant composite development indicator?', *World Development*, vol 19, pp1461–1468

McGranahan, D V (1972) 'Development Indicators and Development Models', *Journal of Development Studies*, April, pp91–102

McGranahan D; Pizarro, E and Richard, C (1985) *Measurement and Analysis of Socio-Economic Development: An Enquiry into International Indicators of Development and Quantitative Interrelations of Social and Economic Components of Development*, UNRISD, Geneva

Miele, F (2003) *Intelligence, Race and Genetics: Conversations with Arthur R. Jensen*, Westview.

Mitchell, G (1996) 'Problems and Fundamentals of Sustainable Development Indicators', *Sustainable Development*, vol 4, pp1–11

Moldan, B (1997) 'The Human Development Index', in Moldan, B; Billharz, S and Matravers, R (eds), *Sustainability Indicators: A Report on the Project on Indicators of Sustainable Development*, John Wiley and Sons, Chichester, pp242–252

Morse, S (2003a) 'Greening the United Nation's Human Development Index?', *Sustainable Development*, vol 11, no 4, pp183–198

Morse, S (2003b) 'For Better or for Worse, till the Human Development Index do as part?', *Ecological Economics*, vol 45, no 2, pp281–296

Morse, S. (2003c) 'Putting the Pieces Back Together Again: An illustration of the problem of interpreting development indicators using an African case study', *Applied Geography*, vol 24, pp1–22

Morse, S; McNamara, N; Acholo, M and Okwoli, B (2001) 'Sustainability Indicators: The problem of integration', *Sustainable Development*, vol 9, pp1–15

Murray, C J L (1991) Development Data Constraints and the Human Development Index, Discussion paper no. 25, May 1991, UNRISD, Geneva

Myers, D (1987) 'Internal Monitoring of Quality of Life for Economic Development', *Economic Development Quarterly*, vol 1, no 3, pp268–278

Narayan, D (1997) *Voices of the Poor: Poverty and Social Capital in Tanzania*, World Bank, Washington DC

Neumayer, E (2000) 'On the Methodology of ISEW, GPI and Related Measures: Some constructive suggestions and some doubt on the "threshold" hypothesis', *Ecological Economics*, vol 34, pp347–361

Neumayer, E (2001) 'The Human Development Index and Sustainability – A constructive proposal', *Ecological Economics*, vol 39, pp101–114

Noorbakhsh, F (1998) 'A Modified Human Development Index', *World Development*, vol 26, no 3, pp517–528

Norton, A (1998) 'Analysing Participatory Research for Policy Change', in Holland, J and Blackburn, J (eds), *Whose Voice? Participatory Research and Policy Change*, IT Publications, London, pp179–191

Odedokun, M O (2000) 'Fulfilment of Purchasing Power Parity Conditions in Africa: The differential role of CFA and non-CFA membership', *Journal of African Economies*, vol 9, no 2, pp213–234

Ogwang, T (1994) 'The Choice of Principal Variables for Computing the Human Development Index', *World Development*, vol 22, pp2011–2014

Ogwang, T (1997) 'The Choice of Principal Variables for Computing the Physical Quality of Life Index', *Journal of Economic and Social Measurement*, vol 23, pp213–221

Ogwang, T (2000) 'Inter-country Inequality in Human Development Indicators', *Applied Economics Letters*, vol 7, pp443–446

Ogwang, T and Abdou, A (2003) 'The Choice of Principal Variables for Computing some Measures of Human Well-being', *Social Indicators Research*, Vol 64, pp139–152

Opschoor, H (1991) 'GNP and Sustainable Income Measures: Some problems and a way out', in Kuik, O and Verbruggen, H (eds), *Search of Indicators of Sustainable Development*, Kluwer Academic Publishers, Dordrecht, pp39–44

Othick, J (1983) 'Development Indicators and the Historical Study of Human Welfare: Towards a new perspective', *The Journal of Economic History*, vol 43, no 1, pp63–70

Peel, D A and Venetis, I A (2003) 'Purchasing Power Parity over Two Centuries: Trends and nonlinearity', *Applied Economics*, vol 35, pp609–617

Plomkin, R (2001) ' "g" is for Ability but its also for Genes', *Times Higher Education Supplement*, 2 November, pp16–17

Preston, S H (1975) 'The Changing Relation between Mortality and Level of Economic Development', *Population Studies*, vol 29, no 2, pp231–248

Qizilbash, M (2001) 'Sustainable Development: Concepts and Rankings', *The Journal of Development Studies*, vol 37, no 3, pp134–161

Quadrado, L; Heijman, W and Folmer, H (2001) 'Multidimensional Analysis of Regional Inequality: The case of Hungary', *Social Indicators Research*, vol 56, pp21–42

Quarrie, J (ed) (1992) *The Earth Summit '92: The United Nations Conference on Environment and Development*, Regency Press, London

Ram, R (1992) 'International Inequalities in Human Development and Real Income', *Economics Letters*, vol 38, pp351–354

Ravallion, M (1997) 'Good and Bad Growth: The Human Development Reports', *World Development*, vol 25, no 5, pp631–638

Rennings, K and Wiggering, H (1997) 'Steps Towards Indicators of Sustainable Development: Linking economic and ecological concepts', *Ecological Economics*, vol 20, pp25–36

Rob, C (1998) 'PPAs: A review of the World Bank's experience', in Holland, J and Blackburn, J, *Whose Voice? Participatory Research and Policy Change*, IT Publications, London, pp131–142

Rogoff, K (1996) 'The Purchasing Power Parity Puzzle', *Journal of Economic Literature*, vol 34, pp647–668

Rushton, J P (1997) 'Race, Intelligence and the Brain: The errors and omissions of the "revised" edition of S. J. Gould's The Mismeasure of Man', *Personality and Individual Difference*, vol 23, no 1, pp169–180

Rushton, J P (2001) 'Black–White Differences on the g factor in South Africa: A "Jensen Effect" on the Wechsler Intelligence Scale for children – revised', *Personality and Individual Difference*, vol 31, pp1227–1232

Rushton, J P (2003) 'The Bigger Bell Curve: Intelligence, national achievement and the global economy', *Personality and Individual Difference*, vol 34, pp367–372

Rutter, M (2003) 'Father of 'g' Tackles "Whys" ', *Times Higher Education Supplement*, 8 August, p23.

Sagar, A D and Najam, A (1998) 'The Human Development Index: A critical review', *Ecological Economics*, vol 25, pp249–264

Sagar A D and Najam A (1999) 'Shaping Human Development: Which way next?', *Third World Quarterly*, vol 20, no 4, pp743–751

Schönemann, P H (1997) 'Famous Artefacts: Spearman's hypothesis', *Current Psychology of Cognition*, vol 16, no 6, pp665–694

Schraeder, P J (2000) *African Politics and Society: A Mosaic in Transformation*, Bedford/St. Martin's, Boston, Mass

Sen, A K (1976) 'Poverty: An ordinal approach to measurement', *Econometrica*, vol 44, no 2, pp219–231

Sen, A K (1977) 'On Weights and Measures: Informational constraints in social welfare analysis', *Econometrica*, vol 45, no 7, pp1539–1572

Sen, A K (1984) *Resources, Values and Development*, Harvard University Press, Cambridge, Mass

Sen, A K (1985) *Commodities and Capabilities*, Elsevier Science Publishers, Amsterdam

Sharma, S D (1997) 'Making the Human Development Index (HDI) Gender-sensitive', *Gender and Development*, vol 5, no 1, pp60–61

Shorrocks, A F (1995) 'Revisiting the Sen Poverty Index', *Econometrica*, vol 63, no 5, pp1225–1230

Simon, D (2003) 'Dilemmas of Development and the Environment in a Globalizing World: Theory, policy and praxis', *Progress in Development Studies*, vol 3, no 1, pp5–41

Sinden, J A (1982) 'Application of Quality of Life Indicators to Socio-economic Problems: An extension of Liu's method to evaluate policies for 26 Australian towns', *American Journal of Economics and Sociology*, vol 41, no 4, pp401–420

Solow, R (1993) 'An Almost Practical Step Towards Sustainability', *Resources Policy*, vol 19, pp162–172

Spangenberg, J H and Bonniot, O (1998) Sustainability Indicators – A compass on the road towards sustainability. Wuppertal Paper no. 81. Wuppertal Institute for Climate, Environment and Energy

Spearman, C (1904) ' "General Intelligence" Objectively Determined and Measured', *The American Journal of Psychology*, vol 15, pp201–293

Spearman, C (1927) *The Abilities of Man. Their Nature and Measurement*, Macmillan and Co, London

Srinivasan, T N (1994) 'Human Development: A new paradigm or reinvention of the wheel?', *The American Economic Review*, vol 84, no 2, pp238–243

Stein, S J (1996) 'Review of Arturo Escobar. Encountering Development: The Making and Unmaking of the Third World', *American Historical Review*, vol 101, no 5, pp1523–1524

Sternberg, R (1987) 'Gee, there's more than g! A critique of Arthur Jensen's views on intelligence', in Modgil, S and Modgil, C (eds) *Arthur Jensen. Consensus and Controversy*, The Falmer Press, New York, Philadelphia and London, pp237–249

Streeten, P (1979) 'Basic Needs: Premises and promises', *Journal of Policy Modelling*, vol 1, pp136–146

Streeten, P (1994) 'Human Development: Means and ends', *The American Economic Review*, vol 84, no 2, pp232–237

Streeten, P (1995) 'Human Development: The debate about the index', *International Social Science Journal*, vol 143, pp25–37

Sudhir, A and Sen, A K (1994) Sustainable Human Development: Concepts and Priorities, Human Development Report Office Occasional Paper no. 8. UNDP, New York

Summers, R and Heston, A (1997) Use of ICP Results: A note on estimates of GDP per capita, Paper presented at a Seminar on the use of International Comparison Programme (ICP) data, Beijing, China 16–20 June

Sweeney, P (1999) *The Celtic Tiger. Ireland's continuing economic miracle*, Oak Tree Press, Dublin

Taylor, M P (1995) 'The Economics of Exchange Rates', *Journal of Economic Literature*, vol 33, pp13–47

Thapa, S (1995) 'The Human Development Index: A portrait of the 75 districts in Nepal', *Asia-Pacific Population Journal*, vol 10, no 2, pp3–14

Townsend, P (1954) 'Measuring Poverty', *The British Journal of Sociology*, vol 5, no 2, pp130–137

United Nations Development Programme (UNDP) *Human Development Reports*, published annually between 1990 and 2001, Human Development Report Office, UNDP, New York

United Nations Economic and Social Council (UNESC) (1999) Evaluation of the International Comparison Programme, Paper E/CN.3/1999/8, UNESC, New York

Vachris, M A and Thomas, J (1999) 'International Price Comparisons Based on Purchasing Power Parity', *Monthly Labour Review*, October, pp3–12

Veenhoven, R (1996) 'Happy Life-expectancy. A comprehensive measure of quality-of-life in nations', *Social Indicators Research*, vol 39, pp1–58

Wallerstein, I (1974) *The Modern World System I*, Academic Press, New York

Wish, N B (1986) 'Are we Really Measuring the Quality of Life? Well-being has subjective dimensions as well as objective ones', *American Journal of Economics and Sociology*, vol 45, no 1, pp93–99

Wolf, S and Spoden, D (2000) Allocation of EU Aid towards ACP-Countries, ZEF – Discussion Papers on Development Policy number 22, Bonn, Germany, March

World Bank (annual) *World Development Reports*, published annually between 1977 and 2004, World Bank, Washington DC

World Commission for Environment and Development (WCED) (1987) *Our Common Future*, Oxford University Press, Oxford

World Economic Forum (WEF) (2000) *Pilot Environmental Sustainabilty Index*. Annual Meeting 2000, Davos Switzerland, WEF, Switzerland

World Economic Forum (WEF) (2001) *2001 Environmental Sustainability Index*. Annual meeting 2001, Davos Switzerland, WEF, Switzerland. Available at www.ciesin. columbia.edu/indicators/ESI

World Economic Forum (WEF) (2002) *2002 Environmental Sustainability Index*. Annual meeting 2002, Davos, Switzerland, WEF, Switzerland. Available at www.ciesin. columbia.edu/indicators/ESI

Zerby, J A and Khan, M H (1984) 'A Comparison of Multivariate Methods for Indexing Socio-economic Development', *Singapore Economic Review*, vol 29, pp47–66

APPENDIX 1
FACTOR ANALYSIS: A BRIEF INTRODUCTION

A simple example of a relationship that could have a clear cause–effect basis is per capita income and life expectancy. It would be logical to assume that greater income could result in better standards of living and indeed better health care either through government taxation or through the payment of private health insurance. Figure A.1 is a plot between these two components of the HDI (data taken from the HDR 2000).

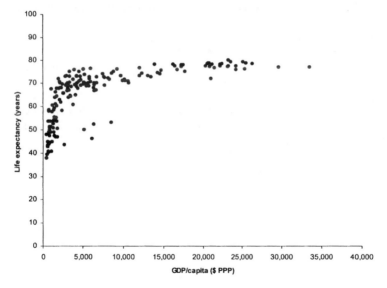

Figure A.1 *GDP/capita as a function of life expectancy*

Life expectancy is presented as years, and GDP is in dollars (adjusted for PPP of course). Note that the relationship between the two variables is not a linear one. As GDP/capita increases, so does life expectancy, but once income reaches $4,000, life expectancy begins to level out. Also note that there are some data points (countries) well outside of the main body of points in the graph.

We can perhaps appreciate the implied relationship between life expectancy and income better by taking the logarithm (base 10) of the income component (Figure A.2).

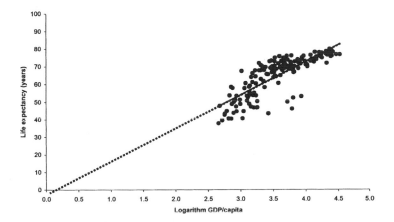

Figure A.2 *Logarithm of GDP/capita as a function of life expectancy*

The logarithm of GDP/capita makes the apparent relationship more linear, as opposed to curved. While the relationship is not perfect, not all of the points are on the line, there is an obvious increase in life expectancy for countries as their logarithm of income increases. The 'best fit' regression line is as follows:

Life expectancy $= -2.56 + 18.8 \times$ logarithm GDP/capita
$R^2 = 68.4\%$
$r = 0.827$

For every increase of '1' in logarithm GDP/capita, the life expectancy increases by 19 years. We can use this fact to generate predicted values for life expectancy for each value of GDP/capita. The results are shown in Table A.1, along with the 'residuals' (the deviations of predicted life expectancy from observed data). The countries in Table A.1 have been ranked in terms of their deviation of predicted life expectancy from observed life expectancy. Indeed, only two of the countries in the table, New Zealand and Hong Kong, have residuals of zero that is their predicted life expectancies exactly match the observed life expectancies. The deviation for some countries is as much as 22 years (Botswana), almost half the observed life expectancy of 46 years. In our example, while the R^2 would be considered to be high, implying some confidence in our fitted model, there is still 31.6 per cent of the variation unaccounted for by the regression line. This raises the question of whether we should concentrate on the fitted line and its parameters (intercept and slope) and try to understand the relationship and its assumed implications, or

Table A.1 *Observed and predicted life expectancy and residuals (observed − predicted life expectancy) for the countries included in the HDR 2000 (data from 1998)*

Country	Real GDP ($/capita)	Life expectancy (years) 1998 observed	Predicted	Residual (O −P)
Tajikistan	1,041	67.5	54.2	13.3
Solomon Islands	1,940	71.9	59.3	12.6
Jamaica	3,389	75.0	63.8	11.2
Armenia	2,072	70.7	59.8	10.9
Cuba	3,967	75.8	65.1	10.7
Albania	2,804	72.9	62.3	10.6
Sri Lanka	2,979	73.3	62.8	10.5
Azerbaijan	2,175	70.1	60.2	9.9
Viet Nam	1,689	67.8	58.1	9.7
Georgia	3,353	72.9	63.7	9.2
Dominica	5,102	76.0	67.1	8.9
Mongolia	1,541	66.2	57.4	8.8
Belize	4,566	74.9	66.2	8.7
Moldova	1,947	67.8	59.3	8.5
Honduras	2,433	69.6	61.1	8.5
Uzbekistan	2,053	67.8	59.7	8.1
Nicaragua	2,142	68.1	60.1	8.0
Costa Rica	5,987	76.2	68.5	7.7
Macedonia	4,254	73.2	65.7	7.5
Yemen Arab Republic	719	58.5	51.1	7.4
Fiji	4,231	72.9	65.6	7.3
Kyrgyzstan	2,317	68.0	60.7	7.3
Sao Tome and Principe	1,469	64.0	57.0	7.0
China	3,105	70.1	63.1	7.0
Samoa (Western)	3,832	71.7	64.8	6.9
Ecuador	3,003	69.7	62.8	6.9
Syria	2,892	69.2	62.5	6.7
Jordan	3,347	70.4	63.7	6.7
Saint Vincent and Grenadines	4,692	73.0	66.5	6.5
Panama	5,249	73.8	67.4	6.4
Madagascar	756	57.9	51.6	6.3
Pakistan	1,715	64.4	58.2	6.2
Cape Verde	3,233	69.2	63.4	5.8
Ukraine	3,194	69.1	63.3	5.8
Myanmar	1,199	60.6	55.3	5.3
Dominican Republic	4,598	70.9	66.3	4.6
Vanuatu	3,120	67.7	63.1	4.6
Bulgaria	4,809	71.3	66.7	4.6
Venezuala	5,808	72.6	68.2	4.4
Philippines	3,555	68.6	64.2	4.4
Lebanon	4,326	70.1	65.8	4.3
Turkmenistan	2,550	65.7	61.5	4.2
El Salvador	4,036	69.4	65.2	4.2
Paraguay	4,288	69.8	65.7	4.1
Antigua and Barbuda	9,277	76.0	72.0	4.0
Bhutan	1,536	61.2	57.3	3.9

Table A.1 *Continued*

Country	Real GDP ($/capita)	Life expectancy (years) 1998 observed	Predicted	Residual (O − P)
Egypt	3,041	66.7	62.9	3.8
Indonesia	2,651	65.6	61.8	3.8
Grenada	5,838	72.0	68.2	3.8
Trinidad and Tobago	7,485	74.0	70.3	3.7
Chile	8,787	75.1	71.6	3.5
Morocco	3,305	67.0	63.6	3.4
Croatia	6,749	72.8	69.4	3.4
India	2,077	62.9	59.8	3.1
Suriname	5,161	70.3	67.2	3.1
Mali	681	53.7	50.7	3.0
Peru	4,282	68.6	65.7	2.9
Nepal	1,157	57.8	55.0	2.8
Greece	13,943	78.2	75.4	2.8
Saint Lucia	5,183	70.0	67.3	2.7
Uruguay	8,623	74.1	71.4	2.7
Algeria	4,792	69.2	66.6	2.6
Comoros	1,398	59.2	56.6	2.6
Barbados	12,001	76.5	74.1	2.4
Poland	7,619	72.7	70.4	2.3
Iran	5,121	69.5	67.2	2.3
Tunisia	5,404	69.8	67.6	2.2
Romania	5,648	70.2	68.0	2.2
Colombia	6,006	70.7	68.5	2.2
Bangladesh	1,361	58.6	56.4	2.2
Ghana	1,735	60.4	58.3	2.1
Kazakhstan	4,378	67.9	65.9	2.0
Mexico	7,704	72.3	70.5	1.8
Spain	16,212	78.1	76.6	1.5
Bolivia	2,269	61.8	60.5	1.3
Thailand	5,456	68.9	67.7	1.2
Malaysia	8,137	72.2	71.0	1.2
Lithuania	6,436	70.2	69.0	1.2
Guyana	3,403	64.8	63.8	1.0
Israel	17,301	77.9	77.1	0.8
Libya	6,697	70.2	69.4	0.8
Benin	867	53.5	52.7	0.8
Cyprus	17,482	77.9	77.2	0.7
Slovakia	9,699	73.1	72.4	0.7
Latvia	5,728	68.7	68.1	0.6
Malta	16,447	77.3	76.7	0.6
Mauritius	8,312	71.6	71.1	0.5
Japan	23,257	80.0	79.5	0.5
Iraq	3,197	63.8	63.3	0.5
Guatemala	3,505	64.4	64.1	0.3
Turkey	6,422	69.3	69.0	0.3
Sweden	20,659	78.7	78.6	0.1
Tanzania	480	47.9	47.8	0.1

▶

Table A.1 *Conntinued*

Country	Real GDP ($/capita)	Life expectancy (years) 1998 observed	Predicted	Residual (O−P)
New Zealand	17,288	77.1	77.1	0.0
Hong Kong	20,763	78.6	78.6	0.0
Italy	20,585	78.3	78.5	−0.2
Portugal	14,701	75.5	75.8	−0.3
Maldives	4,083	65.0	65.3	−0.3
Czech Republic	12,362	74.1	74.4	−0.3
Canada	23,582	79.1	79.6	−0.5
France	21,175	78.2	78.8	−0.6
Belarus	6,319	68.1	68.9	−0.8
Australia	22,452	78.3	79.2	−0.9
Slovenia	14,293	74.6	75.6	−1.0
Congo Dem. Rep. Of the	822	51.2	52.2	−1.0
Argentina	12,013	73.1	74.1	−1.0
Saudi Arabia	10,158	71.7	72.8	−1.1
Netherlands	22,176	78.0	79.1	−1.1
UK	20,336	77.3	78.4	−1.1
Iceland	25,110	79.1	80.2	−1.1
Eritrea	833	51.1	52.3	−1.2
Sudan	1,394	55.4	56.6	−1.2
Brunei Darussalam	16,765	75.7	76.9	−1.2
Oman	9,960	71.1	72.6	−1.5
Estonia	7,682	69.0	70.5	−1.5
Switzerland	25,512	78.7	80.3	−1.6
Finland	20,847	77.0	78.6	−1.6
Hungary	10,232	71.1	72.8	−1.7
Bahamas	14,614	74.0	75.7	−1.7
Germany	22,169	77.3	79.1	−1.8
Bahrain	13,111	73.1	74.9	−1.8
Nigeria	795	50.1	52.0	−1.9
Seychelles	10,600	71.0	73.1	−2.1
Norway	26,342	78.3	80.5	−2.2
Cambodia	1,257	53.5	55.7	−2.2
Belgium	23,223	77.3	79.5	−2.2
United Arab Emirates	17,719	75.0	77.3	−2.3
Brazil	6,625	67.0	69.3	−2.3
Ireland	21,482	76.6	78.9	−2.3
Russian Federation	6,460	66.7	69.1	−2.4
Kenya	980	51.3	53.7	−2.4
Austria	23,166	77.1	79.5	−2.4
Papua New Guinea	2,359	58.3	60.8	−2.5
Niger	739	48.9	51.4	−2.5
Korea, Rep.	13,478	72.6	75.1	−2.5
Haiti	1,383	54.0	56.5	−2.5
Cameroon	1,474	54.5	57.0	−2.5
Lesotho	1,626	55.2	57.8	−2.6
Singapore	24,210	77.3	79.9	−2.6
Saint Kitts and Nevis	10,672	70.0	73.2	−3.2

Table A.1 *Continued*

Country	Real GDP ($/capita)	Life expectancy (years) 1998 observed	Predicted	Residual (O−P)
Senegal	1,307	52.7	56.0	−3.3
Mauritania	1,563	53.9	57.5	−3.6
Swaziland	3,816	60.7	64.8	−4.1
Kuwait	25,314	76.1	80.2	−4.1
Denmark	24,218	75.7	79.9	−4.2
Lao PDR	1,734	53.7	58.3	−4.6
US	29,605	76.8	81.5	−4.7
Congo	995	48.9	53.8	−4.9
Guinea-Bissau	616	44.9	49.9	−5.0
Djibouti	1,266	50.8	55.8	−5.0
Chad	856	47.5	52.6	−5.1
Luxembourg	33,505	76.8	82.5	−5.7
Ethiopia	574	43.4	49.3	−5.9
Burundi	570	42.7	49.3	−6.6
Qatar	20,987	71.9	78.7	−6.8
Togo	1,372	49.0	56.4	−7.4
Mozambique	782	43.8	51.8	−8.0
Burkina Faso	870	44.7	52.7	−8.0
Equatorial Guinea	1,817	50.4	58.7	−8.3
Malawi	523	39.5	48.5	−9.0
Gambia	1,453	47.4	56.9	−9.5
Sierra Leone	458	37.9	47.5	−9.6
Rwanda	660	40.6	50.4	−9.8
Central African Republic	1,118	44.8	54.8	−10.0
Zambia	719	40.5	51.1	−10.6
Côte d'Ivoire	1,598	46.9	57.7	−10.8
Guinea	1,782	46.9	58.6	−11.7
Angola	1,821	47.0	58.7	−11.7
Uganda	1,074	40.7	54.4	−13.7
Gabon	6,353	52.4	68.9	−16.5
Namibia	5,176	50.1	67.3	−17.2
South Africa	8,488	53.2	71.3	−18.1
Zimbabwe	2,669	43.5	61.9	−18.4
Botswana	6,103	46.2	68.6	−22.4

Source: HDR, 2000

whether we should concentrate on the 'outliers' – the points not on the line, and indeed they are some countries a long way from the line.

Therefore, there are two questions we need to ask with this analysis:

1   Does the R^2 value of 68.4 per cent suggest that for some countries there is a relationship between GDP/capita and for others there is not? While one can learn much from the underlying trend in the graphs, it is also important not to ignore those countries that do not fit the line.

2   Does a high R^2 value really imply that the dependent variable is being influenced by the independent variable? A high value for R^2 does not necessarily mean that the two variables are related as cause–effect. They could both be related to a third variable, or perhaps through a chain of variables, or indeed not at all.

Here it is arguably even worse, as we are simplifying indicators which themselves are highly simplifying. Ideally, of course, we should do both – explore what the underlying relationship is telling us, while at the same time being aware of the outliers and why they are where they are.

A further obvious limitation to our analysis is that we have only explored the relationship between two of the HDI components: life expectancy and GDP/capita. How can we pull all three of them together into an analysis? One way of dealing with this is to calculate all of the correlation coefficients for the matrix of components. Using the HDI data from the HDR 2000 (some of the raw data are in Table A.1), it is possible to generate the following matrix of correlation coefficients (Table A.2) between the three partial indices (note that each coefficient has a perfect correlation with itself – a value of 1).

	LE	ED	GDP
LE	1	0.7841	0.827
ED		1	0.77
GDP			1

There are statistical techniques that allow correlation coefficient matrices to be reduced (simplified) even further. In this case we are looking for some underlying linkage or relationship between them. One approach is referred to as factor analysis. Table A.2 is the same list of correlation coefficients but with some additional analysis designed to extract out underlying factors. It is a bit like algebraic techniques of extracting out common multipliers:

$$A = 2B + 6BC + 10BD$$

is the same as

$$A = 2(B + 3BC + 5BD)$$

the '2' has been extracted out as a commonality within the three multipliers. Indeed, we can go further and extract out a second commonality from the $(B + 3BC + 5BD)$ part of the equation as follows:

$$A = 2B(1 + 3C + 5D)$$

The first step in a factor analysis is to add up all the correlation coefficients for each of the three partial HDI indices (life expectancy, education and

Table A.2 *Factors analysis for the three components of the HDI in 2000. Extraction of the first factor*

The correlation matrix (r's)	LE	ED	GDP	Sum of r's for component	Note	Factor loadings for component	Note
LE	1	0.7841	0.827	2.6111	ie $1 + 0.7841 + 0.827$	0.937	ie 2.5871/square root (7.7612)
ED		1	0.77	2.5536	ie $0.7841 + 1 + 0.77$	0.917	ie 2.5871/square root (7.7612)
GDP			1	2.5965	ie $0.827 + 0.77 + 1$	0.932	ie 2.5871/square root (7.7612)
Sum of the above				7.7612			
Average value				2.5871			
				Proportion of total variation		0.862	ie $\dfrac{(0.937^2 + 0.917^2 + 0.932^2)}{3}$

Adjusted r's

	ED	GDP
LE	-0.075	-0.046
ED		-0.085
GDP		

Source: HDR, 2000

GDP/capita). For the life expectancy component (LE), this means adding up the correlation with itself (1.0), with the education (ED) component (0.7841) and with GDP (0.827). The result is 2.6111. Once this is done for all three components, the sum yields 7.7612, referred to as the total covariance in the data set.

Factor analysis then determines the contribution of each of the three factors (LE, ED and GDP) to the total covariance. If all three components were perfectly correlated, this value would be 9.0 (3 + 3 + 3), with each component making the same contribution. In practice, where there is no such perfect correlation between all components, the components that are highly correlated (ie with values closer to 1) would contribute more to this total variation than others. The contribution each component makes to the total covariance is referred to as its loading, and it is found by dividing its sum of correlation coefficients by the square root of the total covariance (in our example the square root of 7.7612 is 2.5871).

As can be seen from Table A.2, the factor loadings for all three components are very high – all greater than 90 per cent – suggesting that all of them are making a high contribution to covariance and indeed that all three of them are making more or less the same contribution. Of the three components, the largest loading is for the LE component (94 per cent) and the smallest is for ED (92 per cent). Indeed the contribution that this underlying factor makes to total variation is 86 per cent. Removing this underlying factor from our correlation matrix should result in a significant fall in the value of the correlation coefficients, and the results are shown at the foot of Table A.2. All of the correlation coefficients drop almost to zero, suggesting that there is no linkage left to explore. One pass through the process was enough.

But what exactly has all of this told us? This particular example has not been exceptionally informative and says little beyond what we already know – that all three of the HDI components are related to each other. Indeed, given this conclusion, the reader may ask why we need to have these three components to the HDI given that they are all highly related to each other?

In practice factor analysis, and particularly a more specialized form of it called Principal Component Analysis (PCA) can be used to explore differences in these HDI components between countries or regional groups of countries as well as trends over time. But be careful not to lose sight of the fact that the raw data for these analyses are in themselves highly reduced representations of human development.

INDEX

'ability', and economic development, 161–70
accountability, rise in, 25–6
accounting systems, national, 33–4
  see also Gross Domestic Product (GDP)
actor oriented theory, 26
Ake, Professor Claude, 26–7
anti-development, 26–7
Atkinson formula, 90, 91

'basic needs' approach, 25, 60, 88
Bellagio Principles for Sustainable
  Development, 176, 180
'blueprint projects', 25
Bretton Woods institutions, 23

CHDI (Corporate Human Development
  Index), 112
communism, 21–2
Corporate Human Development Index
  (CHDI), 112
Corruption Perception Index (CPI),
  beta-transformation used in, 141–5
  calculation of, 138–48
  country comparisons in, 134–7, 146–8
  criticisms of, 140
  developing countries in, 138
  distribution of scores in, 139–40
  league table format of, 140
  link between corruption and human
    development, 159–60
  matching percentile methodology of, 142
  sources of data, 133
  survey respondents, 138, 140
country comparisons,
  competitive effects of, 151, 156
  in Corruption Perception Index (CPI),
    134–7, 146–8
  in Environmental Sustainability Index
    (ESI), 127–32
  of Gross Domestic Product (GDP), 40–9
  in Human Development Index (HDI), 89,
    94–8, 110–12
  'national intelligence', 162–70

CPI *see* Corruption Perception Index

data quality,
  discussed at Ispra workshop (2003), 179
  EU funding and, 172–3
  falsification, 31
  of Gross Domestic Product (GDP), 39
  harmful effect of poor, 179
  imputation, 124, 131
  missing data in Human Development
    Index (HDI), 90–1, 107
Dependency Theory, 24–5, 161
developing countries,
  in Corruption Perception Index (CPI), 138
  industrialization of, 23
development,
  'basic needs' approach, 25, 60, 88
  beginning of concept of, 21–4
  'blueprint projects', 25
  broadening the concept of, 83
  definition of, 29
  dependency approach to, 24–5, 161
  free market approaches to, 25–7
  as increase in choices, 86
  industrialization as, 23
  modernization approach to, 21–4
  sustainable *see* sustainable development
  well-being as goal of, 86–7
development indicators,
  choice of, 30–1
  definitions of, 1–2
  effect on policy, 171–3
  falsification in, 31
  perceived as complex, 1–2
  synonymous with economic growth, 2, 22,
    33
Dissimilarity, Index of, 70–1
distribution of scores,
  in Corruption Perception Index (CPI),
    139–40
  in Environmental Sustainability Index
    (ESI), 124–9
  Gini coefficient, 72–8

'Earth Summits', 29, 121
EAW (Economic Aspects of Welfare), 55
'ecological footprint', 119–20
Economic Aspects of Welfare (EAW), 55
economics, equated with development, 2, 22, 33
Economist Intelligence Unit, 133
EDF (European Development Fund), 171–3
EDP (Environmentally Adjusted Net Domestic Product), 54
education,
    component in Human Development Index (HDI), 90
    primary school league tables, 13–18
    university league tables, 6–13
English Premier League, 5–6
environment see sustainable development
Environmental Sustainability Index (ESI),
    components of, 122–3
    country comparisons in, 127–32
    criticisms of, 131–2
    distribution of scores in, 124–9
    imputed data in, 124, 131
    league table format of, 129–31
    logarithm method of, 124–6
    see also sustainable development
Environmentally Adjusted Net Domestic Product (EDP), 54
ESI see Environmental Sustainability Index
European Development Fund (EDF), 171–3
Eurostat (Statistical Office of the European Union), 48
exchange rates, 48

factor analysis, 157, 160, 194–202
falsification see data quality
FAO (Food and Agriculture Organization), 23
Food and Agriculture Organization (FAO), 23
football leagues, 5–6
Freedom House, 133
FTSE 100, 18–20

'g' (general intelligence), 169–70
Gallop International, 133
GDP see Gross Domestic Product
Gender Empowerment Measure (GEM), 100
Gender-related Development Index (GDI), 100–4
general intelligence ('g'), 169–70
Genuine Progress Indicator (GPI), 55, 56–8
Gini coefficient, 72–8
GNP (Gross National Product), 49, 51, 53–4, 105

GPI (Genuine Progress Indicator), 55, 56–8
Great Depression, 33
Gross Domestic Product (GDP),
    calculation of, 34–9
    consumption and, 54–8
    country comparisons of, 40–9
    data quality, 39
    definition of, 34
    expenditure approach to, 34–9
    fixed capital adjustment, 53
    in Human Development Index (HDI), 90
    inflation effect on, 39–40
    PPP adjusted GDP, 41–9
    problems with, 39–49
    'real GDP', 40
    still feature in HDR, 105–6
    US economy, 36–9
Gross National Product (GNP), 49, 51, 53–4, 105

happy life expectancy, 109–12
Haq, Mahbub ul, 86
HDI see Human Development Index
HDR see Human Development Reports
Headcount Ratio, 61–3
Human Development Index (HDI),
    African media coverage of, 152
    alternatives to, 113–14
    Asian media coverage of, 152–4
    Atkinson formula in, 90, 91
    average values (2000–2003), 94–8
    birth of, 87–8
    calculation method, 88–99
    calculation method criticisms, 108–9
    changes in calculation method, 89–94, 98
    components, 87–8
    components averaged in, 89
    components criticised, 109–13
    country comparisons in, 89, 94–8, 110–12
    criticisms of, 106–13
    data quality criticisms, 107
    education component in, 90
    European media coverage of, 151–2
    factor analysis of, 194–202
    GDP/capita component, 90
    inter-country variation reduced in, 107
    intra-country variation hidden in, 108
    league table format of, 87, 89, 98–9, 151, 156
    link between human development and corruption, 159–60
    link between human development and sustainable development, 112–13, 158–9
    logarithm method in, 90, 91

media coverage of 151–6
missing data treatment, 90–1
North American media coverage of, 155
policy impact of, 171–2
regression analyses, 158–60
South American media coverage of, 155
Human Development Reports (HDRs),
GDP still a feature of, 105–6
structure of, 85–6
themes of, 85
Human Poverty Index, 104–5
Hungary, development indicators for, 83–4

ICP (International Comparison Programme),
48–9, 179
ILO (International Labour Organization), 25
IMF (International Monetary Fund), 23
Income Gap Ratio, 63–7
income inequality,
Gini coefficient, 72–8
Index of Dissimilarity (ID), 70–1
Index of Dissimilarity (ID), 70–1
Index of Sustainable Economic Welfare
(ISEW), 55
indicators see development indicators
industrialization as development, 23
inequality,
adjustment in GPI, 57
see also income inequality
inflation, effect on GDP, 39–40
Institute for Management Development, 133
intelligence, and economic development,
161–70
International Bank for Reconstruction and
Development see World Bank
International Comparison Programme (ICP),
48–9, 179
international comparisons see country
comparisons
International Labour Organization (ILO), 25
International Monetary Fund (IMF), 23
IQ, and economic development, 161–70
IQ and the Wealth of Nations (Lynn and
Vanhanen), 161–70
Ireland, transfer-price fixing in, 49, 52, 53
ISEW (Index of Sustainable Economic
Welfare), 55
Ispra workshop (2003), 171, 176–9, 180

Jamaica economic experiment, 24

Kuznets, Simon, 34

league table format,

of Corruption Perception Index (CPI), 140
of Environmental Sustainability Index
(ESI), 129–31
of Human Development Index, 87, 89,
98–9, 151, 156
prevalence of, 3
life expectancy, 109–12, 194–202
Life Product Index (LPI), 113, 115–16
Local Agenda 21 programmes, 121
logarithms,
used in Environmental Sustainability Index
(ESI), 124–6
used in Human Development Index
(HDI), 90, 91

Manley, Michael, 24
Measure of Economic Welfare (MEW), 55,
56
media coverage, 151–6
Millennium Development Goals, 172–3, 183
modernization approach, 21–4

national accounting systems, 33–4
see also Gross Domestic Product (GDP)
National Income, 53
'national intelligence', 161–70
neoclassical economics, 22
neoliberalism, 26
neopopulism, 26
Net Domestic Product (NDP), 53, 54
Net National Product (NNP), 53
non-governmental organizations (NGOs), 26
Nyerere, Julius, 24–5

OECD (Organization for Economic
Cooperation and Development), 48,
131–2, 171
'openness' of economy, 36, 38
Organization for Economic Cooperation and
Development (OECD), 48, 131–2, 171

Participatory Poverty Analysis (PPA), 182
Personal Income, 53
Physical Quality of Life Index (PQLI), 84
Plant, K. C., 182
policy impact of indicators, 171–3
Political and Economic Risk Consultancy,
133
political economics, 22
poverty,
'basic needs' approach, 25, 60, 88
definitions of, 60–1
Headcount Ratio, 61–3
Human Poverty Index, 104–5

Income Gap Ratio, 63–7
Participatory Poverty Analysis (PPA), 182
Poverty Gap Index, 67–9
'poverty line', 60–1
Sen's Index of Poverty, 72, 74–5, 78–81
'subsistence' approach to, 60
see also income inequality
Poverty Gap Index, 67–9
'poverty line', 60–1
power,
    Gender Empowerment Measure, 100
    influence of indicators, 3
    purchasing power parity (PPP), 41–9, 179
PPP (purchasing power parity), 41–9, 179
PricewaterhouseCoopers, 133
primary school league tables, 13–18
Principal Component Analysis, 157
purchasing power parity (PPP), 41–9, 179
'pyramid of indicator sets', 180–2

quality of life, 2
    see also happy life expectancy

Sen, Amartya, 72, 86, 88, 106
Sen's Index of Poverty, 72, 74–5, 78–81
State Capacity Survey, 133
Statistical Office of the European Union
    (Eurostat), 48
Structural Adjustment Programmes (SAPs),
    26
'subsistence' approach, 60
sustainable development,
    Bellagio Principles for, 176
    definitions of, 27–9
    Environmental Sustainability Index,
        121–32
    and Human Development Index (HDI),
        112–13

indicators of, 119–21
link with human development, 158–9
Local Agenda 21 programmes, 121
visual presentation format, 120
and well-being ranking, 112
'Sustainable Human Development', 86, 112

Tanzania economic experiment, 24–5
transfer–price fixing, 49, 52, 53
'trickle down' approach, 33
Truman, President H. S., 22

United Nations, 23
United Nations Development Programme
    (UNDP), 23, 29, 84
United Nations Environment Programme
    (UNEP), 23
United Nations Research Institute for Social
    Development (UNRISD), 84
university league tables, 6–13

Wallerstein, Immanuel, 24
WCED (World Commission on
    Environment and Development), 27
WEF (World Economic Forum), 121, 133
weighting,
    discussed at Ispra workshop (2003), 178
    in university league tables, 12–13
Wolfensohn, Professor James, 132
World Bank, 23
World Bank Development Reports, 34, 84
World Business Environment Survey, 133
World Commission on Environment and
    Development (WCED), 27
World Economic Forum (WEF), 121, 133
World Summits, 29, 121